the
254

HOW TEXAS COUNTIES
GOT THEIR NAMES

By Zachary Taylor Fulmore

Edited by Michelle M. Haas

Copano Bay Press
2012

First published in book form in 1915 under the title *The History and Geography of Texas As Told in County Names.*

New material copyright 2012
Copano Bay Press

ISBN: 978-0-9847372-8-4

AN ALPHABETICAL GUIDE TO THE 254

Author's Preface

Several county names stand out on the map of Texas that were hoary with age a century and a half before the word "Texas" began to develop into geographical significance. These names were probably here before Columbus discovered America. At any rate Coronado and the followers of De Soto found them here with a well established local identity within less than fifty years after that event.

The history of the State begins with the year 1528, during that epoch-making period when Henry VIII was laying his plans for a divorce from Catherine; when Luther was translating the Bible into German; several years before Calvin wrote his *Institutes of the Christian Religion*, and before Michelangelo painted his masterpiece in the Sistine Chapel at Rome.

Queen Elizabeth had not been born, and a quarter of a century had to come and go before Shakespeare first saw the light.

Let us compare it with some of the older dates in American history. It was seventy-nine years before the first settlement at Jamestown, ninety-two years before the Mayflower landed at Plymouth Rock, and more than two hundred years before George Washington was born.

Like the streams on our western confines, the stream of Texas history for nearly three hundred years had an uncertain and unsteady flow, but enough sediment in the form of county names has been left upon its banks to indicate the volume and general trend of the stream.

This book undertakes an analysis of that sediment in so far as the same can be done, by the historical interpretation of these names.

It is made up, in the main, of a series of sketches which outline the origin and history of the county names of Texas, grouped and correlated in such a way as to indicate their places in a general perspective of the state's history. It is not, and does not purport to be, a history of the different counties of the state, nor does it purport to be a history of the state, except in so far as that is involved in county names.

The body of the text was published in the *Galveston and Dallas News*, and in the *Farm News*, in 1912 and 1913, which made it available to more than a hundred thousand readers in and out of Texas. Scores of such readers, a large majority of whom were strangers to the author, wrote letters commendatory of the work, many expressing a desire to see the same published in book form. Thus encouraged, the author has carefully revised the sketches and considerably enlarged the entire work, and now gives it to the public in this form.

Especial attention is called to the county diagram, or genealogical table of our county system. The use of this as a reference will be of value to the busy lawyer, the abstracter of land titles, and the real estate agent. It also furnishes a convenient framework for the political history of every county in the state.

The maps have been compiled with scrupulous regard for decrees, treaties, and laws fixing boundaries, as well as for historical accuracy. They are not copies of other maps, but were drawn by an expert draftsman in the General Land Office of Texas, under the personal supervision of the author with the books defining or creating boundaries constantly before him, and now for the first time they appear in an historical work.

In a work of this character any attempt to give a bibliography would be impracticable. Wherever it was deemed proper, this has been given in the body of the text.

To the scores of men and women who have aided in the collection of data for the work, the author reiterates his grateful acknowledgments.

The work was first undertaken for the purpose of presenting a true picture of the founders and builders of Texas, or, as the father of history so aptly expresses it in the opening paragraph in his great work, "These are the researches of Herodotus of Halicarnassus that the actions of men may not be effaced by time, nor the great and wondrous deeds displayed by both Greek and barbarian be deprived of renown." As the work progressed he was surprised to find so many descendants of the subjects of the sketches, and the pleasure enjoyed in getting in touch with so large and respectable an element of Texas citizenship contributed much toward making it a labor of love.

Z. T. FULMORE
Austin, Texas
January 14, 1915

Introduction

The word "Texas," although in use among the Indians, "from a time whereof the memory of man runneth not to the contrary," did not begin to develop into a definite, geographical name until about the year 1690. The word signified "allies," "friends," "confederates," and was applied to such tribes as allied themselves or formed leagues for their mutual protection and defense. In 1689 there were ten or twelve such tribes, each with a distinctive name, inhabiting a region embraced within the areas of the present counties of Cherokee, Rusk, Houston and Nacogdoches, and designated in a general way as the Hainai Confederacy. In 1689 a chief of the Nebedache tribe, representing the Texas, or Confederacy, visited De Leon, who was in command of an expedition in search of La Salle's old fort and settlement, and sought the friendship of the Spaniards.

Of the tribes composing this Confederacy De Leon wrote: "The Texas are a well governed people and plant large quantities of maize, beans, calabashes, cantaloupes, and watermelons. It must contain about eight hundred heads of families, each one having a large, wooden house, plastered with clay and roofed with lime. They are familiar with the fact that there is only one true God, that he is in heaven, and that he was born of the Holy Virgin. The Indian governor asked me for ministers to instruct them, and it is certainly a pity that people so rational should have no one to teach them the gospel."

In the following year (1690) De Leon and Father Masanet returned with a party and reached the Nebedache village in what is now the northeastern part of Houston

County, near where the San Pedro Creek empties into the Neches River, and there established the Mission San Francisco de los Texas. That region then began to be called "The Texas Province," and for a quarter of a century the country was known by no other name. When Spain determined to occupy the country in 1715, making the capital or headquarters at San Antonio, the country was officially designated as "Nuevas Philipinas," in honor of Philip V, but the name "Texas" had become so firmly fixed in the Spanish mind that Nuevas Philipinas soon fell into disuse and the name Texas has come down to us not only as a geographical term embracing the original territory of Texas, but, following all the changes, political and otherwise, has attached itself to all the territory within the present boundaries of the state. For a more detailed account—probably the most satisfactory study of the subject yet made—of how the name Texas established itself in the geographical consciousness of civilization, see Dr. Bolton's "The Native Tribes About the East Texas Missions," Vol. XI, No. 4, of the *Quarterly* of the Texas State Historical Association, from which this account is mainly taken.

During the Spanish dominion there was very little development of any sort in Texas. The whole population, exclusive of Indians, did not exceed five thousand souls when Anglo-American settlement began in 1822, but during that early period the Spaniards explored practically the whole of Texas south of the thirty-second parallel. They gave names to all the conspicuous features of the gulf shoreline from Sabine Pass to the mouth of the Rio Grande—islands, bays, passes; to all streams emptying into the Gulf and to many of their tributaries; to all the principal mountains, trees, shrubs, flowers, and vines peculiar to the region, as also to birds, fishes, and animals. In various ways nearly all of these have become geographical names, most of them in their original form, in the lower half of the State. The Spaniards not only affixed names, but they gave geographical terms which have survived on our map. We have no sounds, inlets, straits, capes, runs, ponds, swamps, gaps, nor even lakes of any importance, but in lieu of these, passes, points, bayous, lagoons, matagordas, and the like.

After the student has gone over the geography of the United States and has familiarized himself with the names of all forms of land and of water in other sections, he encounters a new set of terms as soon as he reaches the southeastern border of Texas. He no longer reads of inlets, sounds, runs, straits, and the like, but of passes, bayous, lagoons, etc. As an illustration of the absence of such terms north of the thirty-second parallel, while the passway through the Guadalupe Mountains is called Bandera Pass, such passages north of the parallel are called gaps, as Buffalo Gap, etc., the one the Spanish term, the other the Anglo-American term, one being a relic of Spanish activities and the other the first impress of the Anglo-American.

The faithful priests who followed the expeditions of the Spaniards have left mementos of their faith and devotion in names traceable to the Savior, the Virgin Mary, to Peter and the other apostles, and many names from the long list of their saints and feast days, that have survived all the checkered course of our history. Mingled with these are many Indian names, whose origin and history are known only by the expert ethnologist. With the incoming of the Anglo-American the rapid increase of population brought a corresponding increase in geographical names, most of which are Anglo-American.

The list of the twenty-three original municipalities that existed in 1835 and were later made counties, has grown until the number of counties has reached two hundred and fifty-four.

To this list of names the following nations and states have contributed: England, Ireland, Scotland, France, Austria, Spain, Mexico, Canada, and, with the single exception of Rhode Island, every state in the Union east of the Mississippi River. Among these are the names of alumni of nine leading colleges and universities of Europe, twenty-three of America, two of Mexico, and two of Spain.

Four are the names of men who sat on the supreme bench of states before coming to Texas, five of governors of other states before coming to Texas, four of members of the United States Congress, prior to their arrival in Texas. Nine had been members of conventions that framed the constitutions of other states, twenty-five of members of the legislature of other states, while one was president of the convention which framed the first constitution of the Republic of Mexico. Twelve had served under Jackson in his war against the Creeks, and in vanquishing the British at New Orleans, and their tracks are plainly marked from the Appalachians to the shores of the Pacific.

CHAPTER I,
SPANISH PERIOD OF TEXAS HISTORY

The following county names are connected with the history of Texas from 1685 to 1821:

Angelina	1690-1730
Aransas	1746-1749
Bandera	1732
Bexar	1730
Galveston	1789-1795
Garza	1730
Goliad	1722-1795
Guadalupe	1689
Hidalgo	1810-1811
La Salle	1685-1687
Medina	1689
Nolan	1797-1801
Presidio	1702
Refugio	1791
San Augustine	1756-1772
San Jacinto	1756-1772
San Saba	1756-1758
Trinity	1690
Uvalde	1790
Victoria	1810-1839

Mission Concepción, erected near San Antonio in 1731. Her predecessor, Nuestra Señora de la Purísima Concepción de los Hainais, was located in what would become Angelina County.

ANGELINA

This word means "Angel," or "Little Angel," and was given to the stream from which the county took its name. How it came to be fixed upon our geography involves an interesting episode in the history of the early Catholic missions of Texas.

De Leon, on his second entrance into the country in 1690, brought with him soldiers, priests, and the necessary equipment for the establishment of missions. The first mission established was San Francisco de los Tejas. While its exact location has not been fixed, it was somewhere near the northeast corner of what is now Houston County, where San Pedro Creek empties into the Neches River. Further up the country was an Indian settlement known as the Hainai Village, on the western boundary of what is now Nacogdoches County. The holy fathers, in their visits around among the Indian villages, found at this place an Indian girl, who became drawn to them and expressed a wish to learn their language. She was invited to come to the mission and receive instruction. She was warmly welcomed by both priests and soldiers, and soon became enamored of her work and environment. Her studious habits and affable ways so charmed both priests and soldiers that they applied to her the pet name of "Little Angel," and called her native village Angelina's Village, and the stream that flowed by, Angelina's River.

In 1693 it was determined to abandon this Texas mission, but Angelina had not progressed in her work enough to enable her to speak and write the language, so she would either have to abandon the work she had set her heart upon, or abandon her people and her home and cast her lot with the Spaniards in their far-off country. She chose the latter and accompanied the priests and soldiers to the Mission San Juan Bautista, on the Rio Grande. Here she remained for over ten years, pursuing her studies, and became an object of much attention from the explorers and travelers in their journeys back and forth from Louisiana and Mexico. She very naturally became the pride of the church and of state dignitaries and was famous from Louisiana to Mexico. She grew proficient in the Spanish language, joined the church and was baptized. She later returned to her native village and doubtless did missionary work among her people, though there is no record of it. It was decided to reestablish the missions of Texas in 1716, and in that year the Mission San Francisco was reestablished near the old site, and a new mission was established at Angelina's village, doubtless upon her request, as she actively aided in its establishment, and this was called Purissima Concepcion de Acuna.

In 1719 the French invaded that part of Texas and drove away the priests and soldiers, causing another abandonment of missions, but Angelina remained at her post, as will be seen later on.

It was during this year that Belisle sought her out. Belisle was a distinguished Frenchman, who had been placed in charge of a French colony of about 1,000 persons to settle in Louisiana. Like La Salle, thirty-four years before, he sailed too far west and made a landing at Matagorda Bay to procure water for his ships. While the sailors were procuring water, he and four companions went on shore to hunt. They became lost in the woods, and the vessels left them.

When they were reduced almost to starvation, Belisle gave his dog to his companions to eat, but the dog escaped from them and fled to the wilderness. The four companions starved to death, and Belisle was about to share their fate when the dog returned with an opossum in his mouth. After much wandering and suffering he finally reached Angelina's village, half-starved, naked and lacerated from the stripes he had received among some of the savages. He immediately went to the house of Angelina, who, in spite of the fact that the French had driven away the fathers from her mission and her country was now at war with France, received him kindly, dressed his wounds, restored him to health and strength and sent him to Louisiana. The last recorded evidence of this woman was in 1721, when the Marquis of Aguayo was formally received by eight chiefs of the Texas Indians, speaking to them through Angelina as their interpreter.

In 1731 it was decided to move these two missions to the San Antonio River. The Mission San Francisco was moved to the river, about twelve miles below San Antonio, and stone buildings were erected. Its ruins are still recognized as the old Mission Espada; while Angelina's Mission was moved further up the river and is now at the lower suburb of the city of San Antonio, in a fair state of preservation, popularly known as the Mission Concepcion, and bears its silent testimony to the religious zeal of this Indian woman. To Dr. Bolton of the California State University the author is indebted for the essentials of this episode. He gives some interesting facts of her career and the story will be concluded in his words:

"In 1715 St. Denis, while on his way from Louisiana to the Mission San Juan Bautista, accompanied by an escort carrying merchandise, had occasion to stop at the Hainai Indian village, on a stream in what is now East Texas, where he had previously traded. Penicaut, who was with him, and who wrote an account of the journey, says, 'In this village we found a woman named Angelique, who had been baptized by the Spanish priests. She spoke Spanish very well, and as St. Denis was familiar with that language he employed her as chief interpreter.' (Margry Deconvertes et Entablissements des Francais V., 405-500, translated in Bolton & Barker's *With the Makers of Texas.*")

From the Spanish we learn that Angelique, called by the Spaniards Angelina, was baptized at one of the missions on the Rio Grande, but when it occurred does not appear. Since Angelina could speak Spanish well she must have been with the Spaniards some time before the journey of which Penicaut speaks.

Her baptism was evidently the result of the missionary work among the Texas Indians between 1690, when the first mission was established, and 1693, when it was abandoned. Angelina was useful as an interpreter for the Spaniards at the Hainai Village, which stood west of the modern Douglas and the stream that flowed by, which up to 1690 had been called Pascua del Espiritu Santo, soon came to be called Rio de Angelina, or Angelina's River, presumably with reference to this woman. In 1716 the Mission Concepcion was founded at Angelina's Village, and Father Espinosa, who established it, tells of finding her there and employing her as an interpreter. (Diary, 1716.)

Belisle, the lone Frenchman, who made his way overland from the gulf coast to Natchitoches, in 1719, passed through this Hainai Village, and in his narrative tells of his talk with Angelina while there. (Margry VI, 244.)

In 1721 she was still at the village and was one of a party of leading personages, including eight chiefs, who went out to meet the Marquis of Aguayo when he made his famous expedition to East Texas. (Pena, Diary in *Mem. de Nueva de Espana*, XXVIII, 33.)

ARANSAS

The origin of this name dates back to 1746. From Dr. Bolton I have obtained the following account:

> In 1746 Capt. Oribio Basterra made the first recorded Spanish expedition to the lower Trinity. Passing the Trinity southwestward from Nacogdoches, he named a stream, which seems to be the San Jacinto, in the Orcoquisac country, "El Rio Nombrado Nr'a Senora de Aranzazos (the river named Our Lady Aranzazu)." He evidently gave the name himself, and it is apparent that Our Lady of Aranzazu was a saint in whose honor he named the stream, just as the Guadalupe was named Nr'a Senora Guadalupe, Bahia Nr'a Senora de Loreto, etc., and he might have added Nr'a Senora Refugio. The reference is "Diligencias Practicades pr Jn Juagn de Oribio Sobre Establissements al Francisces" 1746, entry for February 23.'

In this connection it is proper to state that "Our Lady" has reference to the Virgin Mary, in whose honor many shrines were raised in various parts of Southern Europe, and in Latin America, and their Texas names, Aransas, Guadalupe, etc., were in honor of the shrine of the Virgin in those places. How the name was shifted to the river now known as the Aransas is only a matter of conjecture. Basterra had been Governor of Texas in 1739 and was afterward a captain in the army, with a fondness for exploring. He was in Texas for more than twenty years, spending much of his time west of the Guadalupe River.

BANDERA

This county took its name from Bandera Pass. The word means "flag." The reason for the application of this name to the pass, which is a natural gateway through the Guadalupe Mountains, is not certainly known. There are three traditions in regard to it, two of which are in entire accord with well-known historical facts and virtually connect themselves with them. The pass is about fifty miles northwest of San Antonio, and was directly on the route from San Antonio to the San Saba Mission.

For many years it was a strategic point for the Indians. Yoakum's *History of Texas* informs us that in 1732 an armed force pursued a band of marauding Apaches, who had made one of their numerous forays to San Antonio. Around and near this pass the Indians had their villages, and when they reached this place they made their stand and fought vigorously but were severely beaten by the Spaniards. A tradition was current among the old Manchaca and other families in San Antonio a hundred years ago as to this battle, with the added statement that the Spaniards, after they had severely chastised the Indians, left their flags planted upon the mountain top as a signal and warning that more punishment would be meted out if they resumed their raids upon the settlements.

The Comanches, a few years later, came down into this region, made war upon the Apaches and soon overcame them. Not content with this, they began their raids upon the settlements, and in 1758 destroyed the Mission of San Saba and its garrison.

The government at the City of Mexico had persistently failed to garrison San Antonio with a sufficient force to protect the settlers. In 1759 they induced the Apaches to join them as auxiliaries and with a force of 500 men, a majority being Apache auxiliaries, marched against the Comanches. Meeting a force of 6,000 Comanches and allied warriors, they retired to San Antonio and disbanded. The only hope for protection of any sort now rested upon their ability to treat with the Comanches, and for this purpose Padre Calahorra and other priests were deputed to make treaties. One of the results was the fixing of a boundary between the regions they were to occupy. The Guadalupe Mountains became the line, and a flag upon the mountain was the sign of the treaty. While the treaty was habitually violated by the Comanches, it afforded the only protection the settlers had in after years.

The circumstances and facts of the tradition, which refer to this treaty, were related to a party of gentlemen who were traveling through that region in 1867. They encamped for the night at the county site, and while there some thieving Comanches crept in under cover of the darkness and stole some horses. As soon as it was found out, the sheriff, with a posse, started in pursuit, riding as rapidly as possible to this pass, through which they knew the thieves would attempt to go, but when they reached the pass they found the Indians had preceded them and had left a red flag planted upon the mountain nearby. They immediately abandoned pursuit and returned home.

Upon being asked why they abandoned their pursuit they replied that the flag meant a fight with an armed force of Comanches in the event they went beyond; that the Comanches claimed the mountains as a line which set aside to them all the region to the north and west of this pass under an ancient treaty with the Spaniards (evidently the treaty above referred to), and any thieving Indian band who could get their stolen property safely across that line, was protected by the whole tribe. They relied upon this old treaty to give legal color to their robberies.

San Fernando Cathedral in Bexar County, as seen in 1905.

BEXAR

This name was given in honor of the Duke of Bexar to the presidio, established in 1718, and to the villa, established in 1731, the two forming one settlement on the San Antonio River at the site of the modern city of San Antonio.

Bexar was a town in Spain, about twenty miles south of Madrid, and was long the seat of a dukedom. The nephew-in-law and principal lieutenant of Cortez was a Duke of Bexar in 1521. In 1604 Cervantes dedicated his celebrated work, *Don Quixote*, to another Duke of Bexar.

The Duke, in whose honor the present name Bexar was given, was born at Madrid in 1713 and was the second son of Philip V, the then reigning sovereign. Upon the death of his elder brother, Louis, he became Prince of Asturias, heir apparent to the throne. His mother died in 1716, and in the same year Philip married his second wife. The intrigues of the young Duke's stepmother to have one of her own children preferred to the throne caused much indignation throughout Spain and France, Philip V being the first Bourbon king of Spain, and in the midst of this general sympathy the settlement of San Antonio took place. He ascended the throne as Ferdinand VI (Fernando) in 1746, and died in 1759.

The County of Bexar and the Cathedral San Fernando de Bexar, fronting one of the main plazas of the city, commemorate his name and title. It was during this period also that the name Nuevas Philippinas was given to the province of Texas, but the name "Texas" had become a geographical name a quarter of a century previously and the name Nuevas Philippinas soon fell into disuse.

Bernardo de Gálvez (1746-1786)

GALVESTON

There were three distinguished Spaniards of this name: Jose de Galvez, Matias de Galvez, and Bernardo de Galvez.

Jose de Galvez, brother of Viceroy Matias de Galvez, was born of poor parents in Velez-Malega in 1729. He was educated at the University of Alcala, and later became private secretary of Marques de Grimaldi. In 1761, while an intendant in the royal army, he was sent to Mexico as visitador general, with instructions to inspect and reorganize the administration. In 1764 he was given powers superior to those of the viceroy, and before his return to Spain, in 1771, he supervised the expulsion of the Jesuits from Mexico and sent out the Portola expedition to occupy Alta California. He also recommended the establishment of the intendant system in Mexico and the organization of the Provincias Internas, which reforms were carried out after his return to Spain. In 1768 he was made a member of the Council of the Indies, and later became Ministro Universal de Indies, which position he held until his death, in 1787. He was also given the title of Marques de Sonora.

Matias de Galvez, forty-eighth viceroy of Mexico, was a brother of Jose de Galvez. In 1783, after having served as governor and captain-general of Guatemala, he was promoted to the vice-royalty of Mexico. He died the next year. In recognition of the services he had rendered, the king decreed that no residencia should be held, or, as we would say in America, public business was suspended in his honor.

Bernardo de Galvez (Conde de Galvez), forty-ninth viceroy, was a son of Matias de Galvez, forty-eighth viceroy. Before going to Louisiana he had been a dashing soldier in Durango and Chihuahua. (His career in Louisiana can be learned from Gayarre's *Louisiana*.) At the time of his father's death, in 1785, Bernardo was captain-general of Havana, as well as of Louisiana and Florida. He reached Vera Cruz May 26, 1785, and took possession of his office in Mexico June 17. He was accompanied by his young and beautiful wife, Felicitas Saint Maxent, a French woman, a native of New Orleans. His inauguration was brilliant, as was his whole career.

His short rule was marked by two calamities in the form of a famine (1785) and an epidemic (1786). He instituted important military reforms, continued building the great highway to Acapulco, and rebuilt the palace of Chapultepec. Because of his great popularity, he was feared at court in Spain, some even predicting that he would make Mexico independent.

Becoming suddenly ill, on November 8, he delivered the civil rule to the regent, retaining the military command. He died November 30, 1786, after a rule of one year and five months.

During the war between Great Britain and her American colonies he rendered signal service by furnishing supplies, capturing Mobile and Pensacola from the British, and in various other ways. As a mark of appreciation of this service his portrait was presented to the Congress of the United States as one worthy to adorn the capitol, and was accepted in warm words of appreciation. A detailed account of his services to the colonies is given in Winsor's *Westward Movement.* The portrait was destroyed by the British when they burned the capitol, in 1814.

GARZA

This county was named for the Garza family in San Antonio, a family which had been identified with that city for nearly two centuries. On the maternal side they are lineal descendants of Madam Rabaina Betancourt, who came with the first settlers in 1731. Geronimo Garza, the paternal ancestor, came later and married a descendant of Madam Betancourt, and from this marriage sprang a long line of this distinguished ancestry, identified throughout the long history of that city with its civil, military and commercial activities, and is now one of the most highly respected and useful connections of the city.

Their loyalty to Texas as a province of Spain, a State of Mexico, of the United States, and of the Southern Confederacy, inspired the Legislature of Texas, in 1876, to erect a monument to the memory of the family by naming a county "Garza."

GOLIAD

This word means "gigantic," (large) from Goliath of Gath, the giant of the Philistines. Prior to 1829 the presidio and mission and the little settlements around it were known as La Bahia, meaning "the bay."

In 1722 a presidio and mission was established on the site of La Salle's old fort near the bay. It was given the name Nuestra Sanctissima Senora Maria de Loreto la Bahia del Espiritu Santo (our Most Holy Lady Mary of Loreto of the Holy Ghost of the Bay).

It remained but a few years here, when it was moved up the valley to a spot that is now in Victoria County. In 1749 it was moved over to the San Antonio River, the present site, and in the course of time all of the name, except La Bahia, fell into disuse, but it was now far away from the bay, and in 1829 the Congress of Coahuila and Texas concluded to do away with the paradoxical name and, to preserve some trace of the large presidio, named it Goliad.

Remains of Presidio La Bahia, Goliad. Early 20th century, artist unknown. (Painting in the personal collection of Mark Pusateri.)

GUADALUPE

This county was named for the Guadalupe River. This was one of the rivers named by Alonzo de Leon on his first expedition to Texas in 1689, as told in the diary of that expedition: "Thursday, the 14th (April), we moved forward in search of a great river, which the guide told us we should find, and which we reached at 2 in the afternoon...The river has a good ford; its banks are covered with timber. We gave this river the name of 'Our Lady of Guadalupe,' whom we had brought from Coahuila as our protectress, and whom we had painted on our royal standard."

HIDALGO

This county was named in honor of the patriot priest, Miguel Hidalgo. He was born in the province of Guanajuato, May 8, 1753. At an early age he was sent to the College of San Nicolas, at Valladolid, where he became distinguished as a student. He was then sent to the City of Mexico. In 1778 and 1779 he there studied and had conferred upon him the degree of Bachelor of Theology. On his return to Valladolid he obtained, by successive appointments as cura, two of the richest benefices of the diocese, and finally became cura of Dolores, with a stipend of $10,000 to $12,000. He devoted himself to a variety of occupations independent of his clerical duties, and studied the sciences, French philosophical works (being a French scholar) and political economy. He gave critical study to the doctrines propounded in the unorthodox works. This loosened the hold of the church on many of the non-essentials in its doctrines and led him into a detestation of the despotism of the ruling powers.

On the 14th of September, 1810, he issued his famous Grito de Dolores, or war cry for liberty, and launched the revolution which was to free Mexico from the thraldom of Spain. After several victories over the royal troops he was finally defeated in January, 1811, at the battle known as the "Bridge of Calderon." Later he himself was captured and executed at Chihuahua, July 31, 1811. His head was severed from his body, sent to Guanajuato and suspended in an iron cage by the royalists, while his body was buried in Chihuahua, where it remained until 1823, when, by order of Congress, it was transferred, with his skull, to the Cathedral in the City of Mexico in the Chapel las Reyes, the famous burial place of the viceroys and later of the Presidents of the Republic of Mexico. In 1823 a monument was erected in Chihuahua in memory of Hidalgo and other leaders, and in 1863 Juarez raised Dolores to the rank of a city and ordered erected in the principal square a statue to Hidalgo's memory. In 1873 the Congress of Mexico decided that the national flag should be raised on the 8th day of May in commemoration of his birthday, and President Diaz caused the statue to be erected in 1878 at a cost of $40,000.

★ ★ ★

LA SALLE

This county was named for Robert Cavalier Sieur de la Salle, who was born in the village of Rouen, Normandy, November 11, 1643. He was educated for the priesthood, but his aspirations turning in another direction, he went to Canada with the object of discovering an overland passage to China.

After spending several years in exploring Lake Ontario and Lake Erie, he returned to France and obtained from the king, to whom Canada had reverted after the dissolution of the West India Company, the grant of Fort Frontenac, the spot where the city of Kingston now stands. On condition of keeping up that fort, he received a grant of a wide circuit of neighboring country and the exclusive right to trade with the Iroquois Indians, as a check against whom the fort had been built, but his restless disposition was not thus to be satisfied.

He left his fur trade, his fields, his cattle, his Indian dependents at Fort Frontenac and again returned to France to obtain a royal commission to discover the Mississippi River, and also a grant of a monopoly of the trade in buffalo skins. Successful in this mission he returned to Fort Frontenac with men and stores to prosecute his enterprise, accompanied by Chevalier Tonti, a veteran of the Italian wars, who was to be his lieutenant.

This was in the summer of 1678. Before winter he had ascended Lake Ontario and entered the Niagara River. Passing around the falls, he selected a spot at the east end of the Lake Erie, near where the city of Buffalo now stands. Here he built a boat of sixty tons, called the *Griffin*. He equipped it with cordage and sails, and on the 17th of August, 1779, she plowed her way up

Lake Erie, bearing La Salle, Tonti, Father Hennepin, and several other friars of the Recollect order. Thirty sailors, boatmen, hunters, and soldiers made up the remainder of the company. Having entered Detroit, the strait or river at the head of the lake, they passed through it into the limpid sheet of water to which La Salle gave the name Lake St. Clair. Through this they ascended through another strait into Lake Huron, and through the length of that lake by the Strait of Mackinaw into Lake Michigan and into Green Bay, and after a voyage of twenty days cast anchor at its head, thus tracing what is now probably the greatest highway in American commerce, if we embrace the Welland Canal. From here the *Griffin* was sent back to Fort Frontenac, loaded with the most valuable furs, in order that she might bring back supplies, but she was shipwrecked on her homeward passage.

In the meantime La Salle, with his company, proceeded in birch canoes up Lake Michigan to the mouth of St. Joseph's River, where there was a Jesuit mission, and built a fort. He then crossed over to a branch of the Illinois River, down which they descended, and on its banks, below where Peoria now stands, they built a second fort, and called it Crevecoeur (heartbreak) to signify their disappointment at the non-arrival of the *Griffin*, of which nothing had yet been heard.

La Salle then determined to return to Fort Frontenac on foot, and took with him five attendants. Upon his arrival at Fort Frontenac he found things in the greatest confusion, himself reported dead and his property seized by creditors. Tonti, in the meantime, had been attacked by an overwhelming force of Indians and had fled back to Green Bay, and the two forts were entirely deserted.

Upon La Salle's return with supplies and recruits, he built another fort, which he called St. Louis, and again returned to Fort Frontenac, encountering Tonti on the way. He collected a new company at Fort Frontenac and returned to Illinois, and in 1682 rigged a small barge in which he descended to the Gulf. When he reached the mouth of the Mississippi he took formal possession in the name of his king and named the country Louisiana.

He then made his way back to Quebec, leaving Tonti in charge of Fort St. Louis, and returned to France a third time, whither the news of his discovery had preceded him and created great expectations.

His wonderful achievements, under so many difficulties and misfortunes, made him a great favorite of the king, in spite of the representations of the enemies he had made by his harsh temper and domineering disposition in his business transactions, as well as with his subordinates in his exploring expeditions. The king furnished him a frigate and three other ships, on board of which he took five priests, twelve gentlemen, fifty soldiers, a number of mechanics and a small supply of agricultural implements. They were furnished with tools, and in all about four hundred persons designed for a colony at the mouth of the Mississippi River.

Informed of La Salle's departure from France, Tonti left Fort St. Louis, in Illinois, and went down the Mississippi River to the mouth of the Arkansas River.

In sailing for the mouth of the Mississippi La Salle came too far west and landed on the coast at Matagorda Bay in February, 1685, evidently a mistake in calculating longitude from defective instruments, Belisle having made the same mistake thirty-four years later. He built a fort on Garcitas River, some twelve miles west of Lavaca River, naming it Fort St. Louis, with quarters for his colonists. In the vain hope of finding the Mississippi River he made several journeys eastward, and in 1687 was killed by some of his own men, and his bones lie in some unknown spot near the present city of Navasota.

MEDINA

In writing of De Leon's first expedition into Texas, Bancroft (*The North Mexican States,* Vol. I, p. 400) says:

"Leon started from Monclova, March 23, 1689. Crossing the Rio Del Norte above the Salado Junction, he crossed and named on his way northeastward the rivers Nueces, Hondo, Medina, and Guadalupe."

The translated diary of De Leon, given in the *Quarterly* of the Texas Historical Association, Vol. V, tells us that the river was named Medina April 11, 1689, but does not give the person for whom named. The sergeant major of the expedition was one Medina. The author of the tables used in determining latitude and longitude on their journey was Medina, and this was probably the reason for the name given to the river.

NOLAN

The chief interest which centers in this name arises from the exaggerated importance of Philip Nolan's visit to Texas for the purpose of gathering wild horses, and his murder by the Spaniards in March, 1801.

Of his antecedents prior to 1791 we know nothing. Dr. Edward Everett Hale, in *The Real Philip Nolan,* quotes an affidavit to the effect that one Leal became acquainted with Nolan in 1791, and a memorandum of a transaction by which General Wilkinson exchanged $2,000 worth of goods for 12,000 acres of land with one Hunt in 1796, through Nolan as his agent, would indicate that Nolan was at least twenty-one years old, yet Dr.

Hale quotes from a letter received from Hon. Jno. Mason Brown, which stated that Philip Nolan was born in Frankfort, Kentucky. The ground upon which Frankfort is situated was not surveyed until 1773, and Frankfort was not laid out until 1787. The conclusion, therefore, is that Nolan must have been born as early as the year 1764, and was not, therefore, a native of Kentucky, the first settlement in which was not made until 1774.

His connection with General Wilkinson probably began at Lexington, Kentucky, as early as 1785, when Wilkinson established the first dry goods store in that place. Wilkinson, after the close of the Revolutionary War, resigned his office as brigadier general and went to Lexington. He organized the Lexington Light Infantry, the first military company in Kentucky, which years later became famous. The Indians gave great trouble in that region and he frequently commanded this company in expeditions, going up into Ohio once or twice. His frequent absences from his business necessitated the employment of some reliable, competent manager, and it is altogether probable that Nolan became his manager. The commercial transactions of the region, at that time, were carried on by a system of barter, or exchange of goods for buffalo hides and the skins of fur bearing animals, bacon, flour, hams, dried meat and other products of the region. The only practicable way of disposing of such things was to load them into boats and carry them down the river to New Orleans.

In 1786, although at least one such boatload of products had been captured and confiscated at Natchez, Wilkinson determined to try this method of disposing of his goods, and he succeeded. It is more than probable that he took Nolan with him in the hazardous journey and left him as his representative at New Orleans. While Spain had closed the Mississippi River to

American commerce, it seems that both he and Nolan had found favor with the Spanish authorities and that Nolan, without opposition from the authorities, had established the business of bringing horses from Texas and disposing of them.

His experience in such business commended him to Governor Carondelet, who was then organizing a cavalry regiment at New Orleans, to engage Nolan's services in procuring the horses. Nolan's previous visits to Texas, it seems, did not require him to carry passports, but a permit to enter Texas, signed by the general of the department to which Texas belonged, would probably exempt him from paying the tax per head then in vogue. Just what were the contents of this so-called passport we shall probably never know, as the document was upon Nolan's person when he was killed, but we are warranted in assuming that his authority to re-enter Texas and gather horses was ample. His papers were examined at the instance of the Spanish authorities by the proper officers at Natchez, again by the commanding officer at Arkansas Post, and he was adjudged to have the proper authority for re-entering Texas.

Just why Gayoso, the immediate successor of Carondelet, should be so bitterly opposed to Nolan's second expedition, finds its possible solution in the following facts:

The Spaniards, ever since the treaty of 1763, had occupied Natchez and other places on the east bank of the Mississippi by the mere sufferance, first of England, then of the United States. President Adams determined to take possession for the United States, and in 1798, having appointed Wilkinson commander-in-chief of the army, he organized the Mississippi Territory and appointed Winthrop as Sergeant Governor and gave orders to Wilkinson to dispossess the Spaniards from all their posts on that side of the river. This angered the Spaniards and they determined to pursue the retaliatory policy of excluding Americans from Spanish territory, and this was the state of affairs when Nolan was preparing for his second entry into Texas.

His intention to return to Texas was no secret, and armed with the proper documents from the proper authorities he organized an escort, consisting of seven rancheros (Mexican experts in catching wild horses), eighteen young men armed for protection against the savages, and two cooks. Gayoso, without offering any resistance to Nolan's so-called invasion of Texas, annoyed him in all sorts of ways, and to get rid of such annoyance Nolan crossed the river up at Walnut Mills, some distance above Natchez, proceeded on his way to Texas, presented his passports to the officers at Arkansas Post and was permitted, without molestation, to proceed to his destination.

When he had arrived at a suitable place, he erected a blockhouse for protection against the Indians, built his horse pens and had collected about 300 horses. Early one morning in March of 1801, a squadron of one hundred and fifty men rode up and demanded the surrender of himself and his men. He refused to surrender, and so the attack began. He was killed early in the fight.

While on his way to Texas, Nolan was followed by a squadron of horsemen at a safe distance in the rear. While he was stopping at Arkansas Post his trusted guide, one Mordecai Richards, deserted him and returning to Concordia parish made a voluntary affidavit, in which he said Nolan admitted to him that he was going to take his horses back to Kentucky, and as soon as he sold them he would organize a force of men, return and conquer Texas. Upon this flimsy testimony, and

Gayoso's persistent slanders to General de Nava, Nolan was finally murdered.

It is noted that the testimony against Nolan is from Spanish sources alone, except the narrative of Peter Ellis Bean, chiefly devoted to his marvelous exploits in Mexico in later years.

After Nolan's death his rancheros very naturally deserted to the Spaniards. Richards and two others had deserted, and the other members of Nolan's escort were put in irons and finally taken to Chihuahua, where only nine remained, one of whom was executed. No tidings of the fate of the others were ever heard, except of Peter Ellis Bean and David Fero, who rose to the command of regiments in the revolution of Mexico against Spain a few years later.

Nolan's visit has been magnified as the first filibustering expedition in Texas.

The Legislature of Texas, in honor of this, the first American victim in Texas to Spanish treachery, created and named the county for Nolan in 1876.

★ ★ ★

PRESIDIO

This word means "a fortress garrisoned by soldiers." For the protection of some missions established on the Mexican side of the Rio Grande a presidio was erected. Around this a settlement grew up and the name "Presidio" was attached to it. When the territory on the Texas side of the river was organized into a county, in 1875, the name "Presidio" was given to it.

REFUGIO

This county was named for the Mission "Our Lady of Refuge," in honor of the Virgin Mary.

It was established in 1791, in what is now Refugio County, about fifteen miles north of Copano Bay. The mission was established at the instance of Galvez, who desired its establishment for the double purpose of Christianizing the coast Indians of that region and to prevent smuggling. As a mission it was a failure, the record showing, in 1793, that there were only sixty-seven Indians there. The buildings were of stone, but it was in ruins in 1835, when the Texans, who were occupying it, made a spirited resistance, killing and wounding about 200 Mexicans. There is scarcely any visible trace of the mission there now.

SAN AUGUSTINE

In 1756 there was established on the Trinity River a presidio which was called San Augustine de Ahumada, named in honor of Saint Augustine. There was a small mission on Ayish Bayou, which runs south through the modern county of San Augustine, which was connected with the Presidio San Augustine de Ahumada. It was abandoned about the same time (1772).

SAN JACINTO

San Jacinto County was named in honor of the great battle which was fought near the stream of the name, April 21, 1836.

The stream was named in memory of Saint Hyacinth, the anglicized form of San Jacinto. The name is of ancient origin, with a beginning among the myths of ancient Greece in a story which runs as follows:

> One day Apollo saw a shepherd boy making sweet music upon a pipe he was playing. He drew near him and asked, "What is thy name, noble lad?" The lad replied, "Hyacinthus."

> "Thy name is well suited to thee. Let me play upon thy pipe," said Apollo. Apollo made such sweet music upon the pipe that even the brook that flowed down nearby paused in a quiet pool to listen. Apollo finally returned the pipe, saying, "Hyacinthus, I like you. We will be friends, and you shall go with me to the palace of King Admetus."

> "But," said Hyacinthus, "what will become of my sheep? I must not leave them. No, no, Apollo, I cannot go with you."

> Apollo then said to him, "Noble youth, I love you the better, because you prefer duty to pleasure. I go, but tomorrow I will come again."

Apollo came, and for many happy days they played and talked and learned to love each other as the best of friends. One day they were playing a game of quoits, each wishing that the other might win. Apollo picked up the discus and, making a good throw, would have

won but for a sad accident. Zephyrus, the god of the
west wind, blew the discus so that it hit Hyacinthus
on the forehead. Apollo rushed forward and lifted the
head of the youth from the ground, but it was too late.
Hyacinthus was dead. To preserve the memory of his
friend, Apollo caused to spring up on the edge of the
brook that flowed by, the flower which bears his name,
the hyacinth.

The name was kept green in the memory of the Spar-
tans in their religious rites and festivals to impress the
lesson that duty comes before pleasure.

As the ages passed it became a common name among
the early Christians. In the latter part of the twelfth
century there was born of a noble family in Silesia a
son, who, evincing at a very early age great qualities of
mind and heart, was christened Hyacinth. He was carefully educated at Bologna and became converted to the
Dominican teachings. He took the vows of that order
at Rome in August, 1257, and traveled as a missionary
in Northern Europe and to him, more than any other
person, is credited the spread of Christian influences
through that region. He traveled on foot for forty years
among the fierce tribes of that country and achieved
worldwide fame. He died at a monastery in Cracow and
was canonized several centuries later.

The story is that friars from the Presidio San Augustine de Ahumada, on the lower Trinity, explored the
coast during the period, 1751-1772, and coming to this
stream, endeavored to make their way up, but found
it so choked with water hyacinths they were unable to
push their boats through it and called it the hyacinth
stream, honoring it with the name of St. Hyacinth, or
San Jacinto.

That these hyacinths have from time to time been
so dense upon the bosom of the stream as to obstruct

navigation, there are many evidences. The latest is contained in the official report of Capt. J. C. Oaks, in 1908, to the Committee of Rivers and Harbors of the United States Congress, in which he says:

> On August 9, 1907, water hyacinths were discovered in Buffalo Bayou and vicinity, and an allotment of $500 was made, November 4, 1907, to destroy them and prevent them becoming an obstruction to navigation.

SAN SABA

Authors of respectability have defined this as Holy Savior (San Salvador), but a rather careful investigation and inquiries among Spanish scholars and Catholic priests lead to the conclusion that the name comes from San Sabada (Holy Saturday) and that the stream by that name was known among the Spaniards prior to the establishment of a mission near its banks in 1757, and it is more than probable that the stream was discovered on Holy Saturday (San Sabada), and according to custom in naming streams was called San Saba in honor of that day.

Where the mission was established is near the town of Menardville, in Menard County.

The following from Bancroft's *History* contains a brief account of the mission and presidio established nearby:

> It had been decided to establish a presidio with one hundred men on the Rio San Saba. The expedition, including five padres, reached Bejar at the end of 1756 and proceeded in April, 1757, to the new field. The presidio was called in the viceroy's

honor, San Saba de las Amarillas, and the Mission San Saba was located a league and a half distant on the river. The Apaches were pleased and friendly, but declined, under one pretense or another, to congregate at the mission.

The real motive of the Lipanes (Apaches) for the founding of a presidio and missions was to utilize the Spaniards as allies against the Comanches and other tribes by whom they were hard pressed. The northern inland bands, crediting the Apache boast of their new alliance, became bitterly hostile to the Spaniards and formed a league to defeat them. The Apaches gave warning of the approaching design, which caused so much terror at the different forts that but little attention was given to the protection of San Saba. On the 16th of March, 1758, the savages appeared some thousand strong under the command of a Comanche chief at the mission. Too late to effect a surprise, they obtained admittance by pretending friendship, and soon began their work of destruction. The buildings were plundered and burned. The only survivors were Pedro Molina and two or three soldiers, who managed to conceal themselves, and escaped at midnight. Only a few Apaches were present to share the disaster.

TRINITY

Spanish, Trinidad, "the union of three persons, the Father, the Son and Holy Ghost, in one Godhead, so that all three are one God, as to substance, but three persons as to individuality." Adopted as a geographical name in all Latin-American countries.

The Spanish first crossed this stream in 1690 under De Leon and again in 1691 under Teran. The river, from which the county took its name, was probably named on one of these expeditions. The mission of that name was established later.

UVALDE

This county took its name from Uvalde Canyon, named for Juan de Ugalde, governor of Coahuila in 1778, with the additional power of commandante of arms in 1786.

The Apache Indians had been very troublesome on both sides of the Rio Grande, making forays upon the missions and settlements, robbing and plundering and retreating to the canyons and mountain fastnesses, where they had baffled all efforts to subdue them. Governor Ugalde, soon after he had the military power conferred on him, pursued a raiding band and overtook them at this canyon, where a stubborn fight ensued. The Indians were so completely routed that they abandoned this region entirely.

In honor of that event the stream was afterward called the Ugalde (changed to Uvalde) canyon. When the county was organized in 1856, it was named for the canyon.

VICTORIA

Guadalupe Victoria was first President of the Republic of Mexico. The town and municipality of Victoria were named in his honor.

He was a native of Durango, and an active participant in the struggle of Mexico against Spain. As the organized armies of the revolutionists were, one after another, dispersed by the royalists, he organized small bands and kept up a guerilla warfare.

His real name was Juan Felix Fernandez, but during the war he changed it, taking as his first name Guadalupe, in honor of the Virgin patroness of Mexico, and Victoria as his surname to commemorate a victory over the Spaniards. He was an alumnus of the College of San Ildefonso of the City of Mexico, a consistent federalist during his entire career, and was a universal favorite in Mexico, and particularly of Tamaulipas, whose capital bears his name. He was inaugurated President of Mexico October 10, 1824. During his administration there occurred no national outbreak and his career as President was a great success. He retired from office April 1, 1829.

After his retirement from the presidential office Victoria was elected Governor of Puebla, which office he resigned to become Senator for his native state, Durango. In 1839 he was one of the two plenipotentiaries to negotiate peace with France, after which he retired to private life and died March 21, 1843.

His portrait adorns the national gallery in the City of Mexico.

CHAPTER II,
THE ANGLO-AMERICAN COLONIZATION OF TEXAS

With the beginning and rise of the Republic of Mexico, the settlement of Texas may be said to have begun. It had its inception during the Spanish regime, when Moses Austin obtained permission to settle three hundred families, January, 1821. Moses Austin died in June, 1821, and his son and successor, Stephen F. Austin, took charge of the enterprise and carried it to a successful termination.

In order to understand more readily the difficulties under which Austin labored in preserving his rights under the concession to his father, a statement in brief of some of the principal events of Mexican history, affecting his concession, is given.

On the 21st of January, 1821, the concession to Moses Austin was made by royal authority. In August of 1821, Mexico became an independent nation. In May, 1822, Iturbide became emperor and a national legislative body was assembled, called the Junta Nacional Instituyente. In January, 1823, this body confirmed the rights of Austin, but held that Governor Martinez had no authority to make terms as to the quantity of land the colonists should receive.

A national colonization law was passed in January, 1823, and finally decreed by the Emperor in February, 1823. On the 19th of March, 1823, Iturbide abdicated. The original concession to Moses Austin was again confirmed, April 11, 1823. The terms arranged for the distribution of land to settlers between Austin and Governor Martinez were, for 640 acres to the head of a family, 320 for the wife, 150 for each child, 80 for each slave introduced. As this was held to be unauthorized, the quantities substituted were, a *sitio* (a league) or 2.62 miles square for pasturage purposes, and a *labor*, or 177 acres for farming land, called a labor, as that was the part upon which it was contemplated the settlers were to do their labor.

Under this law Austin's rights were secure, with the advantage to his colonists of a sitio and labor, or 4,605 acres, to heads of families, instead of 640, as under the terms he had arranged with Martinez, and 1,107 acres, or one-fourth of a league, to single men.

This law further provided that the empresario, or person who contracted with the executive to introduce settlers, should receive for his services a premium at the rate of five sitios or leagues and five labors (or 23,025 acres) of land for each hundred families introduced, a great advantage to Austin, whose compensation, under the Martinez arrangement was to be paid by settlers.

In February of 1824, the Congress, then assembled, conferred on the respective State Legislatures the power to form colonization laws, and on the 24th of March, 1825, the general colonization law of Coahuila and Texas was decreed regulating the settlement of the country.

As under this law the rights of settlers were created and defined and the Spanish or Mexican land system was engrafted on Texas institutions. Some of its most noteworthy features are here mentioned.

First, settlements were prohibited within ten leagues (26.62 miles) of the coast and within twenty leagues (53 miles) of the boundary of the United States, without the expressed consent of the National Executive. This forbidden area has been very inaptly called the "Littoral and the Border Leagues."

Second, provision was made for the formation of towns, and four leagues (17,712 acres) of land were

granted to each town, an old Spanish law that had its
origin in Chapter XXXV of the Book of Numbers, where
it was provided that each city established for the Levites
should receive a large area around it for common use.

Under this law each empresario was required to select
a townsite, and for Austin's colony San Felipe de Austin
was selected. Gonzales became the town of DeWitt's
colony; Victoria of De Leon's colony; San Patricio of the
Irish colony; Nashville of Robertson's colony. As this is
no longer on the map, its location was in Milam County,
on a high bluff overlooking the Brazos Valley, where the
International & Great Northern Railroad crosses that
river. Each of these townsites were, without exception,
among the most beautiful in Texas.

Under the law, thirty contracts were made, the conces-
sions covering the entire area of Texas, all of Coahuila
east of the Rio Grande, nearly all of Oklahoma, and part
of Kansas, but as nothing was accomplished under most
of the contracts, they are of no historical importance.

There were many other provisions of the law, favorable to settlers, but these are sufficient to enable a clear
understanding of the history of the period.

The names of the empresarios and others immediately
connected with the colonization of Texas from 1822-
1836 commemorated in county names, are:

Austin
Bastrop
Chambers
DeWitt
Edwards
Gonzales
Leon
McMullen
Robertson
San Patricio

Stephen Fuller Austin,
The Father of Texas.

AUSTIN

This county was named for Stephen F Austin, "The Father of Texas." Within the limits of this county, on a high bluff, overlooking the Brazos River, there stands the old village of San Felipe de Austin where some of the most stirring scenes of the colonial days of Texas were enacted.

Stephen F Austin was born in Wythe County, Virginia, November 3, 1793. At the age of six years he went with his father, Moses Austin, to Missouri, at that time in Spanish territory. At the proper age he was sent to a school at New London, in his father's native state, Connecticut. He was prepared for college there and later entered Transylvania University, at the time the only institution for higher education in the United States west of the Allegheny Mountains. After finishing the course he returned home and was elected a member of the territorial legislature of Missouri, which territory was then taking preparatory steps for becoming a State of the Union. The next year he removed to Arkansas Territory and was appointed to the office of Circuit Judge.

In 1821 his father having conceived the idea of colonizing a portion of Texas, Stephen F Austin resigned his office to aid him in his work. He then visited New Orleans with a view to enlisting financial aid, and in arranging for the transportation of supplies by water to the settlers near the coast. He had reached Natchitoches on his way to Texas when he received the news of his father's death. As the responsibility of carrying out the enterprise had already been placed upon him by his father, he proceeded from Natchitoches to Texas with fourteen companions under the escort of Seguin and

Veramendi, commissioners who had been appointed to receive and conduct him into Texas. Upon his arrival at San Antonio he was cordially received by Gov. Martinez and was authorized to examine different sections of land for locating his colony.

After a short time he selected that portion of Texas extending from the Lavaca River to the San Jacinto River and from the old San Antonio Road to the coast, embracing in a general way the region now included within the counties of Austin, Brazoria, Brazos, Burleson, Colorado, Fort Bend, Grimes, Harris, Jackson, Lavaca, Lee, Matagorda, Waller, Washington, and Wharton.

This region had many advantages, among them were its great fertility, ample rainfall for agriculture, two navigable streams centrally situated, ample fuel, wood for building purposes and fine ranges for stock.

The general colonization law of Coahuila and Texas forbade settlements within ten leagues of the coast and to make the titles of his colonists more certain, Austin contracted with the State of Coahuila and Texas, on the 20th of May, 1825, to introduce 500 families. It expressly authorized the settlement of additional families on the vacant land within the bounds of his original or Moses Austin concession, and not comprehended within the bounds of colonies established by other empresarios. The boundaries of this, usually called his Second Contract were:

> Beginning on the West bank of the San Jacinto River at ten border leagues from the coast of the Gulf of Mexico; thence following its course with the right bank of said river to its source; thence on a straight line north to the road leading from Bexar to Nacogdoches; thence with said road westward to a point due north to a point from the headwa-

ters of Labaca Creek; thence on a line due south toward the source of said creek; thence down said creek to the eastern bank of the same, to the boundary line of the ten littoral leagues of the Gulf of Mexico; thence eastward leaving clear the ten littoral leagues parallel with the coast to the place of beginning.

This embraced practically all the land in the original or Moses Austin concession except the space within ten leagues of the coast; in a general way that land is now embraced within the counties of Harris, Montgomery, Walker, San Jacinto, Madison, Brazos, Grimes, Waller, Austin, Fort Bend, Brazoria, Matagorda, Jackson, Colorado, Washington, and Burleson, and parts of Lavaca and Fayette.

Austin's third contract was dated November 20, 1827 and was to introduce one hundred families within the following limits:

Beginning on the eastern bank of the River Colorado at the place where the said river is crossed by the road leading from Bexar to Nacogdoches; thence with said eastern bank of said river upwards the distance of fifteen leagues; thence eastward on a line parallel with said road to the dividing ridge of the waters of the Colorado and Brazos which is the boundary line between this colony and the colony of the Nashville Company; thence with the line of the demarcation of that colony downwards to the road leading from Bexar to Nacogdoches; and thence with this road to the place of beginning.

This embraced the northwestern half of what is now Bastrop County and the portion of Travis, east of the Colorado River and perhaps a small portion of what is now Lee County.

The term "league" is somewhat indefinite. In land measure a league was 2.62 miles square; in ordinary linear measure, three miles. In either case the site of the present capital of Texas was within the bounds of this colonial grant.

Under the colonization law as it then existed the space within ten leagues of the coast might be colonized by the consent of the President of Mexico.

To do away with all uncertainty of his right to colonize this under the original or Moses Austin concession, he made another contract June 8, 1826, consented to by the President of Mexico on the 2nd of July, 1828, and signed respectively on the 12th and 20th of July, 1828. The boundaries of this, although contemplated that it should embrace the area within ten leagues of the coast, was specifically defined as follows:

> Beginning on the left bank of Labaca Creek at the point where it flows into the sea; thence following along the coast of the Gulf of Mexico to the point where the San Jacinto Creek flows into Galveston Bay; thence up the left bank of said River San Jacinto the distance of ten leagues; thence to the west on a line parallel to the coast to a point on Labaca Creek ten leagues distant from the coast; thence with the left bank of said Labaca the precise distance or ten leagues to the place of beginning. (The site of the present city of Houston is well within this area.)

On the 25th of February, 1831, Austin and Williams obtained another contract to introduce 800 families within the following limits:

> Beginning on the left bank of Labaca Creek at a distance of ten leagues from the coast; thence with said creek upwards to its westernmost source;

thence on a straight line northeast to strike the road leading from Bexar to Nacogdoches known as the upper road; thence with this road northeast to the River Colorado; thence up said river on the right bank to the mouth of Salt or Red Fork ("Brazos, Salado, and Colorado") where it enters the same about fifteen leagues above the mouth of Pecan or De las Nueces River; thence from the aforesaid Salt Fork on a straight line northeast to the height or dividing ridge of the waters of the Brazos and Trinity Rivers and with said ridge south entirely to the principal or main headwaters of the River San Jacinto; down this river to the line of the ten coast leagues and with said line westwardly to the place of beginning.

It was intended as shown by these boundaries that the contract should embrace all of Austin's colonies except the area within the ten leagues from the coast and all of the Nashville or Robertson Colony, but as nothing was ever done toward the fulfilment of the contract and as the Nashville Company contract later designated as Robertson's, was adjudged to be Robertson's, a further consideration of it is immaterial.

Prior to the adoption of a constitution and the establishment of a regular government for the State of Coahuila and Texas, Austin was entrusted with discretionary power in the management of his colony. He exercised that power with moderation and tact but with firmness and wisdom.

After the organization of the state government he was elected a member of the legislature from Texas and served 1831-1832. He was not in Texas therefore when the troubles arose between some of the settlers at Anahuac and the Mexican garrison stationed there—troubles

that resulted in the Battle of Velasco. He hastened back
to Texas and the difficulties were soon adjusted, Bustamente having in the meantime been overthrown and
superseded by Santa Anna who represented the liberal
sentiment of Mexico.

Among other high-handed measures adopted during
the Bustamente regime was a law passed by the Federal
Congress at the City of Mexico prohibiting the further
introduction of American settlers into Texas. Realizing
what a death blow this would be to the prospects of
Texas, a convention of the people was called to meet
at San Felipe to take steps to have it repealed, and to
further other policies necessary to meet the demands of
a growing population. The convention met, and Austin
presided over it. It resulted in nothing practical in the
way of accomplishing the purposes for which it was
called and in 1833 another was called to meet in the
same place. This convention memorialized the government of which Santa Anna was now the head, among
other things, to sever Texas from Coahuila and make
it a separate state, to repeal the decree forbidding further introduction of settlers from the United States into
Texas and other matters. Austin and two others were
commissioned to go to the City of Mexico and present the memorial to Santa Anna. Austin alone went,
but, accomplished nothing beyond securing a repeal of
that law; this he accomplished with the aid of Lorenzo
de Zavala and other friends in that city. At that time
there was an epidemic of cholera in that city as well
as in Texas. In October of that year Austin, although
he had not succeeded in getting Santa Anna's consent
to erect Texas into a separate state, wrote to a friend in
San Antonio advising the people to establish Texas as a
separate state and on the 10th of December he left for
Texas.

His letter to San Antonio having become known in Mexico, he was, while on his way home, arrested at Monterrey and carried back to the City of Mexico, and on the 15th of February, 1834, was incarcerated in a dungeon. On the 12th of June he was removed to another more comfortable prison. In the meantime he demanded a trial.

His case was submitted to some official who turned it over to the Federal Judge, and he sent it to the Supreme Court, which disclaimed jurisdiction. Finally in July, 1835, without a trial, he was released from prison and arrived in Texas September 1st, 1835.

Santa Anna's high-handed usurpations by this time had so aroused the people of Texas that they were organizing in all parts of the state for defense. A general consultation was called to be held at San Felipe in October, 1835. Austin was elected a member of this body, but was called to Gonzales on the 11th of October and unanimously chosen commander of the Texas forces then organized to resist Santa Anna.

The revolution being now well under way the Consultation appointed Austin, William H. Wharton and Branch T. Archer commissioners to visit the United States to solicit aid for the Texans in their struggle and on the 24th of November Austin resigned his commission in the army and left on his mission. He remained in the United States doing efficient work until early in the summer of 1836 when he returned to Texas. He permitted his name to be used as a candidate for the Presidency of the Republic, but was defeated by General Houston. In the organization of his cabinet Houston tendered the first place to Austin, who accepted it, and in October entered upon his duties as Secretary of State. In this position he acquitted himself with great credit and displayed consummate ability.

In his instructions to the representatives of the Republic at Washington he outlined what nine years later formed the principal basis of most of the articles of annexation. While in the midst of his arduous labors he became ill and died December 27, 1836.

On the day of his death the following order was issued:

WAR DEPARTMENT, COLUMBIA, DECEMBER 27, 1836.

The father of Texas is no more. The first pioneer of the wilderness has departed. General Stephen F. Austin, Secretary of State, expired this day at half-past twelve o'clock, at Columbia.

As a testimony of respect to his high standing, undeviating moral rectitude, and as a mark of the nation's gratitude for his untiring zeal and invaluable services, all officers, civil and military, are requested to wear crape, on the right arm, for the space of thirty days. All officers commanding posts, garrisons or detachments will, as soon as information is received of this melancholy event, cause twenty-three guns (one for each county in the Republic) to be fired, with an interval of five minutes between each; and also have the garrison and regimental colors hung with black, during the space of mourning for the illustrious deceased.

By order of the President.

WILLIAM S. FISHER, Secretary of War.

A similar order to the navy was issued by S. Rhoads Fisher, the secretary of that department.

Austin's remains were buried in Brazoria County, but were afterwards taken up and reinterred in the State Cemetery of Austin, Texas.

Austin never married, but many of his kindred who had shared his fortunes in Texas survived him to become prominent and useful in the later history of Texas.

BASTROP

The name of the old municipality of Mina was changed to Bastrop in honor of Baron de Bastrop, called by Saudedo, Chief of the Department of Texas in 1827, Don Felipe Henry Neri, Baron de Bastrop.

He was born in Prussia in 1770 and served in the army for a short time. Later he offered his services to the King of Spain, who sent him on a special mission to Mexico and Louisiana. While in Louisiana he secured a contract to colonize over 500,000 acres of land situated between the Mississippi and Red Rivers, but when Spain ceded Louisiana to France and France ceded it to the United States he transferred his claim to Aaron Burr. He then removed to Mexico and finally to San Antonio, where he was acting as an alcalde when Moses Austin arrived at the place in December, 1820, in the interest of his colonial enterprise.

But for Bastrop's influence with Governor Martinez and his intercession for Moses Austin the concession would probably not have been considered at all. He had known Moses Austin when both were citizens of Louisiana.

In 1823 he was appointed commissioner to issue titles to Austin's colonists, but having to wait for surveys, it was not until 1824 that he issued any titles. He was twice elected to the Congress of Coahuila and Texas, and died at Saltillo while serving in that capacity in 1829.

Home of Gen. Thomas Jefferson Chambers at Anahuac, Texas

CHAMBERS

General Thomas Jefferson Chambers, in whose honor this county was named, was born in Orange County, Virginia, April 13, 1802. He was one of a family of twenty children, his father having been married twice. He received a liberal education in his native state, and at the age of twenty-four became much interested in the rising young Republic of Mexico. He visited the City of Mexico and remained there three years, studying the language, laws and institutions of that country. In 1829, he was appointed Surveyor General of Texas, and was made a full citizen of Mexico by Congress.

On February 12, 1830, he with J. A. Padillo, made a contract with the State to introduce eight hundred colonists, but an examination of the situation disclosed that the area to be colonized was within the United States, in what is now Oklahoma and Kansas, so that nothing was done toward the fulfillment of the contract.

He then applied for admission to practice law and was licensed by a special act of Congress. In April, 1834, he was appointed Judge of the Superior Court of Texas at a salary of $3,000 a year. The Treasury of Coahuila and Texas being proverbially empty, he was induced, a little over a year after he was appointed and when his first year's salary was overdue, to accept land in lieu of his salary. At that time the Congress of Coahuila and Texas had fixed the price of public domain at 4 cents per acre to citizens of Mexico, and as he was a full-fledged citizen he was authorized to take land, and an agreement was made with him by which he was to receive land at $100 per league, and the amount due him in June, 1835, was thirty leagues, or 132,840 acres. As this transaction has been criticized unfavorably by some of the historians and a number of his contemporaries, it is due to his memory and to his descendants in Texas to give material facts.

His salary of $3,000 at the end of one year being over-due, he received half (or fifteen leagues) of the amount of land due him. For his previous services as Surveyor General he received five leagues.

The condition of the country after his appointment and other circumstances were such as to render it im-possible for him to hold any court. The validity of this grant to General Chambers was tested by able counsel, and Justice Roberts in the case of Chambers vs. Fisk, reported in the twenty-second volume of Texas Reports, fully sustained the legality of the grant. Eight of the leagues mentioned embraced the land upon which the city of Austin is located. Notwithstanding this, succes-sive congresses of the Republic and legislatures of the State have never compensated General Chambers nor his heirs for the land condemned for the capital city, though the sales of lots yielded large sums to the Re-public and State.

When Texas was invaded by the Mexican armies in 1835, General Chambers went before the Provisional Council and proposed to that body that he would hy-pothecate his lands and raise $10,000 to be used in procuring arms and men for the defense of Texas. His proposition was accepted, and he was commissioned major general for the purpose. He made a report of his commission to the Texas Congress in 1837, stating that he had sent to Texas 1,916 men, had sold $9,035 of bonds and expended $23,621. His report was approved and the treasury directed to settle with him accordingly.

Some of the arms sent in by him were used as late as the Civil War, and two of the cannons are now mounted

at the steps of the Capitol Building at Austin. He took
an active interest in public affairs afterwards, though he
held no political office.

In 1861, he was elected a member of the secession
convention, and in 1863 was a candidate for governor,
but was defeated by Pendleton Murrah. He then retired
to private life at his home in Anahuac and was assassi-
nated there by some unknown person, March 13, 1865.
His body was interred in the cemetery of the Episcopal
church at Galveston.

DeWITT

Green DeWitt was born in Kentucky on the 16th day
of September, 1797. He removed to Missouri in 1819,
first settling in St. Louis County, and later moved to
Ralls County, where he was elected sheriff.

He went to the City of Mexico and later to Saltillo, the
capital of Coahuila and Texas, and on the 15th day of
April, 1825, obtained a contract to introduce four hundred families within the following boundaries:

> On the north, the old San Antonio road, on the east
> the Lavaca River, and from its head a line extended
> in the same direction as the general course of that
> river up to the old San Antonio road; on the west a
> line commencing on said road two leagues west of
> the Guadalupe River and running toward the coast
> at a distance of two leagues west of said river.

This area embraces in a general way the counties of
DeWitt, Gonzales, Guadalupe, Caldwell, and parts of
Comal, Lavaca, Fayette, and Victoria Counties.

After obtaining his contract, he employed James Kerr to select the site for a town, to survey the lands, and manage the establishment of a colony. Kerr selected a beautiful site on the Guadalupe River for the town and named it Gonzales for Rafael Gonzales who was at that time Governor of Coahuila and Texas.

In July, 1826, the little settlement was raided by the savages, who killed several of the settlers, and the place was abandoned. Kerr then moved to the west bank of the Lavaca and established his permanent home there.

Early in 1828 DeWitt, who had been absent most of the time, returned to Gonzales, which had remained unoccupied, and brought his family, consisting of his wife, two sons, and four daughters, and settled there with other inhabitants of the place.

While on a visit to Monclova, he died there May 18, 1835.

EDWARDS

Named in honor of Hayden Edwards, who was born in Stafford County, Virginia, in 1770.

Early in life his parents moved to Kentucky and he was reared there. He was liberally educated and was a man of large means. About the year 1815, he moved to Mississippi, took with him his family and slaves and opened up a plantation on Pearl River. In 1823, he visited the City of Mexico and later made application to introduce eight hundred settlers in Texas. On the 18th of April, 1825, this application was granted to colonize within the following boundaries:

Beginning at the angle formed by a line twenty leagues from Sabine and ten leagues from the coast of the Gulf of Mexico; thence in a northerly direction, passing by the post of Nacogdoches to a point fifteen leagues above it; thence another line west at right angles with the former, to Navasota Creek; thence with said creek downwards to the upper road leading from Bexar to Nacogdoches; thence with said road east to San Jacinto Creek, and down said creek to the point where it is intersected by the boundary line of the ten border leagues, on the coast, which are reserved; from this point on a line east to the place of beginning.

He immediately proceeded to fulfill his contract. As a considerable part of the country to be settled had been occupied by Spaniards and Mexicans, friction soon arose which he was unable to allay. The conflicts which arose finally resulted in what is known in our history as the Fredonian War, the annulment of Edward's contract and his expulsion from Texas. He had thirteen children who settled in Texas, as did several brothers who afterwards became prominent and useful citizens of Texas, His son, Hayden H. Edwards, represented Nacogdoches in the Texas Congress, afterwards in the State Legislature and in the Secession Convention in 1861.

Hayden Edwards, the empresario, died in 1848, leaving many descendants. For a detailed account of the Fredonian War see Foote's *Texas and Texans* and for family data see Brown's *History of Texas*, Volume 1, page 137.

★ ★ ★

GONZALES

Named for the town of Gonzales, after Rafael Gonzales, Governor of Coahuila and Texas in 1825, when DeWitt's colony was first established. Little is known as to his antecedents or his career, beyond the fact that his administration was without particular incident, generally satisfying to the people of Texas.

LEON

This county was named for Martin de Leon, a native of Tamaulipas, Mexico, where he was born in 1765; in 1795 he married in Sota la Marina. In early life he was much engaged in the wars against Tamaulipas Indians. He entered Texas in 1805 and established a ranch on the Aransas River. Not being able to get a grant of land there, he moved to the east bank on the Nueces, but the Indians became so troublesome that he removed to San Antonio. He was a zealous partisan in the revolution against Spain.

In 1816 he moved to Burgos, in Tamaulipas. In 1823, he drove mules from his ranch to New Orleans. He then chartered and loaded the first seagoing craft to arrive at Matamoros. In 1823, he made known his purpose to establish a colony on the lower Guadalupe, and received authority to locate forty-one families upon any vacant land in that vicinity. His grant was ratified October 6, 1825. In 1829, he obtained a contract to settle one hundred and fifty families within an area of ten leagues from the coast, and complied with that contract, founding the town of Victoria. He died of cholera in 1833. There was some friction between the first settlers and those of DeWitt on account of boundaries.

McMULLEN

John McMullen for whom this county was named was born in Ireland in 1796 and was well educated, being a graduate of Trinity University, Dublin. In 1828, he came to Texas and obtained a contract to settle a colony within the following limits:

> Beginning on the left bank of the Nueces with the boundary line of the ten league coast reserve, thence with said boundary to a point ten leagues distant from La Bahia; thence in a straight line to the confluence of the Medina and San Antonio Rivers; thence with the right bank of said river to the old Bexar-Presidio Road; thence with said road to the River Nueces; thence west with said river downward on its left bank to the beginning.

This was known as the Irish Colony, the territory upon which the colony settled embraced in a general way the area of the present counties of San Patricio and parts of Bee, Karnes, Wilson and Atascosa.

Patrick McGloin was his partner in carrying out the contract. McMullen took an active part in the Texas Revolution representing San Patricio in the consultation of 1835 and convention of 1836. In 1849 he removed to California during the gold excitement and settled down there with his family and amassed considerable wealth. He died about the year 1860.

Sterling Clack Robertson (1785-1842)

ROBERTSON

Sterling C. Robertson was born in Nashville, Tennessee, October 2, 1785, Tennessee at that time being a part of North Carolina. He was the son of Elijah Robertson who accompanied Gen. James Robertson to the present site of Nashville and founded that city, Elijah being associated with him in that enterprise. Elijah was a member of the General Assembly of North Carolina in 1789 and represented the political fortunes of that portion of Tennessee up to its admission into the Union as a separate state. He was associated with Thomas Hardeman who was in the same assembly and also a member of the Convention of 1788 which met at Hillsboro and the Convention of 1789, which met at Fayetteville, North Carolina, to deliberate upon a ratification of the United States Constitution.

Sterling C. Robertson was reared in Nashville with all the educational advantages the embryo city afforded. Upon the first call for volunteers he enlisted in the volunteer army of the United States and served against both the Indians and the British, and was finally promoted to the rank of Major and served with that rank on the staff of General Carroll at the battle of New Orleans, in January, 1815.

When Mexico achieved her independence from Spain Robertson's eye was turned to Texas. In 1823, he made an extensive tour through the province and was charmed with the prospect. Upon his return to Nashville, he determined to cast his fortunes with the country. He interested himself and others in organizing a company for that purpose. After the Congress of the new Republic of Mexico had given over the matter of colonization to the states, Robert Leftwich was sent to Mexico to procure a contract to introduce 800 families. The territory sought for the settlement of the colony was embraced in the following notes and bounds:

> Beginning on the west bank of the Navasota Creek at the upper crossing of the old San Antonio road; thence westwardly with said road to the dividing ridge between the Brazos and Colorado Rivers; thence with the ridge of hills northward to strike the old Comanche trace, leading to Nacogdoches; thence with this trace leading to Navasota Creek. Thence down said creek with its meanders to the beginning.

It embraced parts of what is now Brazos and Burleson Counties; all of Williamson, Milam, Falls, McLennan, Bell, Coryell, Limestone, Navarro, a part of Hill and small parts of other contiguous counties.

The date of the concession to Leftwich was April 15, 1825, and was the first contract made to colonize portions of Texas by the State of Coahuila and Texas. For reasons which need not be explained, the contract was made with Leftwich individually but it was in fact the Nashville Company's contract, and so recognized by Coahuila and Texas, as will be seen in the description of Austin's Third or Little Colony, when it is called the "colony of the Nashville Company" in 1827.

Leftwich after securing the concession returned to Nashville where his health began to decline and he finally died. Robertson then took charge of the company's affairs, reorganized the work, establishing his headquarters for offices of the company at a place on the Brazos River near where the town of Marlin now stands. At the same time he settled further down the Brazos and established a village which he called "Nashville" on a high bluff on the right bank of the river just above the present crossing of the river by the International & Great Northern Railway Company. This was to be the objective point of the settlers who were to be distributed from there to such locations as they chose to settle. It was made secure against the Indians and grew to be quite a village.

About ten miles below this point and where the old San Antonio crossed the Brazos was another point called "Tenochtitlan." A few miles above the village of Nashville a river flowed into the Brazos which had been called by the Spaniards San Andress, but as the Spaniards had abandoned the old missions on the San Gabriel and left that region about seventy-five years previously the new settlers found it virtually without a name and called it "Little River." The protracted illness of Leftwich and the delays occasioned by the readjustment of the business of the Nashville Company, Robertson having in the meantime to assume full charge, delayed the introduction of immigrants so that not until 1829 did any settlers come into the colony. The original contract of the company required the fulfillment of the contract within six years from its date; in other words, the contract would expire April 14, 1831. In contemplation of this he secured a renewal of the contract and went actively to work in securing settlers in the colony.

In the meantime a new and most serious complication arose in the decree by the Mexican government forbidding the introduction of any more American settlers into Texas. At the time of the decree Robertson was in the east organizing and equipping at his own expense companies of settlers for his colony and in 1830 and after the date of the decree, a long line of immigrants in charge of Alexander Thomson reached the boundary of

Texas and there learned for the first time that they were forbidden by the decree to settle in Texas. It was wholly impracticable to return to Tennessee or Kentucky. They had disposed of their homes and all their belongings and they concluded to enter Texas and risk the consequences, many of them finding an asylum in Austin's colony.

As Robertson had a valid contract still in existence permitting him to introduce settlers, he took the American view that the government could not destroy his vested rights. Consequently he continued the work of his enterprise.

In the meantime the decree of April 6, 1830, was repealed but now arose a new difficulty.

The Congress of Coahuila and Texas, having been informed of the disobedience to the decree forbidding the introduction of any more settlers from the United States, declared the contract of the Nashville Company cancelled and the region embraced in his contract was given over to Austin and Williams February 25, 1831. It took over three years for Robertson to have this order annulled and the Nashville Company contract restored which was done April 29, 1834. Desiring that settlers already in his colony should not be left to themselves and to carry out his contract at all hazards, he continued to introduce settlers but on the 18th of May, 1835, it was restored to Austin and Williams and matters were in this situation when the Texas Revolution broke out in October, 1835.

The first clash of arms of the Texas Revolution on the 2nd of October, 1835, was at Gonzales, Texas. Robertson at this date was busily engaged in the east, organizing and equipping settlers for his colony in Texas. As soon as the news of a clash of arms reached him he hastened back to Texas and found that an election was soon to take place for delegates to the Convention to meet on the Brazos, and he and his nephew, Geo. C. Childress, were elected delegates to represent the Municipality of Viesca, later known as Milam. He took his seat in that convention participating in all the deliberations, until a day or two before adjournment, when, hearing the news of the fall of the Alamo, he hastened to his colony, had all the important land papers and other evidence of title belonging to his colonists securely packed in a box, placed in a cart drawn by a yoke of oxen, and entrusted the same to his son, then only fourteen years old, with orders to take them beyond the limits of Texas.

He then organized a company and proceeded with all despatch to join the army of Gen. Houston, then on its way to San Jacinto. Whether he overtook Houston in time to participate in that battle is not certainly known. His name does not appear in the official list prepared by Gen. Houston's direction. On the other hand a donation certificate of six-hundred and forty acres of land was issued to him for participation in that battle before the issuance of which, strict proof was required by law.

When matters had settled down after the battle many left the army by permission to look for their fleeing families who had left their homes upon the approach of Santa Anna's army. Robertson left to find his son, who had been sent with the archives of his colony to a place of safety, and after finding him with the archives he returned. At the election in that year he was chosen Senator in the first Congress of the Republic from the Milam District and served in that body until the expiration of his term in 1839. He retired to devote his exclusive attention to his land matters which as we have already seen were in a most complicated condition at the beginning of the Revolution in 1835.

In June, 1837, an act was passed by the Congress of the Republic of Texas authorizing him to institute proceedings in the courts to determine his rights as to the lands as an empresario.

The case is reported in the second volume of the reports of the Supreme Court of Texas. The case was ably briefed and argued on both sides and Chief Justice Hemphill rendered the decision of the court. Among other things the Court says:

> The law of 1834 heretofore referred to, as restoring to him his rights (after the Nashville Company contract had been cancelled by a decree of the Congress of Coahuila and Texas) treats the contract as his (Robertson's) own, and recognizes no other agent for carrying out the project of colonization. He commenced action, shortly after the passage of the law as empresario and continued to act as such; the witnesses recognized him as empresario and his conduct in that capacity is contrasted with that of other like affairs. His activity, energy and expenditures in encouraging emigration are authenticated and he appears to have been unaided by the assistance, pecuniary or otherwise, of others in the establishment of the colony.

> After this contract had subsisted for five years with but little progress toward its completion, it was suspended by the Act of 1830 prohibiting the introduction of immigrants from coterminous countries. In February, 1831, one or two months before the expiration of the contract by its own limitation and years before the suspensory provision of the decree of the 6th of April, 1830, was repealed, the same territory was ceded to Austin and Williams for the purpose of colonization.

The case was tried before a jury and the court refer-ring to the verdict says:

> They find evidence of one hundred families intro-duced previous to the renewal of his contract; two hundred and twenty-nine families agreeably to the titles issued; one hundred prior to March, 1836, and one hundred and twenty-one previous to that time but not recorded in consequence of the clos-ing of the land office, making in all six hundred families.

It appears therefore that Robertson introduced more settlers into Texas than any other empresario except Austin. This decision was not rendered until 1847. Hav-ing in the meantime retired to his plantation on the Brazos in Robertson County a few miles above the present crossing of the International Railway, he died in March, 1842.

SAN PATRICIO

While this is the name of the patron saint of Ireland (St. Patrick) it properly belongs to the Colonial era of Texas history. It is the name given to the town estab-lished by McMullen and McGloin, the empresarios of the Irish Colony before mentioned. The town of San Patricio was granted, besides lots, four leagues of land, and the county subsequently, four leagues additional.

Henry Clay (1777-1852)

CHAPTER III,
THE AMERICANIZATION OF THE MAP OF TEXAS

The immigrants to Texas from the United States began to honor their statesmen and heroes as soon as any sort of organized government began. Their early attachment to their native country was shown in naming the following counties:

Clay	Madison
Fayette	Marion
Jackson	Montgomery
Jasper	Newton
Jefferson	Shelby
Knox	Washington
Liberty	

CLAY

Henry Clay was born in Hanover County, Virginia, April 12, 1777. His father, who was a Baptist minister, died in 1781. His mother was a woman of vigorous intellect and great energy. She reared her family in comparative comfort but Henry Clay's early years were years of much labor and little education.

It was then that he was often seen going to mill on the Pamunky River, mounted on a scrub pony with a meal bag for a saddle and a rope for a bridle, and from this circumstance he became known as "the mill boy of slashes." Up to the age of fourteen, he had received only three years of schooling. He was placed in the store of Richard Denny of Richmond, and a year later he obtained the position of Deputy Clerk in the High Court of Chancery. In 1792, his family removed to Woodford County, Kentucky.

While employed as clerk in Richmond, he attracted the attention of Chancellor Wythe, who was attracted to him and he made him his private secretary and encouraged him to study law, which he afterward did in the office of Robert Brock, Attorney General of Virginia. Having obtained his license to practice, Clay moved to Lexington, Kentucky, in November 1797. He made his first public speech in Lexington in the summer of 1798, on the Alien and Sedition laws, and thus won his first laurels as an orator. 1803 he was elected to the lower house of the Legislature and served until 1806, when he was chosen United States Senator, to succeed General Adair. After serving out that term, he resumed the practice of law. In 1807 he was again elected to the Legislature of Kentucky and was made Speaker of the House, serving in that capacity until 1809, when he was returned to the Senate of the United States to fill out the unexpired term of Senator Thurston.

In 1811 he was elected to the lower house of the United States Congress and chosen Speaker. He was returned and served for thirteen consecutive years, except for two short periods, one in 1814 and another in 1815, when he was one of the commissioners in negotiating the Treaty of Ghent, and in 1820-22, when he returned home and resumed the practice of law. In 1825 he became Secretary of State in the cabinet of the younger Adams, which position he held until 1829. After his term as Secretary of State expired he resumed the practice of law, and in 1831 was elected to the United States Senate, and resigned his seat with the purpose of not re-entering politics, but in 1848 he was again elected to the United States Senate, and was a member of that body until his death, in Washington, D. C, June 29th, 1852.

He was the master spirit of the War of 1812, and a champion of the cause of Greece. He was the author of the "American System" to support internal improvements. He was foremost in securing the Missouri Compromise, and the author of the compromise measures of 1850, which, among other things, adjusted the boundaries between Texas and the United States. He may be said to have been the founder of the Whig party in 1832. He was nominated for the Presidency in 1844, but on the paramount political issue, the annexation of Texas, he was defeated. He became a member of the Episcopal Church on June 25, 1847, and upon his dying bed whispered to the attending clergyman: "I have an abiding trust in the merits and mediation of the Savior."

FAYETTE

This county was named for the Marquis de la Fayette, who was born at the chateau of Chavagniac, in Auvergne, France, September 4, 1797. He was nineteen years old and a captain of dragoons in the French army when the thirteen colonies declared independence.

He warmly espoused the cause of independence in America, and over the protests of friends he made arrangements to join the struggling colonists in December, 1775. Denied any public aid in France, he purchased a ship on his own account and invited his friends to go with him.

At the instance of the British ambassador, orders were issued to seize the ship, and La Fayette was arrested. The ship was sent to Spain, but he escaped from his guards, and was soon on the high seas on his way to America.

After a two months' voyage he landed at Georgetown, S. C, with eleven companions, and immediately went to Philadelphia and asked for a commission as major general, which had been promised him by the American minister in France. He soon felt the embarrassment of a promotion over native officers and then tendered his services on two conditions, viz: That he should receive no pay and should act as a volunteer. These were accepted, and on July 21, 1777, he was appointed major general by resolution of Congress, and on the next day joined General Washington. He took part in the battle of Brandywine and was wounded in the leg, and also fought at Monmouth. He then returned to France, and remained six months. When he came back to America, he rendered active service until the close of the war, then again returned to France. He visited America in 1784 and 1824. He again appeared in public life in 1787, becoming conspicuous in the French Revolution.

After 1797 he retired to the castle La Grange and lived a retired life. In 1824 he revisited the United States and traveled through all the states from Boston to Georgia, and was everywhere received with the greatest demonstration of welcome, and in that year was voted $200,000 and a township of land. In 1830 he took command of the National Guard and served in the second revolution in France. He died at Paris May 20, 1834. His name is spread over all sections of the map of the United States and most appropriately on the map of Texas, as she was aided in her early struggles by so many, who, like La Fayette, came from distant states to aid in her struggle for liberty.

JACKSON

The municipality of Jackson was created by the Consultation in 1835, when Andrew Jackson was President of the United States, and in 1837 was made a county. Andrew Jackson was born in the Waxhaw settlement in what is now Union County, North Carolina. The Waxhaw settlement was so near the boundary line of South Carolina that for a long time the state of his birth was in doubt.

At the age of nineteen he moved to Salisbury, in North Carolina, and studied law, and about the year 1790 he was appointed District Attorney for that portion of North Carolina now known as Middle Tennessee and located in Nashville. He was elected as a delegate to the convention which framed the first Constitution of the State of Tennessee in 1796, and was elected as the first representative of the state in the Congress of the United States. In 1797 he was elected to the United States Senate, but resigned in 1798 to become Judge of the Supreme Court of Tennessee, which position he held until 1804.

At the beginning of the War of 1812 he joined the army and was made a major general of volunteers and fought the Indians and British. On the 8th of January, 1815, he won his greatest military laurels in the Battle of New Orleans. He resigned the position in 1818 and in 1821 he was appointed territorial Governor of Florida. In 1823 he was again elected to the United States Senate, and in 1824 was the leading candidate for the Presidency, but Jackson not having a majority of all the votes, although a large plurality, the election was thrown into the House, and he was defeated. This was greatly to his advantage, and in the next election he overwhelmingly defeated his opponent, John Quincy Adams. He was re-elected in 1832, and after a stormy career in that office he retired to the Hermitage, near Nashville, in 1837, and died there June 8, 1845.

JASPER & NEWTON

These counties were named for twin heroes of the Revolutionary War, and as they are placed side by side on the map of Texas, they are placed together in this sketch.

William Jasper was born in South Carolina in 1750, and enlisted in the Seventh Cavalry, under the command of Captain Dunbar, of Colonel Isaac Mott's regiment, of which Francis Marion was lieutenant colonel. The date of his enlistment was July 8, 1775, and the period for which he enlisted was three years. At the expiration of his term he re-enlisted in the same command. His record as a private soldier was a succession of gallant deeds, and in the month of October, 1776, he was appointed a Sergeant while at Fort Johnson, in North Carolina. From the Charleston Year Book (1889) which gives the diary of Captain Elliot we learn of the estimate placed upon him by the following extract:

> The President, John Rutledge, this day returning his thanks to the Sullivan's Island garrison for their gallant conduct and behavior in defense of the fortress, and taking his own sword from his side, presenting it to Sergeant Jasper, he said, "No doubt he will soon compliment him with a commission."

The story of his rushing through the embrasure and seizing the flag, which had been shot down and fell on the outside, and taking it, in the midst of a hot fire, from the enemy and planting it safely upon the ramparts, is too well known to be repeated here. He was killed while attempting to plant the American colors on the parapets of Spring Hill redoubt at the storming of Savannah, October 9, 1779. The City of Savannah has erected a handsome monument to his memory.

Newton County was named for Sergeant John Newton, who was the son of a pastor of the Baptist church at Charleston, S. C. He was born in that city in 1752. He enlisted in the same command with Sergeant Jasper and was his Alter Ego in all his exploits. He was a corporal and piper in the same company, but survived the siege of Savannah, to be taken prisoner later at the capitulation of Charleston in 1780, and was one of those who succumbed to smallpox shortly afterward.

JEFFERSON

In 1835 a municipality named in honor of the third President was created in the southeastern portion of the present State of Texas. Under the constitution and laws of the Republic it became a county in 1837, with Beaumont as its county seat.

Thomas Jefferson was born at Shadwell, in Albermarle County, Virginia, April 13, 1743. After a short course in the schools of that vicinity he entered William and Mary College, in 1762, and graduated in 1766. He studied law, and in 1769 was elected a member of the Virginia Legislature. He was a delegate to the Continental Congress, which assembled at Philadelphia in 1775. He was made chairman of the committee which drafted the Declaration of Independence and was the author of that document. He served in the State Legislature until 1779, when he was elected governor to succeed Patrick Henry. He held that office two years.

In 1783 he was again elected to Congress and was made chairman of the committee having in its charge the treaty of peace with Great Britain. In 1784 he was appointed minister plenipotentiary to assist Adams and Franklin in negotiating treaties of commerce with the different countries on the continent of Europe, and in 1785 was appointed minister plenipotentiary to France, and served in that position until appointed by President Washington Secretary of State in his cabinet in 1789. On December 31, 1793, he resigned the secretaryship. In 1796 he was elected Vice President when John Adams was elected President, and acted in that capacity during Mr. Adams' term.

On February 17, 1801, he was elected President by the Congress of the United States, the electors having failed to make a choice. He was inaugurated as President on March 4, 1801. In the inauguration ceremonies "he did not ride up Pennsylvania Avenue alone and hitch his horse to the Capitol fence, go into the Capitol and take the oath; but was escorted up Pennsylvania Avenue by a large force of militia and a large concourse of citizens and entered the Capitol amid shouts and cheers of the assembled multitude, the beating of drums and waving of flags. He proceeded to the Senate chamber, took the oath and delivered his address."

In December, 1801, when he sent his first regular message to Congress, he, for reasons which he explained, did not go in person, and this has been followed by his successors down to President Wilson.

He served two terms as President, making many reforms in the administration of the government, greatly
reducing the expenses, paying off a large part of the
debt incurred by the Revolutionary War, and dispensing
with ceremonials incident to the social functions of the
White House. At the expiration of his term, in 1809, he
retired to his estate at Monticello, in sight of the spot
where he was born. With the exception of a narrow escape from capture by the British during the War of 1812
he lived a comparatively quiet life up to his death, July
4, 1826. During that interim he devoted himself to scientific research and to literary labors, outlining a public
school system for Virginia and busying himself with
other matters pertaining to the public welfare, among
which, the crowning act of his career, was the founding
of the University of Virginia in 1825, in plain sight of
Monticello.

He practically demonstrated that the people were ca-
pable of self-government, brought the masses in close
contact with the government and instilled in the minds
of the people principles of government which have ever
since been universally recognized by the various political parties.

One of his first and most important achievements
was the Louisiana Purchase, which, owing to his ideas
of strict construction, he deemed unconstitutional.
But his friend, Wilson Gary Nicholas, insisted that the
treaty-making clause of the constitution permitted the
act, and the constitutional amendment which Jefferson
suggested to meet the case was never submitted to the
people.

He was, perhaps, the greatest publicist and political
philosopher of his day. His *Notes on Virginia*, *Rights of
British-America*, and his *Manual of Parliamentary Law*
are among his principal published works. He was bur-

ied on his estate at Monticello. In 1892 the Congress of the United States had a ten-volume edition of his works published.

NOTE—The claim is made, and two of our standard histories seem to endorse it, that the county and county site were named for Jefferson Beaumont, but the claim does not seem to be sustained by the facts.

The name was first given to the municipality when it was created in 1835. Jefferson Beaumont did not come to Texas until thirteen years later, and when he came did not locate in or near Jefferson County, but settled in Calhoun County, where he lived until 1865, and while temporarily in Jackson County died there in that year.

Henry Millard, who represented that municipality as a delegate to the Consultation in 1835, was one of the original organizers of the municipality, and Beaumont was named in compliment to his wife, whose maiden name was Beaumont, probably a relative of Jefferson Beaumont, and it is possible the claim that it was named for Jefferson Beaumont came in this way.

KNOX

This county was named for General Henry Knox, who was born in Boston, Massachusetts, in 1759, made a brigadier general of the Continental Army in 1776, and in 1781 a Major General, and became Secretary of War in Washington's first cabinet. He died on October 25, 1808, at Thomaston, Maine.

LIBERTY

This word has become a geographical name eighty-eight times in the various States of the Union. Following a custom that began with the Revolutionary War, the inhabitants of this region named their first town Liberty, and from this the county took its name.

MADISON

James Madison was born in Orange County, Virginia, March 16, 1751. He was prepared for college by private tutors, and in 1768 entered the sophomore class at Princeton College and graduated in 1771. He then studied law and in 1773 began the practice of his profession in his native county. He was elected a member of the Virginia Legislature in 1774. In 1778 he was chosen a member of the Executive Council, and in 1779 was elected a delegate to the Continental Congress and served in that body continuously until 1784, when he was sent as a delegate to the convention at Annapolis, Maryland, which was assembled for the purpose of devising a plan to regulate commerce between the states.

In 1787 he was elected a delegate to the Constitutional Convention which met in Philadelphia. He was a member of Congress from 1789 to 1797. In 1793 he was tendered the position of Secretary of State, made vacant by Jefferson's resignation, but declined to accept it owing to his important duties as a member of Congress. In 1798 he again became a member of the Virginia Legislature. In 1801 he was appointed Secretary of State by President Jefferson, and at the close of Jefferson's administration was elected President of the United States, and served two terms, retiring in March, 1817.

After his retirement from the arena of national politics he was chosen a member of the State Convention of Virginia, called to revise the state constitution. He took an active interest in the local affairs of his county, being at one time president of an agricultural society. He died at his home in Orange County, Virginia, June 28th, 1836.

He was a man of varied learning. He was not only familiar with the science of his profession, but had a critical knowledge of the classics, of the French and Italian languages, and had studied Hebrew. He had studied closely the writings of the French philosophers. He was lawyer, naturalist, scientific farmer, ethnologist, and brought all of his varied knowledge to his aid in his greatest accomplishment, political science.

It was at his instance that the convention was called to meet at Annapolis, which led to the convention at Philadelphia which framed the Constitution of the United States. He was the admitted leader of that body and drew up the plan of government upon which its work was based. By his published essays, which make up the greater part of the "Federalist," he became the chief agent in accomplishing its adoption, and from 1789 to 1797, as a member of Congress, led in those measures that put it in successful operation.

The "Federalist" and the "Madison Papers" are quoted and relied upon by the Supreme Court of the United States in all questions involving constitutional construction. The verdict of posterity justly accords to him the title "Father of the Constitution."

★ ★ ★

MARION

Gen. Francis Marion was born near Georgetown, South Carolina, in 1732. He became distinguished in the War of the Revolution while in command of the forces in South Carolina, eluding the superior forces of the British and making constant war upon the Tories. His command was familiar with the swamps of that region and they were made the hiding and camping places of himself and men, and for this reason he obtained the title "Swamp Fox." He was conspicuous for bravery at the siege of Savannah, at Fort Moultrie and other hotly contested engagements.

He served in the State Senate of South Carolina, and was a leader in all measures contemplating leniency to the Tories. He received from that body a solid gold medal as a token of appreciation for his services in the Revolution. He died on his plantation near Georgetown, South Carolina, February 27, 1795.

MONTGOMERY

This county was named for Richard Montgomery, who was born in Ireland, December 2, 1736, and settled at King's Bridge, New York, in 1773. In 1775 he was elected a delegate to represent Dutchess County, New York in the First New York Provisional Assembly. In the same year he was appointed brigadier general, and was killed at Quebec December 31, 1775.

SHELBY

This county was named for Isaac Shelby, who was born December 11, 1750, at Hagerstown, Maryland. He was a surveyor in Western Virginia (now Kentucky) in 1774; was in his father's company at the battle of Point Pleasant, Virginia; was made Captain in 1776, and commissary in 1777.

In 1779 he became a member of the Virginia Assembly; he was commissioned a Major by Governor Jefferson; he was made a colonel and defeated Ferguson at the battle of King's Mountain in October, 1780; was a member of the North Carolina Legislature in 1781 and 1782 (Tennessee then being a part of North Carolina). In 1788 he settled at "Traveler's Rest," in Kentucky.

From 1792 to 1796 he was governor of Kentucky, and in 1813 he joined General Harrison in his campaign against the Indians. In 1818 he was a commissioner with General Jackson to treat with the Cherokees. Shelby County, in Kentucky and a college in Shelbyville were named in his honor. He died in Lincoln County, Kentucky, on July 18, 1826.

WASHINGTON

George Washington was born at Bridges Creek, on the Potomac River, February 22, 1732. At the age of nineteen he was appointed Adjutant General of one of the districts of Virginia, with the rank of Major. At the age of twenty-one he was sent by Governor Dinwiddie to visit the French in the Ohio Valley on an important mission. Also at the age of twenty-one he was promoted to the rank of colonel.

When twenty-seven he was married to Mrs. Martha Custis, a wealthy widow, who was the mother of two children by a former marriage. Five years later he was elected a member of the House of Burgesses of Virginia, and served in that position until the convention at Williamsburg in 1773. In 1774 he was sent as a delegate to the Continental Congress at Philadelphia, and in 1775 was chosen Commander-in-Chief of the Continental Army. He commanded the armies throughout the war for independence.

On December 23, 1783, he resigned and retired to Mount Vernon, his home. In 1787 he was sent as a delegate to the national convention which framed the Constitution, and was chosen president of that body. He was unanimously elected President of the United States, and inaugurated April 30, 1789. He was unanimously re-elected in 1793 and retired March 4, 1797. In July, 1798, he was appointed lieutenant general, but had no occasion to serve as such. He was a Free Mason of high rank.

On December 11, 1799, he contracted a severe illness from exposure. His physician resorted to bleeding to relieve him, and on December 14 he died at his home at Mount Vernon, Virginia. His name is on every state map in the Union.

Mifflin Kenedy (right) and Richard King

CHAPTER IV,
THE PIONEERS OF TEXAS

The following list of county names by no means represents this large class of early Texans, as will be shown from the various sketches preceding and following. The list will show the character of their struggle with the Indians from 1823 to 1881, when the savages finally left the state.

There is no more comprehensive characterization than the following in Theodore Roosevelt's *Winning of the West*:

> The warlike borderers who thronged across the Alleghenies, the restless and reckless hunters, the hard, dogged, frontier farmers, by dint of grim tenacity, overcame and displaced Indians, French, and Spaniards alike, exactly as fourteen hundred years before Saxon and Angle overcame and displaced the Cyrmic and Gaelic Celts.

> They warred and settled from the high hill-valleys of the French Broad and the Upper Cumberland to the half tropical basin of the Rio Grande, and to where the Golden Gate lets through the long-heaving waters of the Pacific.

> The fathers followed Boone, or fought at King's Mountain; the sons marched south with Jackson to overcome the Creeks and beat back the British; the grandsons died at the Alamo, or charged to victory at San Jacinto.

It will be seen, however, that states in different sections of the Union furnished their quota of the men who assisted in conquering the wilderness.

Counties named in honor of these men are:

Armstrong	Harrison	McLennan
Borden	Hill	Parker
Brown	Hopkins	Parmer
Caldwell	Johnson	Smith
Coleman	Kenedy	Starr
Collin	Kerr	Sterling
Coryell	Kinney	Tarrant
Denton	Loving	Taylor
Gaines	Maverick	Throckmorton
Hall	Menard	Titus
Harris	Montague	Wilbarger

ARMSTRONG

This county was named for "The Armstrong family." There is nothing in the act creating the county, or in the journals of the Legislature, to indicate what particular Armstrong family was meant. There are six different families by the name, some of which held important public positions. James and Cavitt Armstrong were members of the convention that framed the Constitution of 1845, and James R. Armstrong, a member of the Secession Convention, in 1861, and James Armstrong was again a member of the convention that framed the Constitution of 1867. Frank C. Armstrong arose to the rank of brigadier general in the Confederate Army. It would be obviously impracticable to give a sketch of all these.

BORDEN

This county was named in honor of Gail Borden, Jr. He was the son of Gail Borden, Sr., and Philadelphia (Wheeler) Borden, and was born at Norwich, New York, November 6, 1801, and received nearly all his educational training in the schools of that place.

In 1814 the family moved to Kentucky to a place opposite Cincinnati, and Gail, Jr., with his younger brother, cultivated a farm on the site which is now occupied by the city of Covington.

From there the family moved to Indiana in 1816, locating on the banks of the Ohio River, ten miles below the town of Madison, where young Gail remained until he was twenty-one years old. His health having become seriously impaired, he concluded to go south, and to that end loaded a flat boat and went with it to New Orleans. After disposing of his cargo he went over into the piney woods of Mississippi and there engaged in teaching school and surveying land, and was married there.

In 1829 he went to Texas, whither the family of his father had previously removed, and engaged in farming and stock raising, and in 1833 was sent as a delegate to the convention of that year. He was then employed by Stephen F. Austin to supervise the official surveys in his colonies and had charge of the Land Office of the colony under the direction of Samuel M. Williams, the Colonial Secretary of Austin.

In October, 1835, in connection with his younger brother, Thomas H. Borden, and Joseph Baker, he established a newspaper at San Felipe called the *Telegraph and Texas Register*, and continued its publication there until March 24, 1836, when, on account of the approach of Santa Anna's army, he moved it to Harrisburg, on Buffalo Bayou. The Mexican army under Santa Anna reached Harrisburg on the 14th of April, just as the paper was ready to go to press. It was seized by order of Santa Anna, the type pied, and presses and all thrown into the bayou.

After the Battle of San Jacinto he purchased a new press and new type and reestablished the paper at Columbia, where the First Congress of the Republic assembled, and it was published there until April, 1837, when it was removed to Houston, the temporary capital of the Republic.

President Houston appointed Borden to the position of Collector of Customs at Galveston in 1837. He gave up this position in 1839 and accepted the agency of the Galveston City Company, which he held for about twelve years. The leisure afforded him while in this position gave him opportunities for bringing into play his genius for invention. His first achievement along this line was the invention of the meat biscuit, which was exhibited at the World's Fair in London in 1852, and won for him the Great Council Medal and an honorary membership in London Society of Arts. The pemmican made by him was used by Dr. Kane on his Arctic expedition.

Depending largely with this convenient form of army ration, upon the patronage of the government for the army and navy, he invested all his means in its manufacture, but army contractors thwarted his plans, and he became bankrupt. Emerging from this, penniless, he began life anew when over fifty years old, and turned his attention to condensing milk, and in 1853 applied for a patent on his invention. After meeting with many difficulties he finally obtained a patent, in 1856, after having sacrificed about two-thirds of his interest in it. Progress was slow at first, but when the Civil War began in 1861 the demand for the product greatly exceeded the supply. From that time on business grew by leaps and bounds, until now (1913) there are over one hundred and thirty plants scattered over eleven states, supplied by twelve thousand farmers, with milk from over two hundred and fifty thousand cows, and turning out more than three hundred million cans of condensed milk annually. With condensed milk other dairy products are manufactured, the plant at Elgin, Illinois, being one of the largest manufactories of butter in the world.

In the meantime Borden had turned his attention to condensing the juices of meat. At first this extract was made at Elgin, Illinois, but competitors who purchased cheap beef from South America caused him to establish a plant in Colorado County, Texas, where good and cheap beef could be obtained, and while engaged in the business there died January 11, 1874. His body was taken to New York and buried in Woodlawn Cemetery.

He had also succeeded in condensing tea, coffee, and cocoa and fruit juices, reducing the last to one-seventh of its original bulk. It is interesting to compare his method for convenient army rations to the methods used by the Japanese in their war with Russia. In the prosecution of his enterprise he amassed a great fortune and dispensed it with a beneficent hand in various ways. He was a man of earnest Christian character, liberal in all his dealings and loyally attached to Texas. His younger brother, James P. Borden, was a participant in the Battle of San Jacinto, serving as first lieutenant in Baker's company of Burleson's regiment, and was later appointed first Commissioner of the General Land Office of Texas.

Gail Borden, Jr. (1801-1874)

BROWN

Henry S. Brown, the father of John Henry Brown, the Texas historian, was born in Mason County, Kentucky, March 8, 1783. His father's family removed to St. Charles County, Missouri, about 1810. The Indians were very troublesome in that region and he volunteered in a military company just then organized to drive them from the country and had his first war experience at the battle of Fort Clark (Peoria). He was married in 1814, and began trading between St. Louis and New Orleans. In 1819 he moved to Pike County, Missouri. He was a friend of Moses Austin, and visited Texas about 1823, and in 1824 returned with a stock of goods for the Indian and Mexican trade. In 1825 he organized a company of men to go in search of his brother, who had been captured by Indians, and after a fruitless search, going over three hundred miles into the interior, he returned to the Brazos. In July, 1826, his brother returned from captivity. Brown engaged in merchandising, trading with the settlers at San Antonio and on the Brazos. From time to time he commanded organized bodies in pursuit of Indians. In one of these expeditions he pursued the savages as far as the county which bears his name. When trouble arose in 1832 with Mexican authorities he organized a company and was in command at the Battle of Velasco. He was an active member of the convention of 1832. He died of cholera during an epidemic of that disease at Columbia, Texas, July 26, 1834.

CALDWELL

Mathew Caldwell ("Old Paint") was born in Kentucky,
in 1798. His father's family removed to Missouri in 1818.
From Missouri he came to Texas in 1833 and settled
in what is now Sabine County. He represented that
municipality in the convention of 1836, and was one
of the signers of the Declaration of Independence. He
later removed to Gonzales and participated in a number of engagements with Indians, being in command
of a company of Rangers in 1838 and 1839. In 1840
he was one of the commanders in the battle against
the Comanches at Plum Creek, near the present town
of Lockhart. In 1841 he commanded a company in
the Santa Fe Expedition, was captured and carried to
prison in Mexico and released in July, 1842, In September, 1842, he was chosen commander of a force of two
hundred men to meet the invading force of the Mexican
General Woll. The historian, Brown, says:

> At sunset on the 17th (September) they marched
> for the balance of the night over the country with-
> out any road, and about midnight took position
> on the east bank of a creek a little below where
> New Braunfels is now situated, and camped there
> until the 18th, just one week after Woll had taken
> San Antonio. Woll's force consisted of 400 cavalry,
> 1050 infantry, and two pieces of artillery. Caldwell
> dispatched Hays and his scouts to challenge the
> Mexicans to attack them, thinking that 202 Texans
> could whip 1450 Mexicans in this position. In a
> few moments they were charged by 400 Mexicans.
> About one o'clock Woll arrived with 800 men and
> two pieces of artillery. After a desperate struggle of
> twenty minutes the Mexicans fell back and at sun-

set retired to San Antonio, and the next day began their retreat to the Rio Grande.

After the pursuit of Woll, Caldwell returned to Gonzales and died there December 28, 1842.

COLEMAN

Robert M. Coleman, in whose memory this county was named, was born in Kentucky in 1799 and came to Texas in 1832.

His experience in Indian warfare in Kentucky prompted his appointment as captain of the first ranging company of Texas doing service on the extreme frontier of Bastrop County and the region north of what is now Williamson, Burnet, and other regions exposed to the Indians, as far east as the headwaters of the Navasota River. When trouble began with Mexico, in 1835, he resigned his position to accept a place as a member of the Consultation, and again was elected a member of the convention of 1836 from Bastrop. He served in that body, and became one of the signers of the Declaration of Independence. When the convention adjourned he hastened to join the army, becoming a volunteer aide on the staff of General Houston, and served as such in the Battle of San Jacinto.

He was drowned in the Brazos at Velasco in 1838. One year later his widow and son were killed by Indians at their home in Bastrop County.

COLLIN

Collin McKinney, in whose honor this county was named, was born April 17, 1776, in New Jersey. In 1780 he removed with his father's family to "Crab Orchard," in what is now Kentucky. Here he became accustomed to Indian warfare. In the winter of 1823-24 he left Kentucky and located near where the city of Texarkana is situated, and from there, in 1831, removed to Hickman's Prairie, in what is now Bowie County. While residing there was elected a member of the Constitutional Convention in 1836, and was a signer of the Declaration of Independence. In 1840 he removed to what is now Collin County, which was named in his honor and the county seat was named McKinney. He represented this county two terms in the Legislature and then retired from public life. He died at his home in Collin County September 8, 1861, and his body was buried near Van Alstyne.

CORYELL

James Coryell, in whose honor Coryell County was named, was born in Tennessee in 1796. When quite a young man he went to Illinois, and from there came to Texas about the year 1828, traveling down the Mississippi River to New Orleans, and from there to Velasco and on to San Antonio. In 1831 he joined a company made up by the brothers James and Rezin P. Bowie, for the purpose of finding the old San Saba silver mines. He survived the famous Indian fight which took place while on their way and returned to San Antonio. Later on he came over to the Brazos, near where Marlin is now situated, making his home with the family of Arnold Cavitt.

In 1835 Coryell went with Cavitt to survey and locate land on what is now called Coryell Creek, in Coryell County. Early in 1836 he joined a company for defense against the Indians. While stationed at Viesca, near the falls of the Brazos, Coryell, with some companions, had gone about half a mile on the road to Perry's Springs, when they found a bee tree which they cut down, and were sitting around eating the honey and talking. In a short time they heard a noise as of sticks breaking. They looked up and saw twelve Indians. Coryell had told the party that he had been sick and was unable to run. Coryell rose to his feet. One of the guns in the party was empty, one failed to fire and Coryell's was the only one left. Those who had no guns ran, and Coryell and the Indians fired at each other at the same time. Coryell fell, grasping some bushes. They then came up and scalped him. Berry, one of the party whose gun had failed to fire, tried it again, but it failed again and he made his escape. There were six men in the party, but Coryell was the only one killed, May 27, 1837.

He was an experienced frontiersman, an excellent backwoodsman and a brave soldier.

DENTON

John B. Denton, the son of a Methodist minister, was born in Tennessee in September, 1806. In early life his parents moved to Indiana, where his father soon died. He was then apprenticed to a blacksmith, who took him to Arkansas about 1822. At the age of 17 he left the blacksmith and during the few next years was licensed to preach, and married.

As an orator he soon became famous. On December 10, 1836, by appointment of the Methodist Episcopal conference of Missouri, he came over into Texas and settled near Clarksville, in Red River County. Receiving an insufficient support from the missionary society of the church, he studied law, and in six months was licensed to practice and was engaged in the practice, supporting himself and family while he kept up his missionary work.

In May, 1841, General Tarrant made a campaign in the west against the Indians and had Denton as his aide. Moving out as far as Village Creek, in what is now Tarrant County, they encountered the savages and defeated them in a desperate battle. There were a number of Indian villages at several places on the creek and the object of the campaign was to drive them off and destroy their villages. The place where this fight took place was on the creek in sight of the present crossing of the Interurban Railway between Fort Worth and Dallas.

After the fight Denton was sent out with ten men to scout the country, and going east his men were attacked from ambush just as they were entering one of the forks of the Trinity, and Denton was killed. After he was shot, his men took his body from his saddle, and after wrapping it with a blanket, carried it to the prairie on the south side of the creek and buried it. The settlers and old frontiersmen, in 1860, exhumed the remains and buried them on Chisholm's Ranch, and in 1901 the Old Settlers' Association of Denton County again exhumed the remains and reburied them in the courthouse square in Denton, amid imposing ceremonies, and erected a suitably inscribed monument to his memory. His oldest son, Dr. A. N. Denton, was a member of the Thirteenth Legislature, and from 1885 to 1888 was Superintendent of the State Lunatic Asylum at Austin, Texas.

GAINES

James Gaines was born in Culpepper County, Virginia, in 1779. He was a brother of Gen. Edward Pendleton Gaines. He accompanied his brother, then a lieutenant in the United States Army, to Nashville in 1803, and aided him in making a survey of the waterway extending from Nashville down the Cumberland River to the Ohio and from there to New Orleans.

He went with the United States troops to Natchitoches and vicinity in 1805 and established a mercantile business and a ferry across the Sabine River near the northeast corner of what is now Shelby County, where the old road leading from San Antonio to Natchitoches crossed that river.

He remained here in business until 1812, when, being in hearty sympathy with the revolution of Mexico against Spain, he joined the Republican Army of the North under Gutierres and Magee, but with many other Americans resigned from the army after the defeat of Elisondo at San Antonio and returned to Gaines' Ferry and resumed business.

In 1836 he was elected as a delegate from Sabine to the Constitutional Convention and was a signer of the Declaration of Independence. In 1839 he represented the county of Sabine in the Congress of the Republic of Texas and later moved to Bastrop County, where he was residing when the gold excitement of 1849 lured him to California. He made that state his permanent home and died there a few years later.

HALL

Warren D. C. Hall was born in Gullford County, N. C, in 1788, studied law and went to Louisiana, locating at Natchitoches. He joined the Republican Army of the North, under Gutierres and Magee, and was made captain of a company in that expedition. Gutierres had escaped the bloody vengeance which Hidalgo, his leader in the revolution of Mexico against Spain, had suffered, and great sympathy was felt in the southwest for the cause of liberty in Mexico. Hall was a warm supporter of the cause and shared in all the engagements against the Royalists in this expedition, but when, under an order from Gutierres, some of the prisoners captured at Alazan Heights were cruelly butchered, he resigned his command and returned to Louisiana. In 1817 he again joined a similar expedition under Aury, but this expedition, after reaching Sota La Marina, returned to Louisiana. He finally removed to Texas in 1835, locating in Brazoria County, and for a time was Adjutant General under President Burnet. He then retired to private life and died on Galveston Island in 1868.

HARRIS

John R. Harris, in whose honor Harris County was named, was born at East Cayuga, New York, in October, 1790, and was reared and educated there. He joined the United States army and served in the War of 1812, commanding a company in the regiment of which his father was Colonel. Both were honorably mentioned by General Scott. He was married to Jane Birdsall in 1816, removed to Missouri, locating near St. Genevieve, where he made the acquaintance of Moses Austin, and became interested in his scheme of colonizing Texas.

Making up his mind to come to Texas in 1821, he carried his family back to New York, there to remain until he could settle. Having made a contract to complete a public building in Vincennes, Indiana, he first went there, and a little over a year later came to Texas. He obtained title to a league of land from the Mexican government in July, 1824, which he located at the junction of Bray's Bayou and Buffalo Bayou. In 1826 he laid out a town which he called Harrisburg, and a year later brought out machinery for a grist mill, sawmill, a blacksmith and carpenter shop, and erected a store, thus forming the nucleus of a town. He also became interested in one of the boats plying between Buffalo Bayou and New Orleans, and in a schooner called the *Rights of Man* which, under command of one of his brothers, ran between Harrisburg and New Orleans, and the Mexican ports. He was appointed Alcalde, and held his court under a magnolia tree, where the cotton compress of Wald and Nevil is now located. While in New Orleans on business, he was taken ill with yellow fever and died there August 18, 1829, leaving a widow and four children. The municipality, afterward established, took its name from the town and when counties were created in 1837 the name Harris was substituted for Harrisburg. The old town is now a suburb of the city of Houston.

HARRISON

This county was named in honor of Jonas Harrison. Although he has many descendants in Texas, few facts as to his career are available. In a document on file in the General Land Office to which is appended his original signature, he stated that he was a native of New Jersey and with his wife and seven children came to Texas in 1821. This was the year of Long's last expedition. With his wife and children he settled conveniently near the Louisiana line in what is now Shelby County and lived there the remainder of his days. He was a man of superior intelligence, popular address and was public spirited. He was a lawyer by profession but living as he did, so many years before there was any organized government or courts, he sustained himself and family on his farm. In 1832 and 1833, he represented his section (Tenaha) in the convention for separate statehood, which appears to have been his last public service. He died in 1837, and his remains were buried on his farm.

HILL

Dr. George W. Hill was born on Hill Creek in Warren County, Tennessee, April 22, 1914. After attending the common schools of that vicinity he took a college course in Wilson County, Tennessee, and from there went to Transylvania University, where he completed a course in medicine. At the age of twenty-three he came to Texas and located in Old Franklin in Robertson County, and began the practice of his profession, and was there married to Matilda Slaughter. At the solicitation of President Houston he accepted the office of Indian Agent and in 1840 or 1841 moved out to Spring

Hill, now in Navarro County. He was elected to the Texas Congress and served for the years 1839, 1840, 1841 and 1842 and in 1843 was appointed Secretary of War by President Houston. He was reappointed by President Jones in 1844 and served until the Annexation. He afterward served in the Texas Legislature.

During all these years he practiced his profession when duty and opportunity called, exposing himself at all times to the many dangers from savages and frontier life and in this way greatly endeared himself to the people. He died at Spring Hill, Navarro County, and his body was buried there, May 29, 1860.

HOPKINS

This county was named for the pioneer family Hopkins of which David Hopkins was the patriarch.

David Hopkins was born in Indiana in 1825 and came to Texas with his parents in 1840 and settled in Lamar, then a part of Red River County, where his parents died. David removed into what is now Hopkins County in the winter of 1843-4 and married Annie Hargrave in 1846. There were several children of the marriage. Shortly after moving down there several members of the family of his father came, among them A. J. Hopkins, who was elected the first County Clerk of the county after its organization in 1848, and died in the same year. When the Hopkins family moved into that region, the settlements were few and much scattered and for several years they were, like most other people on the extreme frontier, greatly harassed by the Indians.

JOHNSON

Middleton T. Johnson, born in South Carolina in 1815, came to Texas in 1839 and located in Shelby County. He represented that county in the last Congress of the Republic of Texas in 1845. At the commencement of the United States-Mexican War he volunteered as a soldier in the United States Army and served throughout the war. In 1848 he was elected lieutenant colonel of Bell's Regiment of Texas Rangers, and put in command of the district of Red River, which extended far out on the northwestern frontier. He served alternately in the Ranger service and in the Legislature up to 1860. In that year Governor Houston commissioned him to raise a regiment for the ranger service, and he was engaged in that service when elected a delegate to the Secession Convention in 1861. He was then commissioned as a colonel of a regiment in the Confederate Army and served throughout the Civil War. He returned to Texas in 1865 and was elected a member of the State convention which assembled in February, 1866, and died while a member of that body in March, 1866.

KENEDY

This South Texas county is named for pioneering rancher Mifflin Kenedy. Born in Chester County, Pennsylvania in 1818 to Quaker parents, Kenedy received his education in the county schools. In 1834, he sailed on the *Star of Philadelphia*, bound for Calcutta, as a cabin boy. In 1836, he was teaching school in Pennsylvania when he made a career change to river navigation. For a decade, he clerked and captained on steamers running on the Ohio, Missouri, Mississippi, Apalachicola and Chattahoochie rivers. During one trip to Florida, he met Richard King, who would later become his partner in both the steamboating and ranching trades. During the Mexican War, Kenedy commanded the *Corvette*, transporting troops and supplies to points on the Rio Grande for the United States Army.

Kenedy began his ranching career in the 1850s with a flock of Merino sheep brought from Pennsylvania to South Texas. For most of the 1860s, he was a full partner in the Santa Gertrudis Ranch with Richard King. Since cattle had yet to become a valuable commodity, Kenedy, in partnership with King, continued to engage in river trade throughout the Civil War, successfully shipping much needed cotton along the Rio Grande.

He was among the first Texas ranchers to fence his lands and in 1869, Kenedy enclosed his 242,000 acre Laureles ranch on three sides with thirty-six miles of fence. In 1876, he partnered with Uriah Lott in the building of a railroad line from Corpus Christi to Laredo, the San Diego & Rio Grande line. After selling Laureles in 1882, he purchased 400,000 acres of land in what is now Kenedy County and created the La Parra Ranch, which he also fenced in. In 1885, he financed Lott's building of the San Antonio & Aransas Pass railway.

In 1852, Mifflin Kenedy took the Mexican widow Petra Vela de Vidal as his wife. She brought six children to the marriage and the Kenedys had six children born of their union. Kenedy died in Corpus Christi on March 14, 1895 and was buried in Brownsville.

★ ★ ★

KERR

James Kerr was born near Danville, Kentucky, September 21, 1790. He was the son of a Baptist minister, and removed with his father's family to St. Charles County, Missouri, in 1808, and in 1812 volunteered in the United States Army and was promoted to the rank of lieutenant. He studied law but never practiced.

He was married in 1819 to the daughter of General James Caldwell, Speaker of the House of Representatives, at St. Genevieve, Missouri. He served several terms as sheriff of St. Charles County, and then removed to St. Genevieve and was twice elected a member of the Legislature from that county, and in 1824 was elected to the State Senate, which position he resigned in 1825 to become general manager of DeWitt's Colony. In the same year he arrived in Texas with his family. Leaving his family on the Brazos, he proceeded to DeWitt's Colony on the Guadalupe. In company with Erastus "Deaf" Smith, he reached the Guadalupe in June and began work.

Soon after his departure from the Brazos his wife and two children died, leaving to his care an infant daughter. He went vigorously to work and before July, 1826, had laid out the town of Gonzales, when settlers began to arrive.

On July 3, during his absence, the Indians attacked the settlement, killing three of his men, and Kerr for a time abandoned the place and moved over on the lower Lavaca River, making his permanent home there, but managing the affairs of the colony. He was a member of the conventions of 1832 and 1833 and in 1835 participated in the engagement at Fort Lipantitian on the west bank of the Nueces River. He was also a member of the Consultation in 1835 and of the Constitutional convention of 1836, which declared independence, and was a member of the Third Congress of the Republic of Texas.

He died at his home on the Navidad River in Jackson County, December 23, 1850.

KINNEY

H. L. Kinney, the founder of Corpus Christi, was born in Pennsylvania in 1813, and came to Texas in 1838. In 1840 he located near the present site of Corpus Christi and went to merchandising. He was elected a member of the First State Constitutional convention in 1845 and represented that section in the Legislature several terms. In 1856 he promoted an expedition to Central America and became a candidate for governor of one of the states of Nicaraugua. He was finally defeated and returned to Texas broken in fortune. He later held several minor offices. He became involved in the difficulties between the Rohos and Crinolines at Matamoros and was killed there in July, 1861.

LOVING

Oliver Loving was born in Hopkins County, Kentucky, in 1813, and was reared and educated there. He married Susan D. Morgan of Muhlenburg County in that state. In 1839 he came to Texas, located in Lamar and in 1840, removed to Collin County, settling near the site of the present town of Plano, where he engaged in farming and stock raising. All supplies of merchandise and all products of the farm were carried in ox wagons to and from Jefferson, and occasionally to and from Houston, and he was engaged much of his time in hauling freight.

In 1850 he hauled supplies for the United States government from Jefferson to Port Belknap (Young County.)

In 1855 he removed to Palo Pinto County, locating in a valley named for him, Loving's Valley. Greatly enlarging his business of raising horses and cattle, sometimes he sent large herds as far east and north as Illinois, and in 1860 drove the first herd of cattle ever sent to Colorado. During the Civil War he removed his family to Weatherford and furnished from his ranch large supplies of cattle and hogs to the Confederate government. In 1866 he formed a partnership with Charles Goodnight and 1867 they started with a herd of steers to New Mexico. While on his way up the Pecos River he was shot by Comanche Indians, and was taken to Fort Sumner, where he died and was temporarily buried. In 1868 his body was removed to Weatherford and reinterred.

MAVERICK

Samuel A. Maverick was born in Pendleton District, South Carolina, in 1803. After attending the preparatory schools of his native state he was sent to Yale College at New Haven, Connecticut, and after finishing the course of study there he went to Virginia and studied law.

In 1835 he came to Texas, located at San Antonio and was there when the Texas Revolution began. Under Ben Milam he took part in the storming and capture of Bexar. Being familiar with the place, he rendered invaluable aid in outlining the course of the storming party. He then adopted San Antonio as his home, and with Juan Antonio Navarro, was sent as a delegate to the convention which declared independence and framed the Constitution of the Republic of Texas in March, 1836.

In 1842, during a session of the District Court in San Antonio, he, with members of the court and other prominent citizens, was captured by General Woll, who made a raid into Texas from the Rio Grande. He was taken to Castle Perote, on the road from Vera Cruz to the City of Mexico, where with a ball and chain he was made to labor on the public works. After his release from prison he returned to San Antonio, and in 1845 represented Bexar County in the State Constitutional Convention, afterward serving several terms in the State Legislature. His last public service was to negotiate a surrender of United States property in San Antonio to the Confederate Government in 1861. He died in San Antonio in 1870, leaving a large family surviving him.

"Maverick" has become an American word and as such has been a subject of misapprehension. The irony of fate has in this case an apt illustration in the following statement of Honorable George M. Maverick, one of the sons of S. A. Maverick:

> Late in the year 1845, Samuel A. Maverick was temporarily residing at Decrow's Point on Matagorda Bay. He was a lawyer with a strong propensity to speculation in land.

> During that period, a neighbor becoming indebted to him in the sum of $1,200, paid the debt in cattle, transferring 400 head at $3.00 per head. There was no market for cattle in those days, the hides only being marketable. He did not want the cattle, but it was a case of cattle or nothing, so he took them and left them in charge of a colored family while he returned to San Antonio. In 1853 the cattle were removed from the coast up to Conquista, fifty miles below San Antonio. Here as before, under the distinguished management of the colored family the

cattle were left to graze, to fatten and to wander away. Mr. Maverick was absorbed in his real estate business in San Antonio. About one-third of the calves were branded, so that in 1865 the entire plant or brand was estimated at only 400 head. To the ingenuous mind the explanation is clear, that the branding of "Maverick's" was "square." The neighbors shrewdly surmised that all unbranded calves and yearlings were mavericks, and the lawful property of the first man who could get his brand upon them, this being at that time the only evidence of ownership. About the year 1856 he sold the entire herd, still only 400 head, to A. Toutant Beauregard, a brother of the distinguished Confederate General, at $6.00 per head. With the exception of this experience, Mr. Maverick never owned any cattle except probably a few milk cows to supply his domestic wants.

MENARD

This county was named for Colonel Michael Branaman Menard, who was born in the village of La Prairie, near Montreal, Canada, December 5, 1805. His parents were French.

At the age of 16 he engaged in the northwestern fur trade in the employ of an American company at Detroit. Later he went to Missouri at the solicitation of his uncle, Pierre Menard, then Lieutenant Governor of the Territory of Missouri and an extensive fur trader, and for several years was the manager of his uncle's business. Becoming attached to the Indians, he determined to remain among them and was elected chief of the principal tribe of the Shawnees, which station he held for several years.

In 1833, Colonel Menard came to Texas and settled near Nacogdoches, where he traded with the Mexicans and Indians. He then became interested with McKinney and Williams in the construction of a mill and trading post on a small stream flowing into the Trinity River near the present line of Polk County, named for him, Menard Creek.

When the Texas Revolution broke out the Mexicans endeavored to incite the Indian tribes on the frontier to overrun and desolate the country. At the solicitation of the Texas government, Colonel Menard went among them, and by his personal exertion prevented an invasion and kept them quiet. He was a member of the convention which declared the independence of Texas and framed the Constitution of the Republic.

In December, 1836, at the first session of the First Congress, Colonel Menard obtained for the price of $50,000 a grant from Congress for a league of land on which the city of Galveston now stands, then unoccupied by a single habitation. He laid out the town and, associating himself with a number of other gentlemen, he formed the Galveston City Company and was its first president, and thus launched the enterprise of the Island City with which he was identified from that date until his death.

He represented Galveston County in the Congress of Texas in 1839 and was the author and powerful advocate of the system of finance by the issue of exchequer bills which, failing to pass that session, was recommended by President Houston the next session and adopted, and provided a revenue that saved the country.

Colonel Menard was a man of rare intelligence and noble character and of the highest order of enterprise and patriotism. He possessed a mind of striking originality, and was most agreeable in business and intercourse. He stood over six feet in height, was of strong muscular build, and possessed undoubted courage. Colonel Menard left a widow, who became the wife of Colonel J. S. Thrasher, and a son, Daniel Menard, all of whom are dead. He died September 2, 1856, of carbuncle. His funeral took place from the Cathedral in Galveston, and his remains were followed to their last resting place in the Catholic Cemetery by almost the entire community.

MONTAGUE

Daniel Montague was a son of Richard Montague. He was born at South Hadley, Massachusetts, August 22, 1798. He received a good education at his home and chose the profession of surveyor and civil engineer.

He left Massachusetts about 1820 and located in Louisiana, where he was a successful surveyor for about fifteen years. Hearing of the fall of the Alamo and the massacre at Goliad, he left his family in Louisiana and hastened into Texas, but finding upon his arrival that San Jacinto had been won and Santa Anna a prisoner, he returned to Louisiana and settled up his business affairs.

In the fall of 1836 he came to Texas with his family and settled at "Old Warren" on the Red River in what is now Fannin County. He was appointed the first surveyor of the old Fannin land district. As the surveyors were the most hated among all the newcomers by the Indians, his scalp became the special object of their ambition. It became necessary for him to organize the settlers against the Indians and he was engaged much of his time in active Indian warfare. He promptly joined the army in 1846, and commanded a company in the Mexican War. When not engaged in military service, he was surveying lands, locating land certificates in that vast region extending from Fannin County out as far as the present county of Haskell, and in this way accumulated a large landed estate.

At the close of the Civil War in 1865, like many other prominent Texas citizens, he took up his abode in Mexico, locating in the valley of the Tuxpan River, where he remained eleven years, when learning of the death of his son, Daniel Ross Montague, he returned to Texas, aged and feeble, to spend the remainder of his days with his only daughter, Mrs. Elizabeth Twitty. While on a visit to a friend at Marysville in Cooke County, he was stricken with pneumonia and died December 20, 1876. Throughout his life he was a consistent Christian and active member of the Methodist church.

McLENNAN

This county was named in honor of Neil McLennan who was born on the Isle of Skye, Scotland in 1788. In 1801 or 1802 he removed to Robeson County, North Carolina, where he lived with his family on a farm until 1816 when he removed to Florida. In 1835 he, with his wife and children, two brothers, and a brother-in-law and one other family procured a schooner and, putting their families and effects into it, sailed for Texas, landing at the mouth of the Brazos and proceeded up the river to Fort Bend. From there they went overland to Robertson's Colony, and obtained land on Pond Creek.

In 1836, Laughlin McLennan and wife and all his children except two were killed by Indians. About the same time they burned the mother of Neil McLaughlin, his two children being carried away captives. In 1838, John McLennan Sr., another brother, was killed by Indians near Nashville on the Brazos. While returning to the settlements from a surveying expedition with George

B. Erath, he first saw the valley of the Bosque. He exchanged his Pond Creek place for the certificates which he located on the Bosque River in 1839 and settled there the next year. He built the first dwelling, a log cabin, in McLennan County. There he reared his family, living a quiet life, except when engaged in fighting the savages which infested that county for ten years later. He died in 1867.

His son, Neil McLennan, Jr., born in 1828, died in 1893, at Waco, Texas.

PARKER

The Parker family came from Illinois in 1833 and settled near where the present town of Groesbeck, in Limestone County, is situated. They, as usual with the first settlers, built a log fort for protection against the Indians. The little settlement, thirty-five in number, of whom only five were able to bear arms, were in their fort when on May 19, 1836, several hundred Comanche Indians came and inquired for a waterhole where they could camp and also asked for a beef.

Benjamin Parker, being then in his seventy-ninth year stepped out to show them the waterhole, and was instantly shot down. The Indians then rushed into the fort, killing Silas Parker, Samuel Frost, and Robert Frost and wounding Mrs. Sarah Parker. They made prisoners of Mrs. Rachael Plummer, and her son, James P. Plummer, two years old, Cynthia Ann Parker, eight years old, and John Parker, six years old, and Mrs. Kellogg. The others escaped and after wandering in the wilderness several days reached the Brazos in what is now Grimes County.

Mrs. Kellogg was in captivity for six months, Mrs. Plummer for over a year. A short time after her capture

Mrs. Plummer gave birth to a child, the crying of which so annoyed the savages that they killed it in a most cruel manner in her presence. She was then delivered over to an old squaw who treated her most demeaningly. She supposed that both her father and son had been killed but they, being in the field at work, had escaped.

One day when some distance from the Indian camp, though in sight of it, the old squaw attempted to beat Mrs. Plummer with a club, but she wrenched the club from the old squaw's hands and with it felled her to the ground. For this act of bravery the Indians patted her on the shoulder and praised her greatly. She received better treatment from this time on, and in time she was sold to a Santa Fe trader, who took her to Missouri, whence she finally made her way back to her friends in Texas. After six years of captivity her son was restored to his people only to find that both his parents were dead.

Cynthia Ann Parker was among the savages for nearly a quarter of a century and became the wife of a chief. In 1860 she was captured by Captain L. S. Ross (later Governor of Texas). She was sent to the settlements. The venerable Isaac Parker, an uncle, went to the camp and she was identified as the long lost niece. She returned with him and soon learned her native language, which she had forgotten. She died, leaving several children by the Indian chief. Her son, Quanah Parker, after whom the county seat of Hardeman County is named, remained with the Indians and became a chief. Isaac Parker was a member of the Third, Fourth, Sixth, and Seventh Congresses of the Republic of Texas from Houston County. He was also a member of the first State Constitutional Convention in 1845. After serving several terms in the Legislature from the region now known as Parker County he died in the early 80's at an advanced age near the city of Weatherford.

For the blood curdling horrors of this tragedy and much interesting data about the subsequent careers of this family see *Border Wars of Texas* by DeShields.

PARMER

Martin Parmer was born in Virginia and was educated in that state. In 1796 he removed to Tennessee, where he married Sarah Hardwick and engaged in business in Dickson County.

In 1818 he removed to Missouri and settled upon the extreme frontier of that territory among the Indians. He was a member of the convention which framed the constitution of that state and of the First Legislature of the state after its admission into the Union.

He came to Texas in 1825 and located at Mound Prairie (now near Alto in Cherokee County). He soon became one of the leaders in the so-called Fredonian War in 1827. He was among the Indians again six or eight years and then reappeared in public life as member of the Consultation in 1835, representing Tenaha (Shelby). He was chosen a member of the Constitutional Convention in 1836, representing San Augustine. He died in 1837.

SMITH

General James Smith, in whose honor this county was named, was born in Spartanburg District, South Carolina, September 10, 1792, and was reared and educated there. He volunteered as a private soldier at the age of twenty and served under General Jackson during the War of 1812, his last service in that war being in the Battle of New Orleans. He returned to South Carolina and in 1816 was married to Hannah Parker. Three years later he removed to Lincoln County, Tennessee, and engaged in farming. He was soon chosen leader of a vigilance committee for the protection of the citizens from Indians and the rough characters of what was then a frontier country. It is related that he was equal to every emergency and that he afforded ample protection and security to the community.

He came to Texas in 1834 in advance of his wife and children, who followed in 1835, reaching Texas on January 1, 1836. He settled in Nacogdoches (now Rusk) County on a league and labor (4,605 acres) of land, which he had selected for himself and opened up a farm.

Being desirous of aiding his struggling countrymen, he returned to Tennessee early in 1836 and raised a company of seventy-five volunteers from Tennessee and Alabama. He brought his company to Texas and enlisted in the service. He expended his own money for subsistence and transportation and for the mounts, arms, and ammunition of his men, purchasing at New Orleans five stacks of arms. After Texas had won independence, his company was mustered out of service.

In August and September, 1836, when many of the soldiers, after being discharged, were returning to Nacogdoches in a destitute condition, at considerable expense to himself, Smith supplied their needs. In 1837 and 1838 the settlers in that and adjacent regions were frequently driven from their homes and they always fled to General Smith's residence for subsistence and protection. In 1839 he led a body of troops to aid General Burleson in the Cherokee troubles. In 1841 he was again put in command of troops in what was then the northwestern frontier, and for his valuable services received a vote of thanks from the Congress of the Republic. In 1844, he was commissioned by President Houston to raise a force of men and ordered to repair to the scenes of anarchy then prevailing in Shelby County in the Regular-Moderator War. He assembled 500 men and repaired to the scene, and by his prudent and firm conduct the belligerents were induced to lay down their arms and submit to the law.

He enjoyed the close friendship of Houston, Rusk, Henderson and other leaders of that day. He at one time declined a place in the cabinet of President Houston. His admiration for Governor Henderson may be seen in the following: When the county of Rusk was created from Nacogdoches in 1843, General Smith's plantation being near the center of the county, he offered to donate sixty-nine acres of land for the proposed county site, provided it should be named Henderson and provided further that whenever it ceased to be called Henderson the land should revert to his estate.

After annexation he ceased to take an active part in politics. His farm, adjacent to the town of Henderson, afforded him ample income, though for a short period he engaged in merchandising, and here he spent the remainder of his days. He died on his farm, December 25, 1855, and was buried with military honors, General Rusk officiating. His tomb is of massive brick and stone, twelve feet high, and is still standing and his portrait hangs over the judge's stand in the district courtroom of Rusk County.

In politics he was a faithful disciple of Andrew Jackson and in religion a loyal member of the Baptist Church. He has many descendants, some of whom have taken a leading part in the different walks of life.

STARR

Dr. James Harper Starr in whose memory Starr County was named, was a descendant of Dr. Comfort Starr who came from Ashford, England to Massachusetts in 1635, and located near Boston. Nicholas Starr, grandfather of Dr. James Harper Starr, afterward located at Groton, Connecticut, and was one of the citizen volunteers who fell in defense of Fort Criswold, September 6, 1781. The name Nicholas Starr is inscribed on the monument erected on Groton Heights.

James Starr, one of the sons of Nicholas, was only five years old at the date of the death of his father. Although left an orphan at this early age, he succeeded in obtaining a fair education and established himself as a machinist and wheelwright. On the 13th of September, 1801, he was married to Miss Shaw, daughter of David Shaw of East Meriden, Connecticut, and settled at New Hartford where he resided until 1815 and then moved with his family to Ohio and settled near Worthington, where he died July 8, 1824.

Dr. James Harper Starr was born at New Hartford, Connecticut, December 16, 1809. He had few educational advantages but was a zealous student and conducted the farm for his mother, the older brother having left home to engage in other pursuits. An injury to his knee resulted in the loss of the use of this joint and disabled him from the duties of the farm.

He then attended the Academy at Worthington and taught school at intervals about six miles from Columbus. About that time a medical college was established at Worthington. He attended this college and was one of its first graduates. In the spring of 1832, he went south and located at McDonough in Henry County, Georgia, and later located at Pleasant Grove, in the same county, where he practiced his profession.

On the 1st of February, 1833, he was married to Miss Harriet J. Johnson, daughter of Samuel Johnson. He continued in the practice of his profession until March, 1836, when he left with his family for Texas.

When they reached Perry County, Alabama, he heard of the conditions in Texas and suspended his journey. On the 1st of January, 1837, he again started for Texas and arrived at Nacogdoches January 17, 1837. The Indians were at that time harassing the settlers and Dr. Starr joined one of the companies organized at Nacogdoches and pursued the savages as far as the Tehuacana Hills.

Dr. Starr's brother, Franklin J. Starr, was afterward in one of those campaigns and from exposure during the campaign died July 7, 1837. This deranged the plans of Dr. Starr as he had to take charge of his brother's affairs and look after the family. He then purchased a home in Nacogdoches and lived there for a third of a century. The Indian troubles continued and he kept himself in readiness to repel raids constantly, up to the time of the expulsion of the Cherokees and other Indians from that part of the state.

In January, 1838, he was appointed President of the Board of Land Commissioners for Nacogdoches County, a very responsible position at that time.

The Cordova rebellion broke out about that time and Dr. Starr took an active part in suppressing it, first as a private then as surgeon in the army.

In May, 1839, he was appointed Secretary of the Treasury by President Lamar. He resigned in the autumn of 1840 and returned to Nacogdoches and resumed the practice of medicine. He was a surgeon in the command organized by General Smith to suppress the Regulator-Moderator War. His interests in land matters soon became so large that he gave up his profession and connected with him in his land business, Nathaniel Amory, and continued with Mr. Amory until the Civil War. After the war he associated with him his son and in 1870 they removed to Marshall, and in 1873 he retired from active business and died in Marshall July, 1890.

He was an active sympathizer with the Confederate cause. He was appointed Receiver of the Confederate States Court at Tyler, and also accepted the appointment as agent of the Post Office Department of the Confederacy and was at the head of the department west of the Mississippi after the fall of Vicksburg, with headquarters at Marshall.

STERLING

This county was named for Captain Sterling, of whom we know little or nothing beyond the fact that he was a buffalo hunter and some time in the sixties pitched his camp on a creek in what is now known as Sterling County. Here he hunted buffaloes for their hides. He shipped the hides to Fort Concho and engaged in the business as long as there were buffaloes in the country. He left that country about 1881 and went to Arizona.

TARRANT

E. H. Tarrant was born in North Carolina in 1796. He removed from there when quite young to Tennessee and served under General Jackson in one or two campaigns against the Indians and participated in the Battle of New Orleans, January, 1815.

In 1835, he came to Texas and joined the army and at the close of the Revolution in 1836, joined the Ranger service and commanded the forces of the northwestern frontier. In 1838 he was chosen to represent Red River in the Congress of the Republic, but resigned to engage again in command of the Rangers for the protection of the northwestern frontier. His most notable conflict with the Indians was on Village Creek in 1841 in what is now Tarrant County, at a point where the Fort Worth and Dallas Interurban Railroad crosses that stream between Dallas and Fort Worth. He was, after annexation, several times a member of the Legislature and died in Ellis County in 1858.

TAYLOR

Edward Taylor was one of those typical Tennesseeans that came to Texas, bringing with him his wife, two sons, and two daughters to settle in Robertson's Colony. Arriving at Nashville, on the Brazos in 1833, he went up Little River to the Three Forks, about five miles southeast of the present site of Belton and selected a spot for a home.

He built himself two log cabins with a covered passage between and made a clearing, and was making himself and his family comfortable. The nearest settlement to him was several miles down the river.

One bright moonlight in November, 1835, eleven Indians made an attack upon the house. A stalwart savage presented himself at the door, violently shaking the shutter and demanding admittance. Being refused, he said, "Friend, no want to fight. Open door and give poor Indian tobacco."

Taylor replied that there were ten men in the house; that he would open no door, and had no tobacco for red devils, at the same time punching him in the stomach with a board pushed through the crack. The Indian then left.

Mrs. Taylor threw open the door leading across the hall and called the boys to come to her room, which they did amid a shower of balls and arrows. The doorway was now securely fastened and a table placed against it, upon which the youngest boy, only twelve years old, stood. He was given a gun and instructed to shoot through an open space above the door whenever an Indian came near. A large Indian, who had procured an ax from the woodpile, started toward the door and had reached the place between the two rooms when the child fired and the Indian dropped dead.

Another Indian ran up to drag his body away and the father fired and mortally wounded him. They had now run out of bullets, but there were some coals in the fireplace and Mrs. Taylor and the girls immediately began moulding bullets.

The Indians now set fire to the vacated end of the house and danced with glee in seeing the flames climb up the roof and to the adjoining room. The joists of the roof over the passage had suspended to them large pieces of fat bear's meat. The burning room soon began to cook the meat, and blazing sheets of oil fell upon the wounded savage and set him afire. Mrs. Taylor, seeing this from the inside and listening to the agonizing howls of the savage said, "Howl, you yellow brute! Your meat is not fit for the hogs but will roast for the buzzards."

Seeing that the house was about to be consumed, Taylor expressed a wish to go out and surrender, but Mrs. Taylor would not consent. Fortunately there was a supply of homemade vinegar and plenty of milk in the house, and with it she declared she could put out the fire. She mounted a table, from which she could reach the roof, and the boards not being nailed, she began to tear them away, making open space far in advance of the flames. She mounted the table and had her daughters pass her the fluid with which she soon quenched the flames.

During all this time the savages were yelling and shooting arrows at her and while many entered her clothing she escaped unharmed. Mr. Taylor and his oldest boy were also during this time shooting at the Indians as they came within reach, wounding one severely. When Mrs. Taylor came down from the roof she discovered an Indian in the outer chimney corner trying to start a fire. Seizing a shovel she threw it full of coals into his face. Seeing their plans defeated, with two of their braves barbecued, they retired and held council of war and decided to retreat.

THROCKMORTON

Dr. William Edward Throckmorton, in whose honor this county was named was the son of a revolutionary soldier, and was born in Virginia in 1795. He was reared and educated there and graduated in medicine in 1817. He practiced medicine there several years and was married to Elizabeth Webb. About the year 1821, he moved to Tennessee and located at Sparta, where he practiced his profession until 1837 when he removed with his family to Arkansas and located at Fayetteville. There his wife died leaving five children, one of whom was James Webb Throckmorton, who became governor of Texas, in 1866.

In 1840 he was married a second time and in the winter of 1841-2 moved to Texas and settled on the east fork of Trinity River about ten miles north of the present town of McKinney. He and several other parties who came with him were the first settlers of that region which was at that time infested with Indians, who robbed, murdered and committed many outrages upon the settlers. This was about five years before the County (Collin) was created. He practiced medicine there and in the settlements within reach until his death in 1843.

TITUS

This county was named for A. J. Titus, a native of Tennessee. He was born in Rutherford County on March 4, 1823. His father was a native of Pennsylvania, and at the close of the Revolutionary War moved to North Carolina, and from there to Tennessee in 1800. In 1832, James Titus, the father, was employed by the United States Government to assist in removing Choctaw and Chickasaw Indians to Indian Territory. Young Titus accompanied them and stopped about fifteen miles north of the site of the present town of Clarksville in Red River County. After visiting various parts of Texas they returned to Tennessee, and in 1839 they came to Texas and settled twelve miles east of the site of the present town of Clarksville and opened up a farm and also established the first post office in the county. A. J. Titus was an active advocate of annexation; opened the first road from Red River County to Jefferson, then the head of navigation. He built the first Presbyterian church in that part of Texas and organized the A. J. Titus Lodge of Masons. He was a Royal Arch Mason and Knight Templar. He was a soldier in the Mexican War. Later he was a member of the Legislature. Between 1846 and 1855, the year of his death, he spent the larger part of his time in Austin and Washington. He was one of the most public spirited and useful citizens of the state.

WILBARGER

Josiah Wilbarger, was born in Rockingham County, Virginia, September 10, 1801, and with his father's family moved to Bourbon County, Kentucky, in 1818. In 1823 the family moved to Pike County, Missouri, where he was married.

With his brother, Mathias, he came to Texas in 1829. In the spring of 1830, Stephen F. Austin came to his "Little Colony" on the upper Colorado with two surveyors and some immigrants who had already been there and selected locations. After Josiah and Mathias had their locations identified and their lines established, they went to work and erected log cabins and opened up farms. The location was at the junction of what is now known as Wilbarger Creek and the Colorado River, in Bastrop County, about twenty-six miles southeast of Austin. They were the first and only outside settlers until July, 1832, when Reuben Hornsby came up and occupied his league of land, on the same side of the river about eight miles from the site of the present city of Austin, his land being mostly beautiful, fertile bottom land.

Hornsby was now the outside settler, and his home became a great place of rendezvous for prospectors and general gatherings of young men who frequently came up and organized into parties to hunt wild game, then abounding all over the country.

Hornsby was a most hospitable man and his wife a most excellent housekeeper. In August, 1833, one Christian and wife and several young men were stopping with Hornsby. Two young men, Standifer and Haynie, had just come from Missouri to look at the country. Early in August Josiah Wilbarger came up to Hornsby's, and in company with Christian, Strother, Standifer and

Haynie rode out in a northwesterly direction to look at the country, carrying their guns, as was the universal custom. When they had gone about six miles northwest they discovered an Indian, who fled to the mountains. They gave chase as far up as where Duval Station of the International & Great Northern Railroad is located, and then abandoned the pursuit.

Returning, they stopped at noon at a spring to rest and eat lunch. This spring is about three miles from the present City of Austin, and in sight of the road leading to Manor. Wilbarger, Christian and Strother unsaddled their horses and staked them out to graze, while Haynie and Standifer left their horses saddled.

While eating they were suddenly fired upon by Indians. Each man sprang to a tree and returned the fire. The party had fired two rounds when a ball struck Christian and broke his thigh bone. Strother had already been mortally wounded. Wilbarger ran to the side of Christian, when a ball from an Indian shattered his powder horn. Wilbarger then primed his gun and sprang behind a small tree, when an arrow from an Indian passed through the calf of his left leg, while his other leg was pierced by an arrow. Up to this time Standifer and Haynie had helped to keep up the fight, but when they saw that Strother was mortally wounded and Christian totally disabled, they mounted their horses and fled.

Wilbarger pleaded with them to take him up on one of the horses, and, wounded as he was, ran to overtake them, when he was struck by a ball from behind which penetrated near the center of his neck and came out on the left side of his chin. He fell, apparently dead. The Indians came up to him, completely stripped him and tore the scalp from his head, all of which he remembered, among other things that the tearing of his scalp from his head sounded like the roar of thunder. The Indians then cut the throats of Christian and Strother, but left Wilbarger for dead.

When Wilbarger regained consciousness the evening was far advanced. He had lost much blood, and his wounds were still bleeding. Consumed by an intolerable thirst, he dragged himself to a pool of water below the spring, slaked his thirst and lay down in the water for an hour. Although this occurred in the month of August, he had become thoroughly chilled. He crawled out to dry land and soon fell into a profound sleep. When he awoke the blood had ceased to flow, but he was again consumed with thirst, and crawled back to the pool and slaked his thirst.

The flies and maggots were now at work on his wounds, and as night approached he determined to go as far as he could toward Hornsby's. When he had gone about a third of a mile he sank to the ground exhausted, crawled under an oak tree, well nigh despairing of life. The next day a relief party started out to hunt for his body and those of Strother and Christian, and he was found, presenting a most ghastly sight, all covered with blood and entirely naked except for a sock on one foot, which the Indians failed to take. Mrs. Hornsby had provided the relief party with a sheet for each of the dead bodies, and Wilbarger was wrapped in one of them and placed on Roger's horse, Hornsby mounting behind, holding him with his arms around him to the Hornsby house. His wounds were thoroughly dressed and bear's oil applied to his scalp. Here he was tenderly nursed until able to be carried home. Although the scalp never grew entirely over his skull, he survived eleven years, dying at his home in 1844. He left surviving him his wife and five children. His brother, Mathias, died a few years later.

CHAPTER V,
POLITICAL ORGANIZATION OF TEXAS &
EVENTS LEADING TO THE REVOLUTION

When the presidential term of Guadalupe Victoria expired, that long series of revolutions began in Mexico, which have continued, with more or less frequency, down to date. One of the results of the first revolution was the elevation of Anastasia Bustamente to the Presidency. During his term of office the first measures hostile to the interests of Texas were adopted. They resulted in armed conflict in 1832 between the Texans and Mexicans, and but for his overthrow by Santa Anna disastrous consequences to Texas might have followed.

Santa Anna, up to that time a loyal republican, now changed his policy, disregarding the Constitution, reorganizing state governments and finally turning his attention to Texas. The following county names represent every phase of the events leading up to the Texas Revolution.

Archer	Grimes	Rusk
Burnet	Hardeman	Somervell
Carson	Hardin	Waller
Childress	Martin	Wharton
Ellis	Mitchell	Williamson
Fisher	Navarro	Zavala
Grayson	Potter	

David Gouverneur Burnet (1888-1870)

ARCHER

This county was named for Branch Tanner Archer, who was born in Virginia in 1780. He studied medicine in Philadelphia, and for some years was a physician and politician in his native state, where he served one or two terms as a member of the Legislature. In 1831 he came to Texas and became a prominent actor in the movements preliminary to the revolution.

He was appointed by the citizens as a commissioner to negotiate with Bradburn at Anahuac for a modification of the orders issued by the military commanders of Texas. This was his first appearance in public life in Texas. He represented Brazoria County in the convention of 1833, and he announced himself in favor of immediate separation from Mexico. With Stephen F. Austin and W. H. Wharton he was appointed as a commissioner in December, 1835, to visit the United States and enlist financial aid and sympathy from that quarter. He was a member of the First Congress of the Republic and was elected Speaker of the adjourned session in 1837. He was for a time Secretary of War in President Lamar's cabinet. Although in feeble health in 1845, he was an active advocate of annexation. He died in Brazoria in 1856.

BURNET

Burnet County was named for David G. Burnet, originally of Newark, New Jersey, where he was born April 4, 1789. He received a liberal education and at the age of sixteen years entered the counting house of Robinson & Hartshorn, New York. Finding this work unsuited to his taste, he joined the expedition of General Miranda to South America. When that expedition failed he returned home and remained there until about 1817, when he removed to Natchitoches, Louisiana. Being threatened with lung trouble, his physician advised him to go into the dry atmosphere of Texas and live outdoors. He went among the Indians of Western Texas and followed their mode of living for a year or two.

Recovering his health he went to Cincinnati, Ohio, where he remained seven or eight years. He came to Texas in 1826 and obtained, on December 22, 1826, a contract to colonize a large tract of country in East Texas. He sold his rights under this contract to a New York company. He was married in New York in 1831 and returned to Texas. In 1833 he was a member of the convention at San Felipe. In 1834 he was appointed judge and held court once or twice. In 1835 he was a member of the Consultation. In 1836 he was elected by the Constitutional Convention President Ad Interim of the Republic of Texas, and held the office until the succeeding October. In 1838 he was elected Vice President of the Republic, and at the end of his term retired to his home near the San Jacinto River. He was appointed Secretary of State in 1846. In 1866 he was elected a United States Senator, but was not permitted to qualify as such. He returned to Texas and died in Galveston December 5, 1870.

CARSON

This county was named for Samuel P. Carson, Secretary of State in Burnet's cabinet. He was born January 22, 1798, at Pleasant Gardens, Burke County, North Carolina. He was a member of the State Senate of North Carolina for two consecutive terms, and in 1826 became a candidate for Congress from the extreme western district of North Carolina. He was opposed by James Graham, Felix Walker and Dr. R. B. Vance, father of the late Senator Zebulon B. Vance. Carson was defeated. During the canvass Vance charged that Colonel John Carson, father of Samuel P., had been untrue to the colonies in the Revolutionary War. He was called upon to retract, and upon his refusing to do so, was challenged to fight a duel, and the challenge was accepted. Carson went over into Tennessee and engaged Davy Crockett to drill him in pistol practice. The duel took place at Saluda Gap, in South Carolina, in 1827. Vance fell at the first fire and died at midnight. While public opinion sustained Carson, he ever afterward regretted the affair.

He was elected to the United States Congress from that district in 1827, and in 1829 and again in 1831. He was a brilliant and fascinating orator; was a trusted friend of Andrew Jackson, but, being a Calhoun Democrat, he became estranged, and in his campaign for re-election in 1833 was defeated, his district being overwhelmingly in favor of Jackson's policies.

His health beginning to decline, he came to Texas in 1834 and selected a location for temporary residence on Red River. During his absence from home his constituency elected him a member of the Constitutional Convention which was held in North Carolina in 1835. He returned to his native state and served in the Constitutional Convention, and when its labors were over came back to Texas, and in March of the next year was appointed Secretary of State by President Burnet. He was immediately sent upon a diplomatic mission to the United States. The only work, however, he accomplished on that mission was to obtain protection for the settlers in East Texas against the Cherokee Indians. As soon as he heard of the victory at San Jacinto he tendered his resignation and went to the mountains of North Carolina and Tennessee to recuperate his health. He returned to Texas late in 1836 and continued to travel in search of health. He died at Hot Springs, Arkansas in 1840.

CHILDRESS

This county was named for George Campbell Childress, author of the Declaration of Independence of the Republic of Texas. He was born in Nashville, Tennessee, January 8, 1804. He was a son of Elizabeth Robertson Childress and James Childress, his mother being a niece of General James Robertson, the founder of Nashville, Tennessee. Through the influence of his uncle, Major Sterling C. Robertson, the empresario, he came to Texas in 1832 and located at Nashville, on the Brazos, in the colony of Robertson.

He was by profession a lawyer, but in the absence of courts he could do little more than act as counselor for the settlers in perfecting their titles to the lands acquired under the colonization laws. In 1836 he was elected a delegate to the convention which declared independence and framed the Constitution of the Republic of Texas. He was a brilliant lawyer and orator, a man of great magnetism, and profoundly versed in political science. These qualities and his record as an ardent advocate for independence commended him to the convention as the proper person to head the committee to draft a declaration. After the adjournment of the convention President Burnet appointed him as a commissioner to go to Washington and present the claims of Texas to President Jackson, the personal friend and Tennessee neighbor of Childress, for recognition as an independent Republic.

Childress went to Washington, but had not arrived when the Battle of San Jacinto was fought. He remained in Washington until the adjournment of Congress and his mission was ended. Later he returned to Nashville and entered the practice of law. In 1840 he committed suicide at his boarding house. He was never married.

ELLIS

This county was named for Richard Ellis, who was born in Virginia in 1782, and was liberally educated in that state. He removed to Franklin County, Alabama, about the year 1813, and engaged in the practice of law and planting. He was elected as delegate to the Constitutional Convention which framed the first State Constitution of Alabama in 1819. He was elected Judge of the Fourth Circuit in 1820. At that time and up to 1832, the Supreme Court of Alabama was composed of the Judges of the different circuits. At the end of his term, in 1825, he removed to the Red River section of Texas and engaged in cotton planting upon a large scale, in what is now Bowie County. He was chosen a delegate to the convention of March, 1836, which declared independence and framed the Constitution of the Republic of Texas, and was elected President of that body and later a member of the Congress of the Republic. After annexation he ceased to take an active interest in political affairs, retired to his plantation and died in 1849.

FISHER

S. Rhoads Fisher, after whom this county was named, was born in Philadelphia in 1795, where he was reared and educated. He removed, about the year 1825, to New Jersey. In 1831 he came to Texas and located at Matagorda, where he engaged in merchandising. In 1836 he was elected a delegate to the Constitutional Convention from Matagorda, participated in all its proceedings and was a signer of the Declaration of Independence. In the organization of the cabinet of the regular government, in 1836, he was appointed Secretary of the Navy by President Houston and resigned that office in 1837. He resumed his business at Matagorda, and died there in January, 1839.

GRAYSON

Peter W. Grayson was born in 1788 in Kentucky, which was then embraced in Virginia. He sprang from a distinguished family in Virginia, which state also has a county named Grayson. He was a man of superior culture and was a lawyer by profession.

He came to Texas in 1832, bringing with him his slaves, acquired two leagues of land in Matagorda County and opened up a plantation to which he devoted most of his time, as there was little to do in his profession. In 1835, when trouble between Texas and Mexico came to a crisis, he repaired to Gonzales and joined the army of Texas and became aide to General Burleson in November. When the provisional government was organized, in March, 1836, President Burnet selected him as Attorney General in his cabinet, to succeed David Thomas, who died shortly after his appointment. Later on, President Burnet sent him on a diplomatic mission to the United States. He succeeded Henderson as Attorney General in Houston's first cabinet.

At the close of President Houston's first term as President, Grayson became a candidate to succeed him, with M. B. Lamar and Chief Justice James Collingsworth as opponents. During the canvass he returned to Tennessee and committed suicide, as did Chief Justice Collingsworth about the same time.

GRIMES

Jesse Grimes was born in North Carolina in 1788. In 1819 he removed to Alabama and engaged in farming. From there he came to Texas in January, 1829, and located in the region that now bears his name and again engaged in farming. His educational advantages in early life were meager, but he was a man of great force of character and of strong native intellect.

He was chosen a member of the convention of 1833 from the municipality of Washington, of which the territory of Grimes County was then a part. In 1835 he was a member of the Consultation; he was also a member of the convention of March, 1836, and a signer of the Declaration of Independence. He was a member of the Senate of the First Congress and President Pro Tem of the Lower House of the Sixth and Seventh Congresses of the Republic of Texas, and Senator in the Eighth and Ninth Congresses. He died on his plantation in Grimes County March 16, 1866.

C. Grimes, a son of Jesse Grimes, was one of the heroes of the Alamo, killed there in the eighteenth year of his age.

HARDEMAN

This county was named for the distinguished brothers, Bailey and Thomas Jones Hardeman, who came to Texas in 1835. They were born in Davidson County, Tennessee, about three miles from Nashville, the former on February 26, 1785, and the latter January 31, 1788. They were sons of Thomas Hardeman, one of the first settlers of Middle Tennessee, a delegate from Davidson County to the convention which assembled at Hillsboro in 1788 to consider the ratification of the Constitution of the United States by North Carolina, and also a member of the convention that framed the first Constitution of Tennessee. He afterward moved down into Southwest Tennessee and was one of the leaders in organizing a new county named in his honor. Here the sons were reared and educated.

Bailey Hardeman studied law in Nashville and located at Bolivar, the county seat of Hardeman County, Tennessee, and was in the full practice of his profession when the Texas Revolution broke out. In company with his brother, Thomas J., he came to Texas in 1835 and located in Matagorda. They had hardly settled down before they entered the active service of Texas. Bailey Hardeman was elected a delegate to the convention which declared independence and took part in the organization of the government ad interim; he was chosen Secretary of the Treasury in President Burnet's cabinet and died about three months later.

Thomas J. Hardeman was married twice, his first wife being Miss Mary Polk, daughter of Ezekiel Polk of Bolivar, Tennessee, and near relative of President James K. Polk. His second marriage was to Eliza DeWitt, daughter of the Empresario DeWitt. Among his children two sons became prominent in the military history of the State, Thomas M. Hardeman having been in the San Jacinto campaign, in the hotly contested Indian fight at Plum Creek and in the Somervell expedition, while William P. Hardeman, after serving in various capacities, rose to the position of brigadier general in the Confederate Army, where he became conspicuous for his bravery in many hard fought battles. Thomas J. Hardeman represented Matagorda County in the Texas Congress in 1837-8, and was the first to suggest that the new capital be named for the Father of Texas. Later he moved to Bastrop County, and served in the State Legislature. He was grand master of the lodge of Masons of Texas in 1850. A few years later he died at his home in Bastrop County, Texas.

Both of these men have numerous descendants in Texas prominent in social, business and political circles.

HARDIN

This county was named in honor of the Hardins of Liberty. The family came to Texas in 1825. There were five brothers, viz: Benjamin Watson, Augustine Blackburn, William, Frank and Milton A. Hardin, sons of Swan and Jerusha Blackburn Hardin. The parents moved from Franklin County, Georgia, to Maury County, Tennessee, in 1807, and resided there until 1825, when they came to Texas and located in what is now Liberty County, on the Trinity River.

Benjamin Watson, the oldest son, became a member of the Ninth Congress of the Republic of Texas in 1844. He also served as sheriff for a number of years. He died January 2, 1850, at his home in Liberty County.

Augustine Blackburn Hardin, the second son, became a prominent citizen shortly after the arrival of the family in Texas. He represented Liberty in the convention of 1833, and in the Consultation of 1835, and in the convention of 1836, which declared independence, being one of the signers of that declaration. After annexation he ceased to take an active part in politics and retired to Liberty County, where he died, July 27, 1871, at the home of his daughter, Mrs. Janet Green, about eight miles north of Liberty. He was buried at the old family burying ground, two miles below.

William Hardin held the office of Alcalde and later of Primary Judge in Liberty County. He then located in Galveston and died in July, 1839.

Franklin Hardin was appointed surveyor of Liberty in 1834, and at the beginning of the revolution, in 1835, he promptly enlisted in the service and was elected first lieutenant in Logan's company of Sherman's regiment and participated in the Battle of San Jacinto. After the battle he tendered the use of his premises adjacent to Liberty for keeping prisoners captured in that battle, and the humane treatment they received there was the subject of special praise by Mexicans in their subsequent reports to their countrymen.

On the 9th of July he organized a militia force and was made captain and in the same year was appointed surveyor of Liberty County. In 1867 he was elected to the Legislature. After this he retired to his home at Liberty and died there in 1878.

Milton Ashley Hardin, the youngest of the brothers, removed to Johnson County and died at Cleburne in 1894.

The Liberty County of the Republic of Texas embraced not only the present County of Liberty, but also the present counties of Hardin, Chambers, Polk, San Jacinto, Tyler and, until 1838, Galveston.

MARTIN

This county was named for Wylie Martin, who was born in Georgia in 1774. He taught school for a short time. In 1812 he was a scout under General Harrison in the northwest; was with General Jackson at the battle of Horse Shoe, and a captain in the United States Army. In 1825 he came to Texas and later was appointed an Alcalde in Austin's colony.

For a time he was the political chief of the Department of Brazos. He was at first opposed to declaring independence thinking it premature. He became a member of the Consultation in 1835. When war seemed inevitable he raised a company and joined General Houston's Army at the Colorado River. He was sent to Fort Bend to guard the crossing of the Brazos, and afterward was sent to the Trinity to aid the fleeing population in crossing that river. He later served in the Congress of the Republic of Texas and died while a member of that body in 1842.

MITCHELL

This county was named for Asa and Eli Mitchell, brothers who came to Texas in 1822. Asa was born in Pennsylvania in 1786, was reared and educated there and was married in 1816. From Pennsylvania he went to Kentucky in 1820. While visiting New Orleans he met Stephen F. Austin and came to Texas and settled in the year 1822 as one of Austin's original 300 colonists. His wife died in 1834. In 1835 he was a member of the Consultation and later a member of the Constitutional Convention of 1836 and a signer of the Declaration of Independence. After the adjournment of the convention, March 17, he joined General Houston's Army and

participated in the Battle of San Jacinto. He first resided
at Velasco, then removed to Bexar, where he resided up
to his death, in 1865. Eli Mitchell, his brother, moved
to Gonzales and died there some time in the seventies.

NAVARRO

This county was named for Juan Antonio Navarro,
who was born in San Antonio February 27, 1795, He was
appointed Land Commissioner for DeWitt's Colony in
1831, and in 1834-5 was Land Commissioner for Bexar
District. He was a consistent Republican and an implacable foe to despotism in any form. He, with Samuel
A. Maverick, was elected delegate from Bexar to the
convention which declared independence and framed
the Constitution of the Republic in March, 1836. He became a member of the Texas Congress in 1838. In 1840
he accompanied the Santa Fe Expedition as a commissioner to treat with the New Mexicans; was captured
and carried to the Castle of Juan d'Ulloa, where he was
kept in close confinement until his release in 1845.

He was an object of special hatred by Santa Anna,
who condemned him to imprisonment for life, though
during his captivity he was offered his liberty and high
office if he would forever abjure Texas. Being a native
Mexican and Texan, his zeal in behalf of Texas aroused
all the ire of Santa Anna. Santa Anna was succeeded by
Herrera, a liberal, in 1845, and he released Navarro. He
arrived at Galveston in February, 1845, after an absence
of four and a half years. Upon his return home he was
immediately elected a delegate to the convention which
framed the first State Constitution, in 1845, and afterward served his district in the State Senate. He died in
San Antonio in 1870, universally beloved and respected

by all patriots in Texas. His father was a native of Corsica, and in compliment to Navarro the county seat was named Corsicana.

POTTER

In Section 2 of Chapter CXIV, Acts of 1878, there is the following language: "The County of Potter is named in honor of Robert Potter, a distinguished Texan in the days of the Republic." Wheeler, in his history of North Carolina, says of him:

Robert Potter was a resident and representative from Granville County. I once thought, after I had prepared a sketch of him, that I would omit it, and pass in silence the name of one who had been a member of this county in the Assembly and the Representative of his district in Congress. But truth demands that not only the good should be noticed, but those who have been notorious for other qualities. This, too, may have a moral effect. It was the custom of the Lacedemonians to intoxicate their servants on certain occasions before their young children, that their young minds, seeing vice in so frightful a mien, might avoid its seductions. Robert Potter was a man of no ordinary powers of intellect. With an address which would have graced the most polished court in Europe, with powers of eloquence that could command the listening auditors, and sway them to his will, and an energy that shrunk from no obstacle or opposition, had his early education been elevated by the piety of the mother of Gaston, his fierce and ferocious temper tamed by parental persuasion, his name might have stood

"High on the dusty rolls which ages keep."

He was a native of Granville. He entered the navy as a midshipman and after a few years resigned and studied law. He entered into public life as a member of the House of Commons from Halifax in 1826. At Halifax his turbulent temper embroiled him in many difficulties. On one occasion, at an election in which Potter was opposed by Jesse A. Bynum, a fracas occurred at which one man was killed and the election broken up. He removed to Granville, from which he was elected to the House of Commons in 1828.

This was an extraordinary period. The financial condition of North Carolina was deplorable. The banks had become neglectful to their duty, and disregarded their charters. Mr. Potter opened the session by a resolution of inquiry. The inquiry produced a committee, of which he was chairman; the affairs of the banks were investigated; much evil and malfeasance were proved. The committee reported a bill to prosecute the banks. This bill, after a long, heated and angry discussion, passed by one vote; but the Speaker (Hon. Thomas Settle) voting with the minority defeated its becoming a law.

This gave Mr. Potter great popularity, and the next year he was elected to Congress in triumph over all opposition. His course in Congress was brilliant and imposing. He was re-elected without opposition, but his career was to end soon in darkness and disgrace. On Sunday, the 28th of August, 1831, moved by

"Jealousy, that green-eyed monster
That doth mock the meat it feeds upon,"

he committed a brutal maim on two relations of his wife. For those outrages he was brought before legal tribunals of the county and fined one thousand dollars and imprisoned six months. After serving an imprisonment of about two years he became a candidate for the Legislature and was elected in 1834.

Wheeler omits an important circumstance, that probably had its influence upon his removal to Texas in 1835. At that stage of our civilization, when poker playing and betting at cards was a favorite method of nocturnal entertainment with many solons, Potter's uniform success in "raking in the pot" caused a suspicion that he was playing the role of the "Heathen Chinee," and a little close watching verified the suspicion. The next day, the failure of Potter to give a square deal, resulted in a resolution by the House expelling him from that body for "cheating at cards."

The distant mutterings of the Texas revolution were then heard all over the East, and Potter shook the dust of North Carolina from his feet and hied himself away to Texas. He had been in Texas only a short time when the people of Nacogdoches sent him to the Constitutional Convention which met at Washington on the Brazos. After becoming a signer of the Declaration of Independence of Texas and participating in all the proceedings of that body, at no time hiding his light under a bushel, the fact that he had been a midshipman in the navy and had a brilliant and imposing career as a member for two terms in the United States Congress, added to his overpowering personality, gave him a place in the cabinet as Secretary of the Navy. At a cabinet meeting, after the Battle of San Jacinto, he vigorously and eloquently insisted that Santa Anna be hanged, but wiser counsels prevailed. From that time, up to October, 1836, he served in this capacity and managed to get hold of a ship. What occurred on that ship is stated in as light form as the circumstances would permit in the case of Lewis vs. Ames, reported in the 44th Volume of Reports of the Supreme Court of Texas. He then moved back to the Red River country, procured a certificate for 4,605 acres as the head of a family in North Carolina, and located the certificate on a beautiful tract of land overlooking Soda Lake, in the present County of Marion, moved on the land and made it his home.

True to his instincts never to be in peace except when in war, he soon became mixed up in the feuds of that region and made deadly enemies, though he had enough followers to elect him Senator to the Congress of the Republic of Texas in 1840. At the adjournment of the last session in which he served he made his will and went home and was killed there March 2, 1842. At his death he was forty-two years old.

RUSK

This county was named for Thomas J. Rusk, who was born in Pendleton District, South Carolina, on the 5th of December, 1803. He studied law and removed to Clarksville, Georgia, where he entered upon the practice of his profession. In 1834 some dishonest agents ran away with the funds of a mining enterprise in which he was interested, and he followed them to Texas. He liked the country and settled at Nacogdoches, where he began his career in Texas. In 1835 the Executive Council appointed him Commissary of the army. In 1836 he was elected a member of the Constitutional Convention, and was later made Adjutant General of the army. He actively participated in the Battle of San Jacinto. Later when Houston left for New Orleans he was appointed Commander-in-Chief.

In the fall of 1836 he was made Secretary of War in the first Cabinet of Houston, but soon resigned to attend to his private affairs. He was elected to the Second Congress in Texas in 1837. In 1839 he commanded a regiment in the war against the Cherokees. In the same year he was appointed by the Congress of Texas Chief Justice of the Supreme Court, to succeed James Collingsworth, deceased. In 1836 he was elected Major General of the militia. In 1845 he became President of the convention that framed the first State Constitution, and in the next year was elected Senator of the United States. This position he filled with credit to himself and great honor to Texas until his death. He died by his own hand on his plantation near Nacogdoches in 1857.

SOMERVELL

This county was named for Alexander Somervell, who was born in Maryland in 1796. In 1817 he went to Louisiana, thence to Missouri, where he engaged in merchandising. In 1833 he removed to San Felipe, Texas, and there engaged in the mercantile business. He took an active part in the Texas Revolution, serving as Major in the campaign around Bexar in 1835 and later as lieutenant colonel of Burleson's regiment, in which capacity he participated in the Battle of San Jacinto. For a time he was Secretary of War in the Burnet cabinet, and was a Senator in the First Texas Congress. He served in the Indian Wars of 1839, and in 1842 was appointed brigadier general and put in command of the forces that pursued the retreating army of General Woll, and this pursuit has since been known as the Somervell Expedition. His forces separated at the Rio Grande and one portion returned with him to San Antonio. The other crossed the river and attacked Mier, and this march is usually called the Mier Expedition. After his return he was appointed Collector of Customs at Saluria, and held the office until annexation, and he was afterwards successively appointed until his death in 1854. He lost his life by drowning while on his way from the Lavaca River to Saluria, in January, 1854.

WALLER

Edwin Waller was born in Spottsylvania County, Virginia, November, 1800. At an early age his father moved to Missouri, where he was reared and educated. He came to Texas in 1831 and located in Brazoria municipality. He took part in the Battle of Velasco in 1832, and in 1833 was appointed Alcalde. He was a member of the Consultation in 1835 and of the Convention in 1836; was also a signer of the Declaration of Independence. In 1838-9 he was appointed one of the commissioners to lay out the plan of the City of Austin and one of the principal streets and the creek, forming the original eastern boundary of the city, bear his name. He was chosen the first mayor of the city in 1840. After the annexation he returned to his plantation in Austin County and for years was Chief Justice of the County and Representative for one term in the State Legislature. He represented the county in the Secession Convention of 1861. About the year 1876 he moved to Austin, but after a short residence returned to his plantation and died there in 1883.

WHARTON

This county was named in honor of the distinguished brothers, William H. and John A. Wharton. They were descendants of an old and distinguished family in Virginia, and sons of William Harris Wharton, a native of Albermarle County, Virginia.

About 1801, shortly after his marriage, the father removed to Nashville, Tennessee, where both sons were born, William Harris Wharton in 1806 and John A. Wharton in 1809. Their father died in 1815, and their mother a short time afterward.

Jesse Wharton, their uncle, who had removed to Nashville from Virginia, took charge of the orphans and directed their education. He represented Tennessee in the lower house of Congress of the United States from 1807 to 1809, and in the Senate of the United States in 1816 and 1817.

After attending the preparatory schools, William H. Wharton entered the University of Nashville.

Henry A. Wise, in his most entertaining volume entitled *Seven Decades of the Union*, says of him:

> At the first commencement of the Nashville University, which occurred soon after our arrival there, a youth, William Wharton, was introduced and delivered an oration which marked him as a man of great promise. He was the pride of Rev. Dr. Lindsley, who then presided over the Alma Mater of many other distinguished alumni of the West. Wharton delivered his salutatory and immediately went off to Texas to join Dr. Archer.

It is possible that a stronger magnet than political ambition lured Wharton to Texas. The beautiful and ac-

complished daughter of Jared E. Groce, the wealthiest
man and the most extensive planter and largest slave
holder in Texas, was budding into womanhood about
this time. She had come to Nashville to school. We do
not know what occurred later except that she became
the bride of Wharton. As soon as he arrived in Texas
he became prominent in political affairs. In 1833 he
was elected a delegate to the convention which met at
San Felipe and was elected chairman of that body. The
memorial prepared by him to Mexico for separate statehood is one of the ablest expositions in the political
literature, of any time, in the history of Texas.

At the commencement of the revolution of Texas
against Mexico, in 1835, he was one of the first on the
ground at Gonzales, and was with the Texas forces until
they reached Bexar. He was then notified that he was
appointed by the consultation as one of the commissioners to the United States, the others being Stephen
F. Austin and B. T. Archer, charged with the important
duty of laying the cause of Texas before the people of
that country and soliciting aid in the struggle.

In December, 1835, he left Texas for the United States,
where he, in most lucid and eloquent public addresses,
set forth the cause of Texas in the summer of 1836, and
upon the organization of the regular government, in the
fall of that year, he was appointed minister to the United
States. He remained in Washington until March, 1837,
when Texas was recognized, and immediately after that
event left for home, leaving Memucan Hunt, who had
been appointed in his stead, in charge.

On his way home he was captured at sea by a Mexican
ship and carried to Matamoros as a prisoner, but soon
made his escape and returned to Texas and was elected
a member of the Senate of the Republic, and was re-
elected in 1838 to the same position. In March, 1839,

while mounting his horse at his plantation in Brazoria
County he was accidentally shot by the premature discharge of his pistol. He left surviving him a son named
for his brother, John A. Wharton, who became major
general in the Confederate Army and was killed at the
close of the war in 1865.

John A. Wharton, after finishing his education, studied law and was admitted to the practice and removed
to New Orleans in 1830 and pursued his profession
there until 1833, when he came to Texas and located
in Brazoria County. He married a daughter of Governor
Johnson of South Carolina.

In 1835 he represented Brazoria in the Consultation,
having first done valuable service on the committee
of safety in Brazoria. He afterward joined the army of
Sam Houston, and was his Adjutant at the Battle of San
Jacinto. After the capture of Santa Anna it was largely
through the influence of Wharton's eloquent appeal to
the army that Santa Anna's life was spared.

At the close of the Texas Revolution he resumed the
practice of law in Brazoria with E. M. Pease (later Governor of Texas) as his partner, under the firm name of
Wharton & Pease, later becoming the firm Wharton,
Pease & Harris.

He served as a member of the lower house of the Congress of the Republic of Texas in 1837, and was returned
in 1838, and died March 17, 1839, while a member of
that body, and was buried with Masonic honors, ex-
President Burnet delivering the funeral oration.

WILLIAMSON

This county was named for Robert M. Williamson, who was born in Georgia in 1806, where he was reared and educated in the common schools. At the age of fifteen he was afflicted with white swelling, which rendered him a cripple for life, causing him to wear a wooden leg, and on that account he was later widely known in Texas as "Three Legged Willie." He studied law and was admitted to the bar in 1827 in his native state, and in 1828 came to Texas and located at San Felipe. Here he learned the Spanish language and familiarized himself with the land laws of Mexico and Spain and was regarded as the best informed man in Texas upon the land laws then governing the country.

He took an active part in all the occurrences leading up to the Texas Revolution. He was made one of the first District Judges of the Republic in 1837. In 1840 he was elected to represent Washington County in the Congress of the Republic, and by successive re-elections held the position until annexation, after which he was elected a member of the First State Legislature. He served in that body until 1849, when he became a candidate for Congress, and was defeated by Volney E. Howard. He then retired to his farm near Independence, and his health gradually declining, he died December 22, 1859.

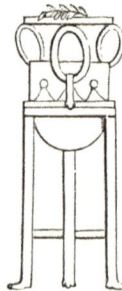

ZAVALA

This county was named for Lorenzo de Zavala. This name was misspelled by the Legislature, and the mistake has been carried in all the official reports as "Zavalla" instead of "Zavala."

This distinguished soldier, statesman and publicist was born in Merida, Yucatan, October 3, 1788, of Spanish parents. In 1794 he was sent back by his parents to be educated in Spain until he was nineteen years old, when he returned to Mexico. At the age of twenty he was elected Secretary of the City Council of Merida, and held the office for six years.

He was in full sympathy with the struggling Republicans of Mexico, and for his openly expressed views and aid to the revolutionists he was imprisoned and confined in the Castle of San Juan d'Ulloa for three years, during a part of which time he was placed in irons. He was released and returned to Merida, where he practiced medicine in 1817, 1818 and 1819. In 1820 he was elected to the Cortes of Spain. In 1822 he returned to Mexico and was elected Deputy to the Constituent Congress, and served in that capacity until the Constitutional convention of Mexico was called in 1824.

He was elected a delegate to that body, was made President of the same, and was the first signer of the first Constitution of the Republic of Mexico. In 1825-26 he was a Senator in the First Congress of the Republic of Mexico. In 1827 he was made first Governor of the Federal District of Mexico. In 1829 he was chosen Minister of Finance of the Republic. In 1830, upon the accession of the tyrant, Bustamente, he left Mexico. Up to this time he and Santa Anna had been friends and co-workers in the Liberal cause. He returned to Mexico in

1833 to witness the waning fortunes of Bustamente and the ascendancy of his friend, Santa Anna. He was then elected to the Federal Congress, and by the unanimous vote of the House of Deputies he was made eligible to the office of Governor of the State of Mexico and held both offices at the same time. In 1834, under the regime of Santa Anna, he was appointed Minister to France.

It was now that Santa Anna threw off his republican mask and made himself dictator. Zavala, always the consistent friend of liberty, refused longer to cooperate with Santa Anna. Instead, he resigned his office and returned to America, locating in Texas in 1835, selecting his home upon a beautiful eminence overlooking San Jacinto River and Bay. He immediately advised determined resistance to the usurpation of Santa Anna. Learning that Zavala had openly espoused the cause of Texas Santa Anna ordered his arrest. This was successfully resisted by the Texans.

He was then elected a delegate to the Consultation at San Felipe, and when the work of that body was over he was elected a delegate to the convention at Washington on the Brazos. He was a signer of the Declaration of Independence. He aided in framing the Constitution of the Republic of Texas and in the formation of a provisional government by that body, and was made Vice-President. At the expiration of his term he retired to his home on the San Jacinto and died November 11, 1836.

This simple record explains Santa Anna's implacable hatred toward him. Amid the rapidly changing scenes of this eminent man's eventful life he gave forth many published addresses and letters in behalf of Republican principles and found time to publish several works. Among his published works is one entitled *Viego Historica de los Revoluciones de Mexico*, published in two volumes. Of this Bancroft says: "Any impartial, un-prejudiced critic will recognize in the author a learned publicist, historian, philosopher, economist and states-man." Another of his published works is *Viego a los Estados Unidas*, of which Bancroft says: "It is a philo-sophic work, showing a deep study of the manners and customs of the American people, and more especially of their political institutions."

His object in publishing this work was to educate his fellow countrymen into a just appreciation of the spirit of liberty as manifested in the institutions of our coun-try. Santa Anna sought by every means in his power to destroy the influence of so great a man in the cause of Texas, going so far as to libel him in published state-ments which he had scattered over Texas; but these had the opposite effect intended with the Texans. His remains were buried on his premises in full view of the battleground where Texas liberty was won.

TEXAS IN 1835

CHAPTER VI,
The Texas Revolution

A brief but accurate and comprehensive detail of causes and events which led to the revolution of Texas against Mexico is contained in the *School History of Texas*, by Barker, Potts, and Ramsdell, to which the reader is referred.

The first conflict of the revolution took place at Gonzales, October 2, 1835. There were no casualties among the Texans. The next was at Goliad, October 9, where one Texan was severely wounded. On the 13th Stephen F. Austin, in command of the forces, proceeded to the vicinity of San Antonio, and on October 28th, a detachment of ninety men, under command of James Bowie and J. W. Fannin, were sent up the river, and at the old Mission Concepcion encountered a force of about four hundred Mexicans and defeated them with a loss of one man killed. The name of that man was Richard Andrews, in whose honor was named the County of...

ANDREWS

Richard Andrews, familiarly known to his comrades as "Big Dick Andrews," because of his immense stature and physical strength, was one of the sons of William Andrews, a soldier of the Revolution.

With his sons he came to Texas in 1818 and established a trading post on the Brazos River, where the town of Richmond is now situated. He fortified the place as a precaution against hostile Indians, opened a store and for many years maintained his family there, trading with the Indians, and successfully resisting all hostile attempts to invade his premises. With this sort of an experience two of his sons, Micah and Richard, became noted Indian fighters.

At the first outbreak of the Texas Revolution they hastened to Gonzales and joined the Texas forces.

At the battle of Concepcion, Richard was killed and was the first man to lose his life in the conflicts of the revolution. His Brother, Micah, though wounded in the same battle, survived to take part in the Battle of San Jacinto as first lieutenant in Captain Jesse Billingsley's company of Burleson's regiment.

About the time this battle took place Stephen F. Austin, who was appointed commissioner to visit the United States with B. T. Archer and W. H. Wharton, to seek aid for the struggling Texans, resigned, devolving the command upon General Edward Burleson. The troops then marched up in the immediate vicinity of San Antonio and invested it.

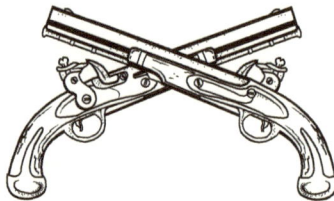

The Storming & Capture of Bexar

The Texans in the interim had been reinforced by two companies from New Orleans, but as the Mexican general, Cos, occupied a fortified place in the city and had sixteen hundred disciplined troops, there was considerable hesitation in attempting to capture the city with the inadequate forces of Burleson. Finally Ben Milam, becoming impatient, proclaimed that San Antonio ought to be taken, and stepping to the front shouted, "Who will follow old Ben Milam?" At the call four hundred men volunteered and began their attack on the 5th of December. The result was that General Cos surrendered his forces on the morning of the 9th.

As a purely military feat this was, perhaps, the most brilliant of all of the battles of the Revolution. Four hundred Texans, under command of Milam, and later Johnson, after making their way through walls and going over the tops of houses for three days and nights, finally captured, in a fortified position, more than four times their own number. They then paroled the Mexicans on the condition that they retire beyond the Rio Grande and not take up arms again to oppose the upholding of the Constitution of 1824, for which the Texans were then fighting, a parole they violated at the first opportunity.

Other smaller engagements, such as the capture of Fort Lipantitlan, on the west bank of the Nueces, the Grass Fight, etc., took place. This victory put the Texans in complete control over all of the territory to the Rio Grande. The names of men participating in that engagement now on our county map are:

Dimmit	Karnes	Milam	Swisher
Glasscock	Lubbock	Ward	

DIMMIT

Philip Dimmit was born in Pennsylvania about the
year 1797, and came to Texas in July of 1822. He was
a merchant and trader, and in 1832 established a store
near the site of the old Fort St. Louis on the Lavaca
River. Here he married a Mexican lady. The place became known as Dimmit's Point. He warmly espoused
the cause of Texas in 1835, and commanded the troops
at Goliad after its capture. In 1841, he moved to the
Nueces River, fifteen miles above Corpus Christi, and
began the erection of a store. Before its completion, he
and his workmen were captured by Mexican raiders
from the Rio Grande and were carried first to Matamoros, then to Monterrey. From there he was started on
his way to prison near Mexico City. He made his escape
at Agua Nueva and was recaptured.

Preferring to die rather than suffer the horrors of a
Mexican prison, he took a large dose of opium, wrote
a letter to his wife, gave directions as to the disposal of
his property, and calmly awaited his death, which soon
afterward occurred.

GLASSCOCK

George W. Glasscock was born April 14, 1810 in Hardin
County, Kentucky. About 1831, he engaged in flatboat-
ing, a part of the time with Abraham Lincoln.

He served with his brother, Gregory, in the Black Hawk
War, in which his brother was killed. In 1833, he went
to Jefferson County, Missouri, and from there removed
to Texas locating at Bevil (Jasper) Municipality, in 1834.
In 1835, as a first lieutenant in Cheshire's company,
Glasscock was in the Grass Fight and at the storming

of Bexar. When not in military service he was engaged in land surveying.

In 1840 he removed from Jasper to Bastrop County, and from there to Travis County in 1844, and located at Webberville, about sixteen miles southeast of Austin. In 1846 he removed to the region where Williamson County now is and aided in the organization of that county. The county site was named Georgetown, in compliment to him. He built the first flouring mill in that part of Texas. In 1853 he removed to Austin and resided there until his death, which occurred February 28, 1868. He took an active interest in building up Georgetown, donating liberally to churches, schools and other enterprises. With the exception of serving as a member of the Tenth and Eleventh Legislatures he never held public office.

KARNES

Henry Wax Karnes was born in Tennessee, September 8, 1812. Early in life his parents moved to Northwestern Arkansas and tried the business of trapping, and he there fitted himself for his subsequent career. He came to Texas about 1828 and secured employment as manager of the large plantation of Jarod E. Groce, on the Brazos River, near the present town of Hempstead. At the first outbreak of the revolution he joined the army. He fought at the battle of Concepcion and was conspicuous for gallantry at the storming of Bexar, December 5, 1835.

Being one of the best scouts in the service, he was elected captain of a cavalry company. This company did much gallant service in many battles. He acted as scout for General Houston on his retreat and kept him informed as to the whereabouts and strength of the enemy, engaging in several skirmishes.

In 1837 he was appointed to take some Mexican prisoners to Matamoros and exchange them for Texas prisoners who had been captured by the Mexicans, but they made Karnes a prisoner. He soon escaped. He joined the ranger service in 1838 and in a combat was severely wounded by an Indian chief. He had red hair, a very strange sight to an Indian. On one occasion, while a prisoner of the Indians, they soaked and scoured his hair, over his protestations that this was its natural color, but they persisted in trying to wash out the color, until convinced by actual demonstration that it was useless. He died in 1840 of the severe wound he had received at the hands of the Indian chief the previous year.

LUBBOCK

Thomas S. Lubbock was born in Charleston, S. C, in 1817. He went to New Orleans at the insistence of his elder brother, F. R. Lubbock, then a merchant at New Orleans and later governor of Texas, and accepted a position with one Holmes, a cotton factor, in 1835.

Shortly after his arrival the struggle in Texas became imminent, and meetings were being held in New Orleans to raise money for the war in Texas. Adolphus Sterne of Nacogdoches attended some of these meetings and informed the people that Texas not only needed money, but men. A company was immediately organized and young Lubbock was the first to enlist. It was agreed that the company would not formally organize in New Orleans, but proceed to Texas and then organize. Accordingly they started for Texas and, arriving late in September, they organized themselves into a military company which they called the New Orleans Grays.

They proceeded on a steamer up the Brazos to Brazoria, and from there marched overland to San Antonio and did gallant service at the storming of Bexar. As the result of this battle was the driving of the Mexicans entirely out of Texas, the company remained at San Antonio for some time. In January, 1836, Lubbock's health beginning to fail, he left the army and returned to the Brazos, where he obtained employment on a steamer, and did not learn that Texas was invaded again until his arrival at Galveston, where he heard the news of the Battle of San Jacinto.

Later he obtained employment from McKinney & Williams, at Velasco. In 1841 he went as lieutenant in command of a company in the Santa Fe Expedition, was made a prisoner and carried to the Santiago Convent in Mexico, and, making his escape by leaping from a balcony, made his way back to Texas.

In 1842 he was again in the army, in the Somervell Expedition. At the breaking out of the war between the States, in company with B. F. Terry, he went to Richmond, Virginia, to get authority to raise a regiment for the war. While in Virginia they participated in the battle of Manassas and were honorably mentioned by General Beauregard for their services in that battle. Obtaining permission to raise a regiment of cavalry, they returned to Texas and organized the famous "Terry Rangers," with Terry as colonel and Lubbock as lieutenant colonel.

On their way to Virginia a special request was made for their service by General Albert Sidney Johnston, and they went to Kentucky. Terry having been killed in a battle at Woodsonville, Kentucky, December 14, 1861, Lubbock was promoted to command of the regiment, but being too feeble in health, he retired to Nashville, Tennessee, where he died in January, 1862.

★ ★ ★

MILAM

This county was named for Benjamin R. Milam, who was born in Kentucky in 1791. He was an active participant in the War of 1812, and after its close he became a trader among the Indians of Texas. He came to Texas in 1816, while the revolution against Spain was at its height, and at once enlisted in the ranks. In 1820 he visited New Orleans, where, in conjunction with Trespelacios he organized an expedition for the capture of Tampico. When Iturbide proclaimed himself Emperor of Mexico Milam joined the party opposed to him. He was captured and thrown into prison, where he remained a year, and was then released by an uprising of the people in favor of the Republican cause. Several years later he obtained, as empresario, a concession for the settlement of a colony on the Red River, where he became acquainted with Richard Ellis. The concession was for land outside of the limits of Texas, and on January 12, 1826, he obtained another concession upon which to introduce two hundred families, the land being within the following boundaries:

> Beginning at the crossing of the San Antonio road, of the Guadalupe River (New Braunfels); thence with said road to the Colorado River; thence up said river to the right bank the distance of fifteen leagues (forty miles); thence in a straight line parallel with the San Antonio road to the Guadalupe River, and thence down the river to the beginning.

He sold out his rights to J. C. Beales, who in time sold to the Bering Brothers, in London, and nothing further was done with it. In 1832 he was at Nacogdoches and participated in the fight against Piedras. In 1835 he procured from the Congress of Coahuila and Texas the exclusive right to navigate the Colorado River. When Santa Anna usurped dictatorial powers in the government of Mexico Milam publicly denounced his cause and was thrown into prison. He escaped and made his way back to Texas.

When near Goliad, hearing the tramp of the forces marching to Goliad, he hid himself in the woods nearby and cried out as they were passing, "Who are you?"

The answer was, "American volunteers bound for Goliad; who are you?"

He replied, "I am Ben Milam, escaped from prison at Monterrey."

He joined the company and participated in the capture of Goliad and went with the company until San Antonio was reached. San Antonio was fortified and defended by four times the number of troops belonging to Texas, and for that reason there was some hesitation in making the attack. Milam stepped out in front and waving his hat, said he was going in to San Antonio, and cried out, "Who will follow Ben Milam?"

With a shout they rushed to his standard and the storming and capture of Bexar were the result. With little more than one-fourth the number of troops at San Antonio they stormed and captured the fortress in San Antonio, taking as prisoners 1600 Mexicans. In the hour of victory, when reconnoitering for a final assault, he was struck by a rifle ball from the enemy and instantly killed, December 8, 1835.

SWISHER

John G. Swisher was born in Tennessee in 1795. He removed to Texas with his family in 1833 and located in Robertson's Colony, where he had many experiences in repelling Indian raids.

At the beginning of hostilities, in October of 1835, he organized a company, was elected captain and was one of those who followed Ben Milam at the storming of Bexar. He was honorably mentioned in the official report of the battle. He was elected one of the delegates from the Municipality of Washington to the Constitutional Convention of March, 1836. He took an active part in all its deliberations. He did not participate in the Battle of San Jacinto, but his oldest son, John M. Swisher, was in the campaign. He moved to Austin and resided there until his death in 1869.

WARD

This county was named for Thomas William Ward, a native of Ireland. He came to the United States and located in New Orleans early in life, and was engaged in business there in 1835, when the Revolution of Texas began.

He enlisted in a volunteer company, afterwards famous as the New Orleans Grays, which had its baptism of blood at the storming of Bexar in December, 1835. He lost a leg in this battle and afterwards became known as "Peg Leg" Ward. He was honorably mentioned for gallantry in that engagement. He was a man of superior intelligence. In April, 1841, while firing a cannon at the anniversary celebration of the Battle of San Jacinto, he lost his arm by the explosure of the gun.

In the fall of that year he was elected Commissioner of the General Land Office of Texas, and held that office until 1848. He was appointed Collector of Customs at Corpus Christi in 1853, and was appointed United States Consul at Panama by President Buchanan in 1857, and served as such until the commencement of the Civil War in 1861.

After the close of that war he resumed his residence at Austin and died there in 1872.

INSCRIPTION
ON THE SHAFT.
NORTH FRONT.

TO THE
GOD
OF THE
FEARLESS
AND FREE
IS
DEDICATED
THIS
ALTAR
MADE FROM
THE RUINS
OF THE
ALAMO

MARCH
6TH
1836
A. D.

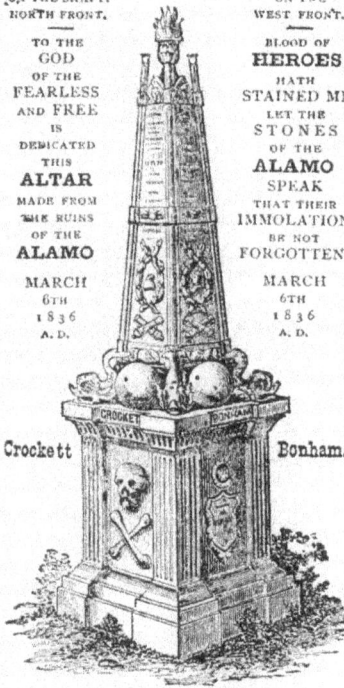

INSCRIPTION
ON THE
WEST FRONT.

BLOOD OF
HEROES
HATH
STAINED ME
LET THE
STONES
OF THE
ALAMO
SPEAK
THAT THEIR
IMMOLATION
BE NOT
FORGOTTEN.

MARCH
6TH
1836
A. D.

INSCRIPTION
ON THE
SOUTH FRONT.

BE THEY
ENROLLED
WITH
LEONIDAS
IN THE
HOST
OF THE
MIGHTY
DEAD.

MARCH
6TH
1836
A. D.

INSCRIPTION
ON THE
EAST FRONT.

Thermopylæ
HAD HER
MESSENGER
OF
DEFEAT,
BUT THE
ALAMO
HAD NONE.

MARCH
6TH
1836
A. D.

Crockett   Bonham.   Travis.   Bowie.

William B. Nangle 1841 Monument to the defenders of the Alamo,
destroyed in the Capitol fire of 1881.

THE ALAMO

While the storming of Bexar was in progress the Governor and Council were in session in San Felipe. The conflict of authority between the Governor and Council resulted in a confusion of military movements. The command of Johnson and Grant was at San Patricio; Fannin was in command at Goliad, and Travis under orders from the Governor took command of the Alamo. He had gathered about him one hundred and fifty men when he wrote the Governor that an invading army of several thousand Mexicans had already reached the Rio Grande, and that San Antonio would be their objective point. He urgently called for reinforcements, but the only reinforcement he received was a company of thirty-two men, on the 23rd of February, making his effective force about one hundred and eighty-five. On the 24th he issued a proclamation addressed, "To the People of Texas and All Americans in the World," in which, among other things, he said, "I am besieged by a thousand or more Mexicans, under Santa Anna. The enemy has demanded a surrender at discretion, otherwise the garrison is to be put to the sword if the fort is taken. I have answered the command with a cannon shot, and our flag still waves proudly from the walls. I shall never surrender or retreat."

On March 6th Santa Anna held a council of war and decided to storm the fort. On Sunday, the 6th, the bugle sounded "no quarter," and the assault was on. The Mexicans soon scaled and broke through the walls, and in a short time every defender of the Alamo lay dead.

The heroism displayed by Travis and his men has been celebrated in song and story, until the name "Alamo" has become the synonym for bravery wherever the English language is spoken. The names of the heroes are chiseled in the granite monument which now stands in the Capitol grounds at Austin, Texas.

Those whose names are on our county map are:

Bailey	Crockett	Kimble
Bowie	Dickens	King
Cochran	Floyd	Lynn
Cottle	Kent	Travis

We have no data on the antecedents of Bailey, Dickens, Floyd, Lynn and King.

George Washington Cottle, Andrew Kent, and George Kimble were heads of families and left their wives and children to go to the relief of Travis on March 1. They had settled in DeWitt's Colony near Gonzales.

BOWIE

This county was named for James Bowie. There are three accounts as to the birthplace of this remarkable man. One account says he was born in Georgia; another ascribes his birthplace to Elliott Springs, Tennessee, and yet another ascribes his birthplace to Edgefield, South Carolina, the date of his birth 1785. That South Carolina was his native state seems most probable.

Early in his life the family removed to Catahoula Parish, Louisiana, and it was there he was reared and educated, along with his brother, Rezin P. Bowie, the inventor of the famous Bowie knife. As young men they were lured by the temptations of the slave trade going on at the time, and in this way they became acquainted with the pirate LaFitte. James Bowie also became connected with Long's expedition in 1819. In 1828 he was naturalized as a Mexican citizen and later married the daughter of Vice Governor Veremendi at San Antonio.

His celebrated Indian fight on the road from San Antonio to San Saba took place in 1831. He was in Nacogdoches in 1832 and took part in the fight with Piedras, afterwards being commissioned to convey the prisoners to San Felipe, whence they were taken to Tampico. In 1835 he joined the army and was second in command at the Battle of Concepcion. After the storming and capture of Bexar he joined the army near Goliad. He there met Houston, who sent him back to San Antonio. There he found Travis in command, but remained there and was killed March 6, 1836, with the others of the garrison.

★ ★ ★

COCHRAN

This county was named for Robert Cochran, who, in the early part of 1835, started from Boston with a small stock of goods and located in Brazoria, and early in February, 1836, joined the army in San Antonio. He was a single man. The only data that could be obtained was from evidence used in litigation over the land granted to his heirs, for which the author is indebted to R. C. Crane, an attorney at Sweetwater, Texas.

CROCKETT

This county was named for David Crockett, who was born August 17, 1786, in Tennessee, then a part of North Carolina, near the present line between that state and North Carolina. His father was an Irishman; his mother was a native of Maryland.

He was of a most pronounced type of the strong individuality characteristic of the mountain population of East Tennessee in his day. He could neither read nor write until eighteen years old. At the age of seven his father removed to Jefferson County, Tennessee, and later in life moved and settled in Franklin County, Tennessee. He went into the Creek War and remained until its close. Returning to his home he lived in great domestic felicity until the death of his wife in 1821. He married a second time and was equally devoted to his second wife. In 1821 he was elected to the Legislature. There he met for the first time Colonel (afterward President) Polk, who, it seems, having a desire to cultivate Crockett's acquaintance, addressed him thus: "Colonel Crockett, I suppose the Legislature will make some change in the judiciary?"

"I suppose so," said Crockett, and got out of the way as soon as possible.

"For," said he afterward, "I did not know what in the thunder the 'judiciary' was."

In 1827, 1829 and 1831 he was successively elected to the United States Congress. Colonel Bailey Peyton, then a member of the lower house, gave the writer the following account of the opening paragraph of his first speech in that body:

"Mr. Speaker, I am skeered, but I don't know what about; I know I can lick any man in this house, and I ain't afeared of none of 'em; still I'm skeered."

He afterwards made a tour of the principal cities of the North, where he was the object of much attention, as a representative of the hardy frontiersmen of the Southwest. As was the case with many frontiersmen of that day, he was an expert with his rifle, was a great hunter and was often called upon by duelists for instructions in marksmanship. In his fourth canvass for Congress he was defeated by a small majority through the influence of the Jackson Democracy. Chagrined over his defeat, and disgusted with political conditions in Tennessee, he picked up his trusty rifle, bade farewell to his family and came to Texas. He took the oath of allegiance at Nacogdoches and hurried on to the theater of war. He arrived at San Antonio too late to take part in the Battle of Concepcion and the storming of Bexar, but joined the forces of Travis in the Alamo, and March 6, 1836, yielded up his life. He left a most interesting autobiography.

★ ★ ★

TRAVIS

William Barrett Travis was born in Edgefield District, South Carolina, August 1, 1809. The place of his birth was near old Red Banks Baptist Church, in what is now Saluda County. A post office at this place has been named Travis. His paternal and maternal ancestors were among the earliest settlers of that region. His grandparents were Barrett and Elizabeth de Loach Travis, and resided in Chester District during the revolution, where Barrett Travis died. The widow, with her four children, moved to Abbeville District and Mark, the father of William Barrett, moved to Edgefield and married Jemima Stallsworth, the mother of William Barrett,

William Barrett was the oldest of eleven children. The parents moved to Conecuh County, Alabama when William Barrett was about six years old, settling on a farm about six miles above Evergreen, the county seat, and young Travis was reared there. An uncle, a Baptist minister, had previously moved there, as did also one of the Stallsworth families, and one of the Stallsworths represented that district in the United States Congress about 1822.

After attending the schools of the neighborhood, William Barrett was sent to the academy of Prof. McCurdy, in Monroe County, a school of considerable reputation in its day.

After attending this school he obtained employment to teach school near Monroeville, county seat of Monroe County, and while thus engaged studied law under Dillett and Parsons. In the meantime he became infatuated with Lucinda Cato, one of his pupils, and was married to her. He then obtained a license and began to practice law, but both soon found that they were not suited to each other and they separated. Travis came to Texas, leaving her and their two children in Alabama. Arriving in Texas he located at Anahuac and began the practice of law in the winter of 1831-2. This was during the administration of the tyrant Bustamente, under whose orders Bradburn had been stationed at Anahuac in command of a company of soldier-convicts, with the ostensible purpose of enforcing the collection of duties on imports.

Patrick C. Jack, a young lawyer, was also a practicing lawyer there at that time. Travis and Jack, with other citizens, were arrested and thrown into prison. There are several accounts of the circumstances leading to their arrest. One (*Texas Almanac*, 1859, page 32) is to the effect that an anonymous letter to Bradburn telling him that a company of one hundred men was being organized on the Sabine to cross the river and forcibly take the runaway slaves he had refused to deliver up to the owners. He investigated, but found no basis for the rumor. Supposing Travis, Jack and others anxious to incite the Texans to a revolt, and of playing a trick on him, he had them arrested.

Another account (Filisola) says: "Early in May, 1832, some of Bradburn's soldiers made an attack upon a woman and that an American being in the neighborhood failed to respond to her cries or come to her assistance, that Bradburn was called upon to punish the culprit, and upon his refusal, they formed a mob, seized the American, tarred and feathered him and drove him through the town with a great noise."

Another account (Yoakum) says: "On one occasion a soldier having committed an outrage, the indignant citizens arrested him and inflicted severe punishment upon him. That Bradburn was harboring runaway slaves from both Texas and Louisiana there seems to be little doubt. This, with the infamies of his convict soldiers, was a constant source of irritation. Travis, Jack and other prisoners were released later after Bustamente was overthrown by Santa Anna. Both Travis and Jack then removed to San Felipe, where they became prominent lawyers. Santa Anna soon threw off his republican mask, and early in 1835 another Mexican officer, Tenorio, in charge of a company, was stationed at Anahuac. His company was also made up of convicts. Smarting under past outrages, Travis organized a company and captured Tenorio and his command, but his act was disapproved by the authorities at San Felipe and Tenorio was released. For this he was ordered to be arrested by the Mexican authorities, but he was never arrested."

Events were now rapidly leading up to the revolution of Texas against Mexico, and Travis was one of the first to join the army. He was in the campaign from Gonzales up to the capture of Bexar on detached service, and made some captures from the Mexicans which were of great service to the Texans. After the capture of Bexar he was detached on scouting service, but in January, 1836, was ordered to take command of the Alamo. Getting news that Santa Anna was on his way to Texas with a large army he began to appeal for reinforcements, there being at that time only one hundred and fifty men at the Alamo. He dispatched J. B. Bonham and two others to Fannin at Goliad. The siege of the Alamo, according to Travis' own statement began on the 23rd of February and continued the 24th, 25th, 26th, 27th, 28th and 29th of February, and 1st, 2nd, 3rd, 4th, and 5th of March, and on the 6th of March the fortress was stormed and every man put to the sword.

★ ★ ★

GOLIAD

Fannin, in command of about four hundred men, found himself almost surrounded by a large force of Mexicans under the command of the Mexican General Urrea, on the 18th of March, and began his retreat to Victoria, but was overtaken near Coleto Creek, about nine miles east of Goliad, and a hotly contested battle took place. On the morning of the 19th a white flag was raised and Fannin surrendered. The prisoners were marched back to Goliad. In the meantime the command of Major Ward was brought in as prisoners and on the 27th of March all who were able to walk, except about a dozen, were marched out and shot. Of those participating in the struggle at Coleto on the 19th, our county map shows the following:

Callahan	Haskell
Duval	Shackelford
Fannin	

CALLAHAN

This county was named for James H. Callahan, who was born near Marion, Georgia in 1812. He came to Texas with the Georgia Battalion in December, 1835, was taken prisoner of war with Fannin's men at Coleto and carried back to Goliad, but his life was spared, as he was a mechanic. It was thought by the Mexicans that his services as such might be utilized by them. After his release he joined the Ranger force and became a captain of the Rangers. In 1856 he became involved in a personal difficulty in Guadalupe County and was killed.

DUVAL

This county was named for Captain Burr H. Duval, who was massacred with Fannin's command at Goliad, March 27, 1836. He came from a distinguished Kentucky family, his father having been a Representative in the United States Congress from 1813 to 1815, and having previously served as captain of mounted volunteers in the War of 1812. In 1822 he was appointed Provisional Governor of Florida.

Burr H. Duval, the subject of this sketch, was born in Nelson County, Kentucky, in 1809, and educated at St. Joseph's College, at Bardstown. Late in the year of 1835 he gathered a company of volunteers and took passage down the river to New Orleans, and from there sailed first to Quintana, at the mouth of the Brazos, where the company formally organized. The company proceeded from there by water to Copano, from which place they marched first to Refugio and then to Goliad. There they joined Fannin's command, where, after the surrender, he was cruelly murdered on the 27th day of March, 1836.

FANNIN

James Walker Fannin was born in Georgia in 1805. He was left an orphan at a tender age and was taken in charge by an uncle, James Walker, and under this name registered as a cadet at West Point Military Academy. He was for a short time after he left there in the United States Army, but resigned and returned to Georgia. He retained his uncle's name and added to it the family name, becoming James Walker Fannin.

In 1834 he came to Texas and engaged in planting on the Brazos. As soon as the war broke out at Gonzales he organized the Brazos Guards and hastened to the west. It was Fannin's company and a few others who were sent forward to select a suitable camping ground for the army near San Antonio, and which fought the battle of Concepcion, in which fight Fannin won the title of "The Hero of Concepcion." When the army was reorganized after Austin's resignation as commander-in-chief, Fannin was sent east to enlist and procure ammunition. The Council at San Felipe, contrary to Houston's orders, ordered him to collect forces at Copano for a descent upon Matamoros.

In January, 1836, Fannin announced that an expedition had been ordered by the Council to Matamoros, and ordered all volunteers to report at San Patricio. The Civil Government at San Felipe was in confusion, with General Houston recognizing the authority of Governor Smith, and Fannin recognizing the authority of the Council. Fannin arrived at Goliad about the 1st of February and the troops were organized there, with Fannin as colonel and Ward as lieutenant colonel. After several intervening contests with the Mexican Army, he collected what troops he could (about 400 men) at Goliad and prepared for defense, but learning that there was a large force of the enemy near he evacuated the town. After stopping at a small creek nine miles east of Goliad to give the teams an opportunity to graze, he resumed his march, and when within two miles of Coleto was overtaken by the Mexican cavalry. Colonel Fannin was wounded in the fight. A white flag was raised in the morning.

The accounts of what occurred are contradictory, some to the effect that terms were agreed upon, providing for the safety of Fannin's army, others that the surrender was unconditional, but all agreeing that there was a surrender. It matters not what the real facts may be, the horrors of the cruelty of the massacre that followed are in nowise mitigated. Fannin's troops were then marched back to Goliad and shot on March 27th.

HASKELL

This county was named for Charles Ready Haskell, who was born near Nashville, Tennessee, September 12, 1817. He was the son of Joshua Haskell and was attending school when the company of Captain Burr H. Duval was organized in Kentucky. He joined the company on its way down the Mississippi and followed its fortunes to that fateful Sunday, March 27, 1836, when he with his entire command was murdered.

SHACKELFORD

This county was named for Dr. John (Jack) Shackleford, who was born in Richmond, Virginia, March 20, 1790. His father, Richard Shackleford, was married three times, his last wife being the mother of the subject of this sketch.

Upon arriving at the age of twenty-one Shackelford left Virginia to seek a new home. He located in Winnsboro, South Carolina, where he married Miss Maria Young, daughter of a Presbyterian minister, and practiced his profession as physician and surgeon. He served for a time in the war of 1812-1815, and in 1818 moved to Shelby County, Alabama, where he was a successful practitioner accumulating considerable land and slaves and engaging in planting. In 1822-24, he was elected to the State Senate from Bibb and Shelby Counties, and being a man of large means, lived and entertained sumptuously. Becoming surety for a cousin who engaged in merchandising and afterward failed, Dr. Shackleford was compelled to sell his lands and slaves to satisfy the debt. In 1829 he was appointed receiver of the Land Office at Courtland, Alabama.

In the late fall of 1835, when he learned that the revolution in Texas had begun, he organized a military company, composed of the best young men in that section, among whom were his oldest son, and two of his nephews. The company was armed and equipped at private expense, and being uniformed in red jeans, was called the Red Rovers. Commanding the company as Captain, Shackleford carried it down to New Orleans and from there by water around to the coast of Texas, landing on the shores of Copano Bay. After a short campaign, the company was surrendered as part of Fannin's command, and after surrender were murdered by the Mexicans.

Dr. Shackleford himself was spared in order that the Mexicans might utilize his services as a physician and surgeon among their sick and wounded. He managed to make his escape in the following June, and as the result of the Battle of San Jacinto rendered his further services unnecessary, he hastened back to his home in Alabama to carry the news of the Goliad massacre to the parents and friends of the young men murdered.

He remained in Alabama and practiced medicine. His wife died in 1854, and he married a second time. He died on the 22nd of January, 1857. His widow survived him many years. The pathetic welcome he received upon his return home is most graphically pictured in Foote's *Texas and Texans*, Mr. Foote having been an eye witness.

As an indication of the profound sensation created in the United States by the massacre at Goliad, the following quotation is taken from a speech made by Hon. Thomas H. Benton in the United States Senate in 1836:

Goliad has torn Texas from Mexico; Goliad has decreed independence; San Jacinto has sealed it! What the massacre decreed, the victory has sealed; and the day of the martyrdom of prisoners must forever be regarded as the day of disunion between Texas and Mexico...

Unhappy day, forever to be deplored, that Sunday morning, March 6, 1836, when the undaunted garrison of the Alamo, victorious in so many assaults over twenty times their number perished to the last man by the hands of those, part of whom they had released on parole two months before, leaving not one to tell how they first dealt out to multitudes that death which they themselves finally received.

Unhappy day, that Palm Sunday, March 27, when the five hundred and twelve prisoners at Goliad, issuing from the sally port at the dawn of day, one by one, under the cruel delusion of a return to their families, found themselves enveloped in double files of cavalry and infantry, marched to a spot fit for the perpetuation of the horrid deed—and there without an instant to think of parents, country, friends, and God—in the midst of the consternation of terror and surprise, were inhumanly set upon, and pitilessly put to death, in spite of those moving cries which reached to heaven and regardless of those supplicating hands, stretched forth for mercy, from which arms had been taken under the perfidious forms of a capitulation.

Five hundred and six perished that morning—young, vigorous, brave, sons of respectable families, and the pride of many a parent's heart—and their bleeding bodies, torn with wounds, and many yet alive, were thrown in heaps upon vast fires, for the flames to consume what the steel had mangled. Six only escaped, and not by mercy, but by miracles. And this was the work of man upon his brother; of Christian upon Christian; of those upon those who adore the same God, invoke the same heavenly benediction, and draw precepts of charity and mercy from the same divine fountain.

Accursed be the ground on which the dreadful deed was done! Sterile, and set apart, let it forever be! No fruitful cultivation should ever enrich it; no joyful edifice should ever adorn it; but shut up, and closed by gloomy walls, the mournful cypress, the weeping willow, and the inscriptive monument, should for ever attest the foul deed of which it was the scene, and invoke from every passerby the throb of pity for the slain, and the start of horror for the slayer.

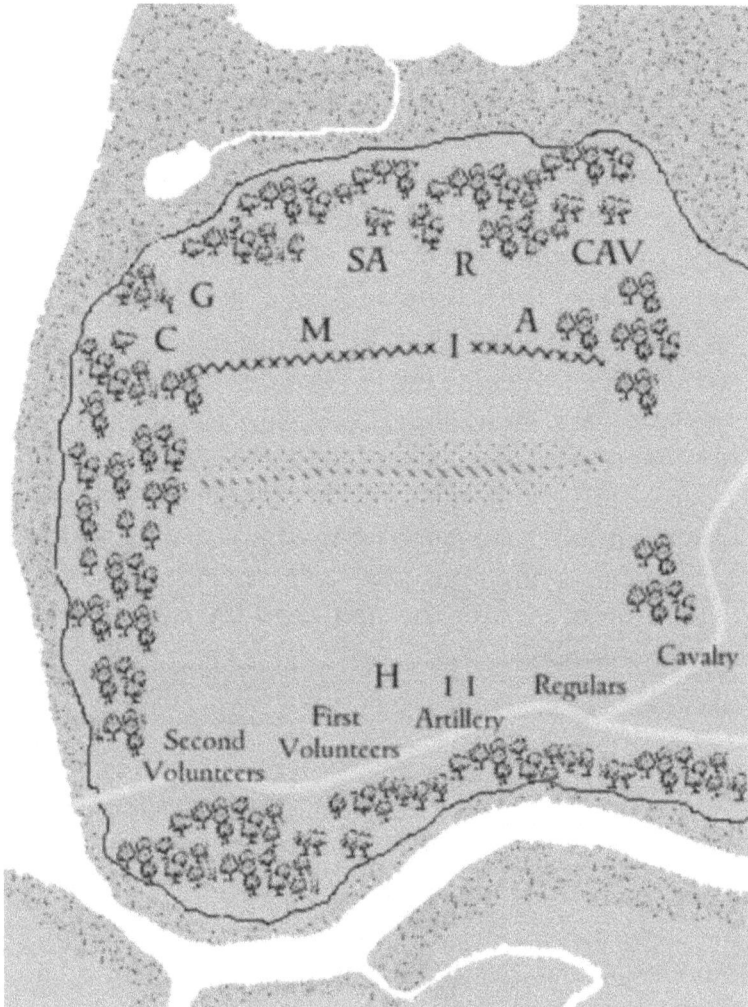

A - Aldama Battalion   R - Mexican reserves
C - Cos' reinforcements   SA - Santa Anna
G - Guerrero Battalion   CAV - Mexican Cavalry
M - Matamoros Battalion   I - Cannon

H - General Houston

The battle lines drawn for the Battle of San Jacinto.
(Illustration courtesy of Mark Pusateri, originally published in *The Soldiers of San Jacinto,* Copano Bay Press, 2008.)

THE BATTLE OF SAN JACINTO

The convention which was in session at Washington on the Brazos elected Sam Houston as commander-in-chief of the army on the 5th of March. He was then a member of the convention but left it the next day and hastened to the relief of Travis. On the 13th, he learned of the fall of the Alamo and the destruction of its garrison and stopped at Gonzales where he organized such forces as he could collect. He took steps to aid the fleeing settlers and on the 5th of April learned of the massacre at Goliad. He also reached San Felipe on that day, and from there marched up the Brazos and encamped nearly two weeks in the bottom.

On the 13th of April, he crossed the Brazos and continued his march reaching Harrisburg on the 18th of April. Going down Buffalo Bayou, one wing of his army encountered the Mexicans, but withdrew and encamped for the night. On the 21st, in command of seven hundred and eighty-three men he attacked Santa Anna's forces, his army rushing into the fray with the battle cry "Remember the Alamo! Remember Goliad!" and after eighteen minutes of stout resistance by the Mexicans, they were thrown into confusion and panic, and the slaughter began. The result was the killing of six hundred and thirty Mexicans, wounding two hundred and eight, and capturing seven hundred and thirty prisoners, among whom was Santa Anna, himself.

Among the participants whose names are on our county map are:

Briscoe	Dawson	Erath	Houston	McCulloch
Burleson	Deaf Smith	Hale	Kleberg	Motley
Cooke	Eastland	Hockley	Lamb	Sherman

BRISCOE

This county was named for Andrew Briscoe, who commanded Company A of the regulars at San Jacinto. He was of English descent, born on November 25, 1810 and reared on the family plantation in Claiborne County, Mississippi. He was educated at Clinton Academy in Hinds County, and attended Franklin University in Kentucky, later studying law under General John A. Quitman at Jackson, Mississippi.

Early in 1835, he shipped a stock of goods to Anahuac, Texas, and resisted the collection of duties. For this he was thrown into prison, but was released by W. B. Travis and his volunteer company. In the fall of that year, Briscoe was captain of the Liberty Volunteers at Concepcion. He was at the storming and battle of Bexar on December 5, 1835 and, as mentioned above, at the Battle of San Jacinto. Afterwards he was Chief Justice of Harris County.

Upon retiring from this office he gave his time to the promotion of a railroad from Harrisburg to the Brazos River, and this survey was later adopted by the line which is a part of the Southern Pacific Railroad system. After a mile or two of road had been graded and the ties placed, the enterprise was abandoned in 1840 as being premature.

In the interim he had married a daughter of John R. Harris, and removed to New Orleans, where he engaged in a banking, brokerage and exchange business. He died there October 4, 1849, and his remains were sent to the old family burying ground on the plantation in Claiborne County, Mississippi, and buried.

BURLESON

This county was named for General Edward Burleson, colonel of the First Regiment of Volunteers at the Battle of San Jacinto. He was born in North Carolina in 1798, and when a mere lad went with his father into the Creek War, acting as his secretary, and thus received his first military lesson under the leadership of General Jackson. The family moved to Virginia, where he was elected lieutenant and colonel of militia. He next removed to Tennessee and was there elected colonel of militia.

In 1831 he came to Texas and settled in what is now Bastrop County, then on the extreme frontier, and was soon called upon to lead his neighbors against marauding Indians. At Gonzales, when Stephen F. Austin became commander of the forces there, Burleson was elected colonel of the only regiment then organized. When Austin resigned Burleson was elected Commander-in-chief, and was holding this position when Bexar was captured. At the reorganization of the army in 1836 he was elected colonel of the first regiment. In 1837 he was elected brigadier general of the militia, and in 1838 was appointed colonel in the regular army. In 1841 he was elected Vice President of the Republic. In 1842, when it was deemed advisable to invade the border states of Mexico, he was the general choice of the troops for the position of commander, but President Houston appointed Alexander Somervell to the position. In 1843 he was a candidate for the Presidency, but was defeated by Anson Jones. In 1846 he served on the staff of General Henderson.

After his return to Texas he located his home at the beautiful spring which forms the San Marcos River. He was elected to the State Senate and was unanimously chosen president of that body. He died in the city of Austin, December 26, 1851. A detailed biography of General Burleson would embrace a substantial history of Indian warfare in Texas from 1831 to his death. A contemporary expresses the opinion that he rendered a larger military service to the state than any other man among the numerous fighters of that period in our history.

COOKE

W. G. Cooke was born in Fredericksburg, Virginia, March 26, 1808, where he was reared and educated. He removed to New Orleans and was in business there in October, 1835. When volunteers for Texas were called for, he immediately stepped forward and enrolled his name. Upon their arrival at San Antonio he was elected Captain of the New Orleans Grays, followed Ben Milam into San Antonio and led his company in the forefront at the storming of Bexar. Later he was on the staff of General Houston and was with him at the Battle of San Jacinto, being appointed Assistant Inspector General in that battle with the rank of Major. After the battle he accompanied General Houston to New Orleans and returned with him to Texas. He remained with the army until 1837, when he settled in Houston and established a drugstore.

In 1839 he was appointed Quartermaster General of the army by President Lamar; on March 19, 1840, was in the Blockhouse Fight with the Comanches and in May, 1841, was appointed one of the commissioners to accompany the Santa Fe Expedition. He was made a prisoner and carried to Mexico, but he was released in 1842 and returned to Texas. In 1844 he was married to Angele Navarro, a niece of Juan Antonio Navarro, in San Antonio, Texas. When the State Government was organized, in 1846 he was appointed Adjutant General. In December 1847, he died at Seguin, Texas.

DAWSON

Nicholas Mosby Dawson was born in Woodford County, Kentucky, in 1808. His parents removed to White County, Tennessee, where he was educated. In 1834 he came to Texas and located near his kinsman, W. M. Eastland, in what is now Fayette County. When news of Santa Anna's invasion reached his vicinity, he volunteered and was elected second lieutenant of Company B of the volunteers and participated in the Battle of San Jacinto.

A short time after the battle he quit the army and resumed business. He was residing in Fayette County in 1842 when Woll made his raid into Texas and captured San Antonio. As soon as the news reached LaGrange, he organized a company and hastened to the front. On the day of the Battle of Salado, while trying to lead his men into the Texans' camp, he was surrounded by an overwhelming force of Mexicans. When about half of his men had been killed, he raised the white flag. It was fired upon and the fight renewed. He finally surrendered his pistol to a Mexican officer. He was then seized by the Mexican soldiers and put to death. There were fifty-three men in his company; thirty-three were slain in battle, fifteen surrendered, five of whom were wounded, and two made their escape.

DEAF SMITH

The real name of this eccentric man was Erastus Smith. He came to be known as "Deaf Smith" by reason of his being partially deaf.

He was born in New York State, April 19, 1787, and in 1798 moved with his parents to the territory of Mississippi and settled near Natchez. His parents were pious Baptists, and reared him with the best influences, moral and intellectual, which the then wild and sparsely settled condition of the country afforded.

In 1817, he wandered away from home and came to Texas alone, but remained only a short time. Four years later he again came to Texas, making his headquarters in and around San Antonio. He spent most of his time rambling alone in that section of Texas.

When DeWitt's Colony was first established, he identified himself with it, and finally married a Mexican lady in San Antonio. He inherited valuable land, in Claiborne County, Mississippi, but paid no attention to it, and died a poor man.

Before the Texas Revolution began, by his lonely wanderings, he acquired such a knowledge of the country as few possessed. But at the breaking out of the revolution it was feared by reason of his Mexican marriage that his loyalty to Texas was a matter of uncertainty. This however, proved a mistake, and he joined the forces of Austin, among the first, at Gonzales. He was detailed on scout duty, for which he was peculiarly fitted, and performed invaluable services, prior to the storming of Bexar, by which time he had become known to all the army.

He was in the first fight at Concepcion, in the storming of Bexar, and marched at the head of Johnson's command, as the Texans made their way into the city, and while on top of the Veramendi house, he was wounded.

Upon the reorganization of the army under Houston, in March, 1836, he was put in command of scouts, and ordered to report the movements of the Mexican army, and aid the fleeing families, and rendered valuable services. His remarkable efficiency and reliability made him a special favorite of General Houston's.

When near Harrisburg, on the San Jacinto campaign, he captured a courier with important dispatches to Santa Anna, and from these he learned that Santa Anna was near the mouth of Buffalo Bayou.

On the morning of the 21st of April he was detailed by General Houston to destroy Vince's bridge, which he promptly did, and on the afternoon of the same day, went into the fight, with a dash and intrepidity that won for him universal praise from the army.

Two or three days after the battle, he was given important orders from Santa Anna to Gen. Filisola to retreat. Later on he was made captain of the Rangers and after one or two small engagements, he retired from the army and located in Richmond, Fort Bend County, where he died, November 30, 1837, and was buried there. A modest monument, in the corner of the Episcopal Church yard, marks the spot where he was buried. It has the inscription, "Deaf Smith, The Texas Spy, died November 30, 1837."

EASTLAND

Thomas B. Eastland was a lieutenant in the United States Army and in 1800 was Quartermaster General for Kentucky. In the War of 1812, he served with distinction under General Harrison. In 1801, he married Nancy Mosby and had five sons and one daughter. William M. Eastland, the son in whose honor Eastland County was named, was born at Woodfarm, Woodford County, Kentucky, March 21, 1806, and was a cousin of Colonel J. S. Mosby, the famous scout and cavalry leader in the Civil War. In early life the family moved to Tennessee and in 1834 he, with two of his brothers and Nicholas Mosby Dawson, came to Texas. They located near LaGrange and engaged in the sawmill and lumber business, and as was the case with practically every other citizen on the frontier, he was frequently called on to repel the Indians. At the breaking out of the Texas Revolution he promptly volunteered and was elected first lieutenant of a company, afterward Company F of Burleson's regiment, and acted in this capacity at the Battle of San Jacinto.

After this, the last battle of the Revolution, he returned home and resumed business. His wife died in 1837, and two years later he was married to Louise M. Smith, daughter of Rev. W. B. Smith, a Methodist minister. When Texas was invaded by General Woll in 1842, he organized a company at LaGrange and marched to San Antonio, but arrived too late to participate in the battle which took place between Texans and the Mexicans.

The Somervell Expedition was then organized and Eastland's company joined it. Upon reaching the Rio Grande, he took his command across and was in the Battle of Mier, where the Texans surrendered December 26, 1842. While on their way to prison, upon arriving at the hacienda of Salado, they rushed upon their guards and escaped, but while in search of water they came to a camp of Mexican soldiers too numerous to contend against, and surrendered. They were taken back to Salado, and informed that they were to be shot, but by the intervention of General Mexia the order was changed so that one man in ten should be shot, and they were to draw by lot to determine which one of the ten should be shot. One hundred and fifty-nine white beans were placed in the bottom of an earthen jug and seventeen black ones upon top of them. The jug was not shaken. Captain Eastland drew the first black bean, and they continued until the last black bean was drawn.

Soon afterward, the ill-fated men were marched into a separate courtyard and shot, March 25, 1843. In 1848 the bones of the murdered men were exhumed and taken to LaGrange and buried, and a monument erected over them.

ERATH

This county was named for George B. Erath, member of Company C, First Regiment of Volunteers. He was born at Vienna, Austria, on January 1, 1813, and was educated at Santa Ana College and the Polytechnic Institute of that city. He came to the United States, landing at New Orleans July 18, 1832, and after traveling through the western states, arrived in Texas and came to San Felipe. In 1834, he hired himself to Alexander Thomson as a chain carrier in surveying land in Robertson's Colony, and was soon promoted to the position of surveyor. In July, 1835, he went into the war against the Indians, and later he joined the company of Jesse Billingsley and fought as a private at San Jacinto. He afterwards joined Hill's company of Rangers and in 1838 was made lieutenant and given a separate command. In all of these commands he saw much hard service and engaged in many Indian fights. In 1838 he formed a company of surveyors, but the Indians were so troublesome that they were forced to do more fighting than surveying. In 1839 he was elected captain of a Ranger company. In 1841 he was made captain of a company of minutemen.

At intervals, during the time, Erath surveyed land to replenish his finances, as the Republic was too poor to equip him and pay his expenses. In 1842 he joined the Somervell Expedition. After his return home he was elected to the Lower House of the Texas Congress in 1843, was re-elected in 1844 and 1845. He was elected to the First Legislature in 1846, and in 1848 he was elected to the State Senate. In 1849 he surveyed and planned the city of Waco. He was appointed major of frontier forces in 1861 and in 1862-3 again became a member of the Legislature. In 1873 he was elected State Senator and served in that capacity until the reorganization of the state government under the Constitution of 1876. This was his last public service. He died at Waco, Texas, May 13, 1891, at the age of seventy-eight.

HALE

This county was named for Lieutenant John C. Hale, killed at the Battle of San Jacinto, April 21, 1836. From proof on file in the General Land Office of Texas, it is learned that John C. Hale came to Texas from Louisiana in 1834 and settled in what is now Sabine County with his family. At the organization of the company of Captain Benjamin Bryant, he was chosen first lieutenant. From H. W. B. Price, a member of the same company,

it was learned that as soon as this company was organized, it was hurried forward to meet General Houston's
army, and met the command as it was crossing the Brazos. The company was promptly assigned a place, and
marched with the army to San Jacinto. Only twenty men
of the company participated in the battle, the remainder
being detailed to nurse the sick and guard the baggage.

HOCKLEY

This county was named for George W. Hockley, who
was born in Philadelphia and reared and educated in
that city. In early manhood he moved to Washington
City and was for a time in the employ of the government. It was here that he first met General Houston,
and it was probably through the latter's influence that
Hockley went to Tennessee about the year 1828. Nothing has been learned of his career in Tennessee.

In 1835 he came to Texas, joined the army in 1836,
and was appointed Inspector General in the San Jacinto
campaign. He commanded the artillery at San Jacinto.
He was appointed Secretary of War in General Houston's second term. In 1843 he was sent by President
Houston to Mexico to negotiate a peace. There is no
evidence that he was in the Mexican War, 1846-7. He
seems to have retired from public life after annexation.
He died in Corpus Christi at the home of his kinsman,
H. L. Kinney, on June 6, 1851, and his remains were buried in the cemetery established during General Taylor's
occupancy in 1845-6.

★ ★ ★

HOUSTON

This county was named for Sam Houston, the central figure in the history of the Republic of Texas. He was born in Rockbridge County, Virginia, March 2, 1793. When he was quite young, his widowed mother removed with her family to east Tennessee, at that time the western limit of civilization. There he spent his time alternately at school and at work on the farm or in a store as a clerk. At one time he left home and spent some time among the Cherokee Indians. In 1813 he enlisted as a soldier in the Creek War, and distinguished himself at the Battle of the Horse Shoe, where he was promoted for gallantry.

He was appointed Indian agent in 1817, resigned and studied law, and in 1819 was made District Attorney of Davidson County and Major General of the militia. He began the study of law in Nashville, and after holding several minor offices in Tennessee, was, in 1823, elected to the lower house of the United States Congress; he was re-elected in 1825 and served until 1827. He was elected governor of Tennessee in 1827 and shortly after his entering upon the duties of the office he resigned and took up his abode among the Cherokee Indians in Arkansas. In 1832, it seems that he was sent on a mission to some of the Indian tribes in Texas, and shortly after his return to Arkansas, he came to settle permanently in Texas.

In 1833 he was elected a member of the convention for separate statehood. In 1834 he was instrumental in defeating a project to introduce Creek Indians into Texas. In 1835 he was elected delegate to the General Consultation, but regarded separation from Mexico as premature. Upon the organization of the provisional government, in November, 1835, he was appointed commander of the forces in the field. He was elected a delegate to the Constitutional Convention, which assembled March 1, and on the 7th he was appointed commander-in-chief of all the military forces of Texas.

He immediately repaired to Gonzales, and learning of the fall of the Alamo and the massacre of Goliad, he organized a small force at Gonzales, and began a retreat eastwardly and finally brought the war to a successful close at San Jacinto, April 21, 1836. In October, 1836, he was inaugurated first Constitutional President of the Republic of Texas.

After his term expired, he was elected to the Congress of Texas two successive terms. He was again elected President in 1841 and in 1846 he became one of the United States Senators from Texas, which office he held until his election as governor of the state, in 1859. He was governor when the state seceded, but being opposed to secession, would not forswear his allegiance to the United States and abandoned the office in the spring of 1861 and retired to his home in Huntsville, Texas, where he died July 25, 1863. His fame became worldwide and his memory is cherished by the people of Texas.

KLEBERG

Robert Kleberg, in whose honor this county was named, was born September 10, 1803, in Herstelle, Westphalia, Germany. He received a collegiate education at the Gymnasium of Holzminden, and then entered the University at Goettingen, and received the degree of doctor juris.

After serving in several judicial positions, he became dissatisfied with the military and administrative despotism prevalent there and decided to emigrate to America in 1834. To use his own words, "I wished to live under a republican form of government, with unbounded personal, religious, and political liberty." Prussia smarted at that time under an offensive military despotism.

On September 24, 1834, he was married to Miss Rosalie von Roeder, daughter of a former officer in the army, and she too wished to emigrate to Texas. Some of the unmarried brothers of his wife and one of her unmarried sisters, well provided with money, clothing, tools, farming implements and other things necessary to commence a settlement, left in advance of the others. The remainder of the family started six months later. In the party were Robert Kleberg and his wife, his father-in-law and his family and several others destined for San Felipe de Austin. At New Orleans they chartered the steamer Sabine and sailed for Brazoria, Texas, and after a voyage of eight days on the Gulf were wrecked on Galveston Island, about ten miles west of the present city of Galveston.

The island was then a wilderness, inhabited only by deer, wolves, rattlesnakes and Indians. Several days after the vessel was beached, the steamer *Ocean* came in sight and seeing their distress signal, anchored near their camp and agreed to take a few of the company to Brazoria, among whom was Kleberg.

Upon their arrival there they found no boats or others means of transportation, and Kleberg and one of the von Roeders went on foot to San Felipe. There they met Captain Moseley Baker and others, and were informed that their advance party had located about fourteen miles southwest beyond some springs which formed the head of a small stream emptying into the San Bernard River, but that two of his brother-in-laws had died and the others were in a small hut and in a pitiable condition. Emaciated by disease and exposure the settlers shed tears of joy upon Kleberg's arrival.

After a few days of rest, Kleberg and his companion, chartered a boat to bring their company from Galveston Island. They found the party in good spirits, and after a stormy voyage, brought them up to Harrisburg, where he engaged comfortable quarters for the family. Leaving the women and children at Harrisburg, the men with wagons drawn by oxen and loaded with their tools, supplies, etc., proceeded to their little settlement and began work, erecting two log houses, ceiling one with oak planks sawed by hand and put ten acres in corn and cotton. They brought their families from Harrisburg, leaving their furniture, among other things a fine piano, valuable oil paintings, music, books, etc., all of which were destroyed in the following April by Santa Anna's army when Harrisburg was burned.

As soon as the news of the fall of the Alamo reached San Felipe and the families of settlers were fleeing to avoid the inhuman cruelties of Mexican vengeance, the Von Roeders and Kleberg and his wife packed up what they could carry in ox carts and went to San Felipe to decide upon a definite program. The crucial moment of Kleberg's life had now come. Should he leave his

young wife and tender infant to work their way out of
the country, or should he go with her to a place of safety
beyond the Sabine? There was little time to consider
the matter. Finally it was agreed that his father-in-law,
the elder Van Roeder, should take charge of the family,
and that Robert Kleberg and young Von Roeder should
join Moseley Baker's company, then forming, and stake
their lives for the independence of Texas.

From that time on they were actively engaged in
Houston's campaign, finally participating in the Battle
of San Jacinto. The only other service in which these
men engaged in that year was in Rusk's command, following the Mexican army to insure its retreat beyond
Rio Grande. Upon their arrival at Goliad, they gathered
the charred bones of those who had been murdered by
the Mexicans by command of Santa Anna, and buried
them with military honors.

At the family parting near San Felipe, Mrs. Kleberg
mounted a pony, took her infant in her arms and started on her journey. When the company was disbanded
the Klebergs returned to their little settlement, which
formed the nucleus of what is now the flourishing
town of Cat Springs in Austin County. In 1848 Kleberg
removed from the Cat Springs settlement to DeWitt
County, near Myersville, where another German settlement was established, and was residing there at the
commencement of the Civil War. He was loyal to the
Southern Confederacy. Being fifty-eight years old, he
was past the age of military service, but he organized a
militia company. His sons, Otto and Rudolph, joined the
Confederate army and served in General Tom Green's
command. Robert Kleberg died full of years and honor
at his home near Yorktown, Texas, October 23, 1888. He
held various offices of honor, but none that required
prolonged absence from his family and home duties.

LAMB

This county was named for Lieutenant George A. Lamb, who was killed at the Battle of San Jacinto, April 21, 1836. He was born in Laurens District, South Carolina, October 3, 1814. He was left an orphan in boyhood and made his home with the Bankhead family. He had a good common school education and was of a genial, happy disposition.

He came to Texas with young Richard Bankhead in 1834, Bankhead was a married man and with his wife and three little girls settled in what is now the western part of Walker County. Bankhead contracted a severe cold from exposure in moving, and died October 20, 1834, shortly after his arrival in Texas, leaving his widow and three little girls in charge of young Lamb, who faithfully discharged his trust. Lamb was frequently called from home to assist in repelling Indian raids. For the protection of the widow and children he arranged a hiding place in the swamp nearby, stocking it with ample provisions until his return. On September 8, 1835, he was married to Mrs. Bankhead.

When volunteers were called for, he enlisted in a company then organizing in that region and was unanimously chosen second lieutenant. The company went promptly to General Houston's aid. After undergoing the hardships of that campaign, Lamb was killed in the first charge of the Texans. Having a presentiment that he would lose his life in the first battle he engaged in, he took all the money he had and his watch and sent all to his wife and step-children with an affectionate message.

McCULLOCH

This county was named for Ben McCulloch, who was born in Rutherford County, Tennessee, November 11, 1811, and came to Texas in the winter of 1835-36. He was a private in the artillery corps at San Jacinto and was placed in immediate charge of the Twin Sisters, two small but famous brass cannons. On the next day he was promoted to a First Lieutenancy for gallantry in the battle.

When the war was over, he settled in Gonzales and engaged in land surveying. In 1839 he was elected to the Texas Congress and served in that body two years, just after he had made his first successful Indian scouting trip. In 1840 he participated in the Battle of Plum Creek. In 1841 Indian raids were so frequent that his services were in constant demand. In 1842 he was elected first lieutenant of Hay's Company of Rangers. Later he resigned, owing to pressing personal matters, but rejoined as a private and was in many hard-fought contests with the Indians.

He promptly joined the United States volunteers at the beginning of the Mexican War and his services as a scout for General Taylor received favorable notice in more than one official report. After that war he was engaged alternately in Indian warfare and surveying land. In 1853 President Pierce appointed him United States Marshal for the Western District of Texas. In 1858 President Buchanan sent him to Utah upon an important mission, the duties of which he performed with great tact and judgment.

At the beginning of the Civil War, 1861, he was commissioned brigadier general in the Confederate Army and ordered to Arkansas. He commanded his brigade at the Battle of Wilson's Creek where the federal general Cecil Lyons was killed. He was himself killed at the Battle of Pea Ridge, March 7th, 1862.

MOTLEY

This county was named for Dr. William Motley, who was born in Virginia, April 9, 1812. When he was a child his parents moved to Kentucky, where he was reared and educated. He graduated in medicine after taking a literary course at Transylvania University in 1834, and came to Texas in 1835, locating at Gonzales. He was a delegate from this municipality at the convention of March, 1836. He promptly joined the army after the adjournment of the convention and was aid to General Rusk at the Battle of San Jacinto, April 21, 1836, where he was mortally wounded. In closing his official report of that battle, General Rusk said, "Dr. William Motley was mortally wounded and soon after his spirit took its flight to join the immortal Milam and others in the better world."

SHERMAN

This county was named for General Sidney Sherman, who commanded the left wing of the cavalry at San Jacinto. He was a descendant of Roger Sherman of Revolutionary fame, having been born in Massachusetts in 1809. During his youth his family removed to Cincinnati, Ohio. In 1835 he was engaged in manufacturing bagging in Newport, Kentucky. Hearing of the Texas Revolution, he left his business and organized and equipped a company of fifty men to engage in the cause of Texas. He arrived at the Brazos in February, 1836, and hurried on to the relief of Travis in the Alamo, but when he reached

Gonzales he learned that the Alamo had fallen. At the organization of the first regiment at Gonzales he was elected lieutenant colonel, and upon the reorganization of the army on the Brazos he was elected colonel. The day before the Battle of San Jacinto he made an attack on the Mexicans. On the 21st he opened the fight and first sounded the war cry, "Remember the Alamo! Remember Goliad!"

Several months later, after hostilities had entirely ceased, he returned to Kentucky, where he had left his family. Before leaving for Texas, he was taken sick with fever and remained in bed ten weeks. Again, while on his way back to Texas, he was taken sick in Louisiana and confined six weeks. He returned to Texas with his family after a few months and settled on San Jacinto Bay. In 1842 he was elected to the Texas Congress.

In 1840 he conceived the idea of rebuilding Harrisburg, which had been destroyed by Santa Anna in 1836. He with others purchased a 4,000 acre tract of land, including the old townsite. He went to Boston and interested capitalists, who organized a company to build a railroad from Harrisburg westward. After six or seven years of unabated effort he succeeded in rebuilding the town and starting the first railway train in Texas. The shrill whistle of the "General Sherman" was the first glad sound of the locomotive upon the solitude of the Texas forests, the first west of the Sabine, and with one exception the first west of the Mississippi. From 1853 to the end of his life his business career was marked by successive misfortunes. He died in Galveston in 1873.

★

THE REPUBLIC OF TEXAS

The Battle of San Jacinto was the final battle of the Texas Revolution, and deserves to be ranked among the most decisive battles of the different wars in America.

On the 19th of December, 1836, the Congress of the Republic of Texas defined its boundaries as follows:

> Beginning at the mouth of the Sabine River and running west along the Gulf of Mexico, three leagues from the land, to the mouth of the Rio Grande; thence up the principal stream of said river to its source; thence due north to the forty-second degree of north latitude; thence along the boundary line as defined in the Treaty between the United States and Spain to the beginning, as shown on the following map.

This map (page 216) also shows the county subdivision of the Republic up to 1825, the location of colonies during the existence of the Republic and other dates.

★

REPUBLIC OF TEXAS and boundaries as claimed by Texas from December 19, 1836 to November 25, 1850.

CHAPTER VII,
THE REPUBLIC OF THE RIO GRANDE

In 1839 there was a movement in Northern Mexico for the establishment of a Republic to be independent of Mexico. President Lamar declined to commit Texas to the move, but many in Texas sympathized with it. A force of about 600 Texans joined the movement and marched into Mexico to be betrayed by the Mexicans. The names of persons in that enterprise now on the map are Cameron and Zapata.

CAMERON

Ewen Cameron was born in the highlands of Scotland in 1811. He came to Texas in 1837 and immediately allied his fortunes with the Republic. The first opportunity which presented itself for active service came in 1839. In furtherance of the cause of those liberal Mexicans who were still struggling against the tyranny of their government, he organized a company of which he was elected Captain, and commanded it in a battle known as the Battle of Alcantra, in which they were victorious. The revolution was a failure.

Cameron then returned to Texas. Two years later he organized a company, and commanded it with conspicuous gallantry in the Battle of Mier. With the entire command he was surrendered a prisoner. While on their way to prison the Texans, led by Cameron, rushed upon their guards and made their escape, but after a series of horrible sufferings among the mountains of Mexico they gave themselves up to the Mexican soldiers. At the

Haciendo Salado seventeen of the men were shot. Cameron, after drawing a white bean at this lottery of death, was ordered shot by Santa Anna later on. When he was taken out he bared his breast to his executioners, and his body was pierced by many bullets. His execution occurred April 25, 1843.

ZAPATA

This county was named for Colonel Antonio Zapata, a native of Mexico and a wealthy stockman. He owned a large cattle ranch on the Rio Grande in the region which is now Zapata County. He was an ardent Republican. He was colonel in command of forces in the army which was raised to further the interest of the Republic of the Rio Grande. He was captured at night while on his ranch, and was taken out and shot. His head was severed from his body and stuck on a pole somewhat after the fashion of the Royalists' treatment of the patriot Hidalgo.

CHAPTER VIII,
THE TEXAS NAVY

MOORE

This county was named for Commodore Edwin Ward Moore, a native of Virginia. At the breaking out of the revolution in Texas he was a lieutenant on the United States sloop *Boston*. He resigned his commission and was appointed captain in the Texas Navy. During President Houston's second administration there occurred between Moore and the president a serious misunderstanding, the details of which may be learned in the *Quarterly* of the Texas Historical Association of April, 1910. By the terms of annexation he was entitled to a transfer to the United States Navy, with the same rank which he held in the Texas Navy, but there were complications which prevented this and he retired from naval service. He went to Virginia, but returned to Galveston, Texas, in the employ of the Buchanan administration. Later he returned to his native state and died there in 1865.

CHAPTER IX,
EARLY STATESMEN OF TEXAS

The work of the early statesmen of Texas admits of no extended comment in a review of this character, but there are several prominent features of it that cannot be passed over.

The first and foremost is our homestead law. "It is peculiarly an American institution," says Thompson, in his work on homestead and exemptions. If anything similar to it exists in any other country, we are not aware of it. The earliest homestead law, of which the writer has any knowledge, was an act of the Congress of the Republic of Texas, passed January 26, 1839. Since the passage of this act, the protection of the homestead became a favorite object with all legislatures of Texas. When the state adopted a new constitution, on entering the American Union in 1845, that instrument guaranteed, for the first time, a family homestead. Vermont led in 1849 in following the example of Texas, and today, with probably not an exception, every state in the Union has a homestead law.

The next feature to be noticed is the twelfth article of the Declaration of Rights in the Constitution of the Republic, which provides that "no person shall be imprisoned for debt in consequence of inability to pay." This, too, has been followed first by the Congress of the United States in 1839, and the statutes of all the states are today unencumbered by this relic of medieval barbarism.

The other feature is the simplified system of pleading, based upon the abolition of the distinction between law and equity in our courts, especially the doing away with the action of ejectment with John Doe, and Richard Roe and the casual ejector. Texas led in this, and in all the States of the Union there has been similar action.

These were immense strides in the work of civilization, worthy of the pride of every patriotic Texan. Among these, the following are on our county map:

Anderson	Henderson	Jones	Wilson
Bee	Howard	Kaufman	Wood
Bell	Hunt	Lamar	
Crosby	Irion	Rains	
Hamilton	Jack	Van Zandt	

ANDERSON

This county was named for Kenneth L. Anderson, who was born in Hillsboro, North Carolina, September 11, 1805, and was educated in the celebrated Bingham School in his native county. He removed to Shelbyville, Tennessee, about the year 1829. After practicing his profession at that place until 1837, he removed to Texas and located at San Augustine. He was appointed District Attorney in 1842, and later was elected a member of the lower branch of Texas Congress, of which he became Speaker. He was one of the most eminent lawyers of the Republic, and at different times formed partnerships with General Rusk and Governor Henderson. He was Vice President of the Republic in 1844, and died while on his way home from a session of Congress at Washington on the Brazos. He was buried at Fanthorps, in Grimes County on July 3, 1845. The name of Fanthorps was afterward changed to Anderson in his honor.

BEE

This county was named for Barnard E. Bee, who was born in Charleston, South Carolina in 1787. He was educated in the law and served on the staff of Governor James Hamilton of South Carolina. Bee was also prominent in the nullification troubles of that state.

He came to Texas and joined the army in the summer of 1836. He was elected as one of three commissioners to accompany Santa Anna to Washington, D. C. in order that the Mexican dictator might, in the presence of President Jackson, renew the promises he had made to the Republic of Texas in regard to recognizing her independence. The promises were renewed in General Jackson's presence, but they were never complied with.

When the commissioners reached New Orleans, Santa Anna was in want of funds and drew his draft upon his bank in Vera Cruz for $2,000. By the endorsement of Colonel Bee, he obtained the money. Upon his return to Vera Cruz, Santa Anna repudiated the draft upon the plea that he was a prisoner under duress. Colonel Bee made good the draft, and after waiting for some time was paid back by the Republic of Texas.

He was Secretary of War under President Houston, and Secretary of State under President Lamar, and later Minister to the United States from the Republic of Texas. He was subsequently commissioned as Minister to Mexico. When his credentials were sent to Mexico, Santa Anna politely returned them, with the statement that he would be delighted to receive Colonel Bee as his friend, but never as the official representative of the rebellious province of Texas. Bee opposed to annexation and after that event was consummated, he returned to South Carolina, where he died in 1853.

While General Hamilton P. Bee was speaker of the
House of Representatives of Texas the county of Bee
was named in honor of his father. To another son, Colonel Barnard E. Bee Jr., a graduate of West Point, who
was killed at the first battle of Manassas, the world is
indebted for the prefix "Stonewall" to the name of General T. J. Jackson.

BELL

This county was named for Peter Hansborough Bell,
who was born in Culpepper County, Virginia, in 1808,
and was reared and educated there. Upon attaining his
majority, he removed to Petersburg, Virginia. He was
engaged in business there when in March, 1836, learning that the Texans were hard-pressed in their struggle
for liberty, he set sail and arrived off the mouth of the
Brazos in the first days of April.

As nearly all the inhabitants had fled from that section
upon hearing of the approach of Santa Anna, there was
no communication with the interior, and he was presented with the alternative of either re-embarking and
sailing back to the United States or plunging through
the wilderness on foot to find Houston's army. He set
out on foot, following the course of the river, and on the
12th of April found Houston's army just as it was leaving the Brazos. He immediately enlisted, marched with
the army to San Jacinto, and participated in the conflict
as a private in Captain Karnes' Cavalry Company. He
remained in the army for some time and then attached
himself to the ranger service, and was thus engaged
when he was appointed Inspector General in 1839.

After the expiration of his term he again joined the
ranger service and in 1845 was commissioned a captain

of rangers and was in this service when the Mexican War began. In 1846 he enlisted in the volunteer service of the United States and was in Taylor's army. Upon the organization of Hays' Second Regiment it was divided, part going to the army of General Scott under Hays and the remainder, under Bell, as lieutenant colonel, was assigned to duty on the Rio Grande. After the conclusion of the war he returned to Texas.

In 1849 he was candidate for governor against Governor Wood, who was asking for a second term. He defeated Wood, served as governor, and was re-elected Governor in 1851. Some months before the expiration of his term, in 1853, he was elected to the United States Congress and served until 1855, when he was re-elected and served until 1857.

He then married Mrs. Ella Eaton Dickens, daughter of Hon. William Eaton of North Carolina, moved to North Carolina, and was living there on his plantation in 1861 when the Civil War began. He was tendered a commission as a colonel in the Confederate Army by President Davis, but declined it. He was now fifty-three years old, and added to this, shared the feeling of many of his neighbors that the policy of secession was of doubtful expediency in the first place, and in the second place the odds were too largely against the South. He was a silent and sad spectator of that four year's conflict and at its close witnessed the destruction of his fortune.

He lived a retired life the remainder of his days. In 1891 the Legislature of Texas voted him an annual pension for life. He died March 8, 1898, and was buried in the cemetery at Littleton, Warren County, North Carolina, by the side of his wife, who died in the preceding year. Upon the brick vault over their remains is the following inscription: "Peter H. Bell, ex-Governor of Texas, died March 8, 1898, age 90 years. Died July

16, 1897. Ella Reeves Bell, wife of ex-Governor Bell, in her 62nd year."

Of him, Brown, the Texas historian says, "He was a man of splendid physique, and combined with true courage, was distinguished by kind and genial characteristics. It is believed that he had not personal enemy in Texas."

CROSBY

This county was named for Stephen Crosby, who was born in South Carolina in 1808. He went to Alabama about 1830 and engaged in steamboating, and continued in this until about 1845 when he came to Texas and accepted the position of chief clerk in the Land Office, to which position he was elected in 1853 and in 1855. In describing the Democratic convention of 1857 Governor Lubbock says in his memoirs:

> There was some fun in nominating the Commissioner of the General Land Office. The convention was really anxious to nominate Captain Stephen Crosby, the incumbent of the office, and without doubt one of the most popular officers and men in the State. He had, however, strayed off from the Democratic party and joined the Know Nothings. He was shelved by the pledge prescribed by the convention and ran as an independent, but was defeated, but was re-elected in 1859, and under successive elections served until removed by the military authorities in August, 1867.

Crosby died in Austin, Texas, in 1869.

HAMILTON

This county was named for General James Hamilton, lawyer and governor of South Carolina. He was born May 8, 1786, in Charleston. He served with distinction in the war of 1812 on the Canadian frontier. In 1823 he was a member of the South Carolina Legislature; in 1825, he was elected to the Congress of the United States, and was re-elected in 1829. In 1831, he was elected Governor of South Carolina.

He became interested in promoting the cause of Texas independence in 1838 and was appointed commercial and diplomatic agent to Europe by President Lamar. He negotiated treaties of commerce and navigation with England and the Netherlands. While in this service he sacrificed most of his private fortune. He declined the command of the army of the Texas Republic, and declined the seat from South Carolina in the United States Senate made vacant by the death of Senator Calhoun in 1850.

In 1857 he started to Texas in the hope of obtaining financial relief for the losses he suffered while in the service of the Republic, but was lost in the wreck of the steamship *Opelousas*, on which he was a passenger. He was a highly cultured man and was one of the founders of the *Southern Review*.

HENDERSON

This county was named for J. Pinckney Henderson, the first governor of the State of Texas. He was born March 31, 1809, in Lincoln County, North Carolina. He attended the university of that state at Chapel Hill in 1830, and then studied law, removing to Mississippi and settling at Canton, where he practiced his profession until he came to Texas.

In 1836 he raised a company of volunteers and brought them to Texas, arriving at Velasco in June. At the inauguration of President Houston in October, 1836, Henderson was appointed Attorney General and later became Secretary of State. In 1837 he was Minister to England and France, and negotiated treaties of commerce and navigation with these countries. He returned to Texas in 1840 and resumed the practice of law with Thomas J. Rusk and Kenneth L. Anderson as partners. He was sent in 1844 as special Minister to the United States.

In 1845 he was elected first governor of the State of Texas. During the Mexican War he temporarily abandoned his office and became commander-in-chief of the Texas forces with the rank of Major General. For his gallantry at Monterrey he was presented a sword by the United States Congress. In 1857 he was elected United States Senator to succeed Senator Rusk, but died June 4, 1858, at Washington, D. C, before taking his seat, and was buried in that city.

★ ★ ★

HOWARD

Volney Erskine Howard was born in Oxford County, Maine, October 22, 1809. He had the usual experience of a bright New England boy, laboring on the farm and attending school alternately. He entered Bloomfield Academy and afterward Waterfield College. Upon the invitation of an uncle, who was practicing law, he went to Mississippi in 1832, but upon his arrival there he learned that his uncle had just died. He at once began the study of law and located at Brandon, where he was elected a member of the Legislature and in the same year was elected to carry the electoral vote to Washington. While in that city he was married to Catherine Elizabeth Gooch, a native of Massachusetts, a lady of rare accomplishments.

Upon his return to Mississippi he was appointed reporter for the Supreme Court and compiled seven volumes of Howard's Mississippi Reports, During this time he purchased *The Mississippian* and made it the leading Democratic newspaper of the Southwest. In 1840 he was nominated as the candidate of the Democratic party for a seat in the United States Congress, and although he ran one thousand votes ahead of his ticket, he was defeated by his Whig opponent, Governor Tucker.

During his career the Union Bank monopolized the politics of Mississippi. He voted against the bill by which the state guaranteed the bank's issue and predicted the insolvency of the bank and the repudiation of the state's obligation by the friends of the bill, in the event of its passage, a prediction that became true in a few years. He was severely criticized by the press and as severely retorted through his paper and on the stump.

In the midst of public discussion on the subject Howard was chosen by the Democratic party to answer the challenge of Sargent S. Prentiss to a joint discussion at Jackson. This meeting has always been regarded as a famous event in the political history of Mississippi. Partisans of the respective sides both claimed that their champion won the victory, but all admitted that Howard carried his end of the discussion with matchless skill and ability. It was during this stormy period that Hiram G. Runnels, president and manager of the bank, challenged Howard to fight a duel. The challenge was promptly accepted, and the duel was fought at Columbus. Howard was shot, the ball striking a rib and coursing around the breast. As he had predicted, the bank became involved and the question of repudiation came before the Legislature. Repudiation was vigorously opposed by Howard, but the measure carried, greatly to his disgust.

He immediately afterward shook the dust of Mississippi politics from his feet and moved to New Orleans, where he began again to practice law. Just at this juncture, the annexation of Texas to the United States was assuming tangible shape, and late in December, 1844, he removed with his family to San Antonio, and within a short time after his arrival there was elected a delegate to the first State Constitutional Convention in July, 1845. He took an active part in the convention, and at the first election for state officers and a legislature, he was chosen senator from San Antonio. On the 27th of February, 1846, Governor Henderson appointed him to the position of Attorney General, but he declined to qualify and kept his place in the State Senate.

In 1849 he was candidate for the United States Congress to succeed Timothy Pilsbury, also a native of Maine, and was opposed by Judge Williamson ("Three-legged Willie") a very popular man, but he defeated Williamson and served two terms in Congress. He achieved a national reputation by his speeches on the compromise measures of 1850, especially the features directly affecting Texas.

At the expiration of his term he was appointed by President Pierce attorney to the Land Commission of California, but served only a few months, when he located in San Francisco and began the practice of law. In 1856 the "Vigilantes" were at the height of their power in San Francisco. Howard was an outspoken, uncompromising advocate of the supremacy of the law and strenuously opposed the policy of the Vigilantes. The Governor issued his proclamation, ordering them to disband, but they defied his order. He called out the militia and put Howard in command, but their strength was too great to be overcome by the militia.

The enmity to Howard, resulting from his course, was so great in San Francisco that he removed to Sacramento in 1858, and in 1861 located in Los Angeles, where he devoted himself to the practice of law for about ten years. He accepted the office of District Attorney for several terms and was a member of the convention that framed the Constitution of California. He was elected Judge of Superior Court of Los Angeles in 1880, and while holding this position was nominated to a place on the Supreme Bench, but declined, owing to advancing years and the necessity of having to be away from home. His term as district judge expired in 1884, when he reached the age of seventy-five years. He then retired and died in 1889.

Memucan Hunt, Jr. (1807-1856)

HUNT

This county was named in honor of General Memucan Hunt, who was born in North Carolina, in Granville (Now Vance) County, August 7, 1807. Memucan Hunt, grandfather of the subject of this sketch, was a member of the Provincial Assembly of North Carolina in 1774, and again in 1776, and in 1777 was appointed first State Treasurer, and held the office ten years. William Hunt, father of General Memucan Hunt, was a major in the Revolutionary War.

General Hunt was reared on his father's farm. At the age of fourteen he entered Bingham School at Hillsboro, North Carolina. After finishing the course, he returned home and assisted in the management of his father's business. At twenty-two he entered a commercial partnership, doing business at Weldon and Norfolk. In 1834 he was a leader in the internal improvements conventions held at Hillsboro and Raleigh, and late in that year removed to Mississippi and took charge of a plantation and slaves his father had given him, and was engaged in a large and lucrative business when the Texas Revolution broke out.

Early in 1836 General Thomas J. Green, a brother-in-law of William H. and John A. Wharton, was in Mississippi raising troops for Texas, under authority of the Consultation of Texas. J. Pinckney Henderson, another North Carolinian, had but a short time before removed to Mississippi and had begun the practice of law at the county seat of Madison, and both he and Hunt warmly sympathized with the cause of Texas.

When news of the tragedies of the Alamo and Goliad reached them, they immediately joined Green. Hunt was offered a brigadier general's commission upon their arrival in Texas. Several hundred men were soon mustered in, and they proceeded by boat to New Orleans, and then to Velasco, Texas, arriving there in June, 1836, eight weeks after the Battle of San Jacinto.

Although the revolution ended with the victory of San Jacinto, Mexico was threatening another invasion, and President Burnet offered Hunt a commission as major general, to serve only in case a renewal of the war, with power to appoint subalterns, and he appointed, among others, J. Pinckney Henderson, a Brigadier General and Dr. Ashbel Smith, Surgeon. In the interim, Hunt, through agents in Mississippi, Tennessee, and North Carolina, organized and equipped troops at his personal expense, issuing stirring appeals to the people of those states.

On December 25, 1836, there being no further apprehension of an invasion from Mexico, he resigned and started back to Mississippi, but was urged by President Houston to accept the position of Minister from the Republic of Texas to the United States, to act with W. H. Wharton. In the last hours of President Jackson's administration, they succeeded in having the United States recognize the independence of Texas. Wharton immediately returned to Texas and Hunt remained in charge of the interests of Texas until August 1837, when he left for a business trip to Mississippi. Just prior to his departure he was banqueted by Calhoun, White, and other members of the United States Senate and lower house of Congress.

Lamar succeeded Houston as President in 1838, and appointed Hunt Secretary of the Navy. He then secured the services of a number of the better young officers of the United States Navy who resigned their commissions and joined the Texas Navy. The brilliant exploits of this short-lived navy are among the precious relics of the history of the Republic.

In 1839 he was appointed to act with a commissioner from the United States to adjust the eastern boundary line between that country and Texas, and concluded a treaty in the same year. During President Houston's second term as President he was appointed Inspector General of the Army. In 1842 he was Adjutant General in the Somervell Expedition. In 1846 he enlisted in the Mexican War and was tendered a position on the staff of General Henderson, but failing health compelled him to return to Texas in 1846.

After annexation he retired from public life and devoted his energies to recuperating his fortune which he had sacrificed for Texas. He had expended $28,000 in cash and personally obligated himself for $5,000 more, and in the interim had sacrificed his planting interests in Mississippi. The Legislature of Texas, without a dissenting vote, allowed his claim and paid it in lands, and he thus became a large land owner, but unsettled as it was, the land was of little value.

In 1850 he was married to Annie Taliaferro Howard of Galveston. He obtained the first charter for a railroad from Red River through central Texas, to the coast and devoted the remainder of his life to this enterprise. He served one term in the Legislature (1852), and in 1853 was appointed commissioner to represent the United States in adjusting the southwestern boundary. He continued actively promoting his railway enterprise, enlisting capitalists in New Orleans, New York, and Boston, and in 1856, while in New Orleans, he became suddenly ill and returned to Galveston. Upon the advice of physicians that he seek a higher altitude, he left Galveston for Tennessee, and, gradually growing worse, died at the home of his brother, in Tipton County, in that state, June 5, 1856.

IRION

Robert Anderson Irion was born in Paris, Tennessee, July 7, 1806, where he was reared and educated until ready for the university. He graduated from Transylvania University, Kentucky, in 1826, studied law, and entered upon his profession in his native state. He came to Texas in 1833 and located at Nacogdoches. He was elected a member of the first senate of the Republic of Texas. In 1837 he was appointed Secretary of State in General Houston's cabinet. After serving out his term, he returned to the practice of law at Nacogdoches. When General Houston was inaugurated the second time, he was tendered the office of Secretary of State, but declined and lived the remainder of his life at Nacogdoches, where he died in 1860.

JACK

This county was named for William H. and Patrick C. Jack. Wheeler's history of North Carolina, in giving an account of the adoption of the Mecklenburg Declaration of Independence says: "It was forwarded to the Continental Congress, at Philadelphia, by Captain James Jack, and a copy, also, to Samuel Johnson, moderator of the Provincial Congress, at Hillsboro, on August 25, 1775."

After the close of the war of the Revolution, Patrick Jack, son of Captain James Jack, removed to Wilkes County, Georgia, and became a prominent citizen of that state, serving as a member of the Legislature, and in 1812 commanding a company in the war with Great Britain. He reared a family in Wilkes County, Georgia. Among his children, William H. Jack, Patrick C. Jack, and Spencer H. Jack became prominent in the early history of Texas.

William H. Jack was born April 12, 1806, and was reared and educated in Georgia, graduating at the University of that state in 1827. He studied law and removed to Tuscaloosa, Alabama, and began the practice of law in 1828. In the following year he was elected a member of the Legislature of Alabama.

In 1830 he removed to Texas and located at San Felipe and began the practice of law. In 1832 his brother, Patrick C. Jack, and others, having been imprisoned at Anahuac by the Mexican authorities, he organized a party for their release, which was accomplished later. He was the author of the famous Turtle Bayou Resolutions. In 1835 he joined the Army of the Republic, taking part in the principal campaigns and performed his last military service as a private soldier at the Battle of San Jacinto. Shortly afterward he was appointed Secretary of State in Burnet's cabinet and served as such until October, 1836. During that time he was elected a member of the lower house of the First Congress. He was afterward a member of the Senate of the Seventh and Eighth Congresses, and was Chairman of the Judiciary Committee. He died of yellow fever at Galveston, August 24, 1844.

Patrick C. Jack, brother of William H., came to Texas in 1832 after having located and practiced law for three years in Jefferson County, Alabama. Upon his arrival in Texas he located first at Anahuac and later at San Felipe and began the practice of law. For protesting against the arbitrary conduct of Bradburn, Mexican commander at Anahuac, he was imprisoned, but was soon released, as above mentioned. At the beginning of the revolution, in 1835, he promptly volunteered and commanded a company at the storming of Bexar. In December, he was elected a member of the lower house of the Second Congress of the Republic (1838-1839) and in 1841 was appointed District Judge of the Sixth District, in which position he served until he was stricken with yellow fever in Houston, where he died August 4, 1844.

As these sketches are restricted to men for whom counties have been named, we can do no more than to merely mention Spencer H. Jack, a no less distinguished member of the family, and Thomas M. Jack, son of William H. Jack, the princely gentleman and scholar, the erudite lawyer and finished orator, the gallant soldier and genial gentleman beloved of all who came within the sphere of his magnetism.

JONES

Dr. Anson Jones, last President of the Republic of Texas, was born at Great Barrington, Massachusetts, on the 20th day of February, 1789. He was licensed to practice medicine in 1820, and after several years in the practice went to Venezuela.

In 1833 he came to Texas and settled in Brazoria. He joined Captain R. J. Calder's company as a private. Later he was made surgeon of the Second Regiment, and in that capacity served at the Battle of San Jacinto, leaving his medical post long enough to take part in the battle as a private. In 1836 he represented Brazoria in the Texas Congress. In 1838 he was appointed Minister to the United States, and while absent was elected to the Senate. In 1842 was made Secretary of State by President Houston, and at the close of his term was elected President of the Republic.

His last remarks in the ceremonies attendant upon the change of Texas from a Republic to a State of the Union are justly regarded as one of the finest specimens of

Texas oratory. After annexation he retired to his country home, and for eleven years remained in private life. In 1857 his friends brought him forward for the United States Senate, but he was defeated, and on the 7th of January, 1858, he committed suicide by shooting himself at the old Capitol Hotel in Houston.

KAUFMAN

David Spangler Kaufman, in whose honor this county was named, was born at Boiling Springs, Pennsylvania, December, 1812. He attended the common school there, entered Princeton College and graduated in 1833. He then moved to Natchez, Mississippi and there studied law and was admitted to the bar. He then located at Natchitoches, Louisiana, and began the practice of his profession.

In 1837 he moved to Nacogdoches, Texas, and in 1838 was elected to the lower house of the Texas Congress and served in 1839-43, and in the Senate of the Texas Congress from 1843 up to annexation. He was chosen Speaker of the Lower House in 1839 and again chosen in 1840. In 1845 he was appointed Charge D' Affairs at Washington. He moved to Lowe's Ferry on the Sabine in that year. At the first election for members of the United States Congress he was chosen to represent the eastern district of Texas, re-elected in 1847 and 1849, and on the 31st of January, 1851, died and was buried in Washington.

He was a lawyer of exceptional ability, especially gifted as an orator. During the debate on the Cherokee Land Bill, a measure championed by Sam Houston, then a member of the Texas Congress, Kaufman represented the opposition with conspicuous ability and later in the lower house of the United States Congress he won his laurels in the debates on the Compromise Measures of 1850.

LAMAR

Mirabeau B. Lamar, second President of the Republic of Texas, was born in Louisville, Georgia, August 16, 1798. In early life he was the private secretary of Governor Troupe. In 1835 he visited Texas and declared his intention of becoming a citizen. He returned to Georgia to make his arrangements. Hearing that the revolution had begun, he hurried back to Texas. He reached the army encamped on the Brazos, enlisted as a private and was in the Battle of San Jacinto, and was especially commended for gallantry by General Houston. Soon after the battle he was invited to President Burnet's cabinet and made Secretary of War.

At the first election he was chosen Vice President of the Republic, and at the second election was chosen President to succeed General Houston and served two years. In 1847 he was made Post Commander at Laredo. In 1851 he was married to Miss Maffitt, sister of the celebrated Confederate Naval Commander, and settled in Fort Bend County on his plantation. In 1859 he was appointed as Minister to Argentine Republic, but his health failing, he returned home and died, December 19, 1859, and was buried at Richmond, Texas.

RAINS

This county was named for Emory Rains, a native of Warren County, Tennessee, where he was born May 4, 1800. He came to Texas in 1826 and settled in Red River (Lamar) County. Later having located in Shelby County, he represented Shelby and Sabine Counties in the Senate of the Republic during the Second Congress in 1837 and in the Constitutional Convention of 1845. After annexation he represented Shelby County in the Legislature and held several minor offices. He died March 4, 1878, in the county that bears his name.

VAN ZANDT

Isaac Van Zandt, in whose honor this county was named, was born July 10, 1813, in Franklin County, Tennessee. He was the son of Jacob and Mary (Isaac) Van Zandt. His father was the youngest son of Jacob Van Zandt, who, about the year 1800, moved from North Carolina to Tennessee and settled in Franklin County. His maternal grandfather, Samuel Isaac, moved from South Carolina, to Lincoln, an adjoining county, about the same time. Both grandfathers were soldiers in the Revolutionary War, Isaac having been one of Marion's men.

Our Isaac Van Zandt's early education was only such as was afforded by the country schools, ill health interfering with this much of the time, but his fondness for reading good books largely compensated his lack of school work. He early became a member of the Primitive Baptist Church and so continued through life.

At the age of twenty he married Francis Cook Lipscomb, a cousin of Judge Lipscomb, of the Supreme

Court of Texas. About this time he began merchandising with his father at Salem, a nearby village. His father
soon afterwards died and the business was closed. He
then converted all his holdings into money, went north
and purchased goods, and began merchandising at Cof-
feeville, Mississippi. It was during the "flush times" in
Mississippi, and he went down in the general financial
crash.

In 1838 he started for Texas, but did not arrive until
late in 1839, having spent most of the time at Camp
Sabine, an abandoned military post, where he was ill
most of the time. He made a brief trip into Texas and
returned with the news that he had been offered two
hundred dollars by a Mr. Shoemaker to settle up some
business for him. He then (December 1839) moved his
family into Texas, and after going into an unfinished
log-house he later purchased a place near Elysian Fields
in Harrison County. He lived here until his appointment
as Minister to Washington.

After his return to Texas he took up his abode at
Marshall, which town he helped to lay out in 1842. He
was licensed to practice law in 1840. In this year, while
yet not entitled to vote, he became candidate for Congress and was elected by two-thirds majority over his
opponent, and while a member of that body opposed
Houston's Cherokee Land Bill. He was re-elected to
Congress the next year. In 1842, although only twenty-
nine years old, he was appointed by President Houston
Minister Plenipotentiary to the United States and made
the trip to Washington, by private conveyance. He spent
the greater part of 1842 and 1843 in Washington. It was
during this stay in Washington, that he, in company
with J. Pinckney Henderson, had frequent conferences
with John C. Calhoun, the result of which was a treaty
of annexation which was rejected by the United States

Senate. In 1844 he was on the *Princeton* with President Tyler and party when the bursting of a gun killed Mr. Upshur and Mr. Gilmer, members of Tyler's cabinet.

He returned to Texas in 1844 and was elected to the Constitutional Convention of 1845 and led the forces in favor of inserting the Homestead Clause in the constitution. After this he resumed the practice of law, and in 1847 was a candidate for governor, but it was not his to complete the race, as death ended his career before the election. He died of yellow fever at Houston, October 11, 1847, at the age of thirty-four years three months and one day. At his death his family consisted of his wife and five children. This family circle continued unbroken for sixty-one years, until the death of his widow, April 8, 1909, at the advanced age of nine-three years.

WILSON

James C. Wilson, born in England in 1816, was a man of superior education and intelligence. He came to Texas in 1837 and located in Brazoria County. When General Woll captured San Antonio and a number of prominent citizens, a proclamation was issued calling for troops. Wilson joined the company of Captain Reese from Brazoria. Following the fortunes of his company, which was in the Mier Expedition, he was made a prisoner and marched to Mexico City. He made his escape from prison, returned to Texas, and in 1844 was elected District Clerk of Brazoria County. He held this office until after annexation, when he moved to Matagorda County, which he represented in the Senate of Texas. In 1856 he was appointed Commissioner of Claims. At the end of his term he joined the itinerant ministry of the Methodist Episcopal Church and died at Gonzales in 1861.

WOOD

This county was named for George T. Wood, who was born in Georgia in 1815, and came to Texas in 1838, locating in Liberty County. He engaged in planting and performed some service as a ranger. He represented Liberty in 1841 and 1842 in the Congress of the Republic, and was later commissioned brigadier general of the militia. At the beginning of the Mexican War he enlisted and was made colonel of a regiment that participated in General Taylor's campaign. After the war was over, he returned to Texas and represented his district in the State Senate. In 1847 he was elected governor of the state, but held the office only one term, having been defeated by P. Hansborough Bell in 1849. He then retired to private life and died in the part of Liberty County now embraced in San Jacinto County in 1856.

CHAPTER X,
The Early Jurists of Texas

The lawyer of this generation who is familiar with the system of jurisprudence that has been developed, from its inception in 1836, cannot fail to be impressed with the preeminent ability of the lawyers and judges whose constructive genius laid the foundation so deep and broad and withal so much in harmony with those principles of justice and good practical judgment that must forever remain their most enduring monument. Of those who have been commemorated in county names are:

Brewster	Gray	Lipscomb	Webb
Collingsworth	Hansford	Mills	Wheeler
Dallam	Hartley	Ochiltree	
Donley	Hemphill	Oldham	
Franklin	Hutchinson	Roberts	

BREWSTER

Henry Percy Brewster was born in Laurens District, South Carolina, November 22, 1816. At the age of nineteen, while on a visit to Alabama, he heard of the fall of the Alamo and the massacre at Goliad. He hurriedly made his way to New Orleans and embarked in a vessel for Texas. He arrived at Velasco in the early spring of 1836 and proceeded to the headquarters of the Texas Army and enlisted as a private in Captain Briscoe's Company. He was made private secretary to General

Houston, participating in the Battle of San Jacinto. He accompanied the General to New Orleans in May and, returning to Texas in August, was made Secretary of War in Burnet's cabinet.

After retiring from that position, and just as he arrived at the age of twenty, he began the practice of law at Brazoria and from the outset was recognized as a most brilliant and thorough young lawyer. In 1840, he was appointed District Attorney. After holding that office until 1843, he resigned and resumed his practice. He immediately went to the forefront of his profession and eschewed political preferment. He was engaged in much of the most important litigation in the state of the succeeding ten years.

In 1846 he was Attorney General of Texas, succeeding J. W. Harris. In 1855 he moved to Washington and continued the practice of law there until the breaking out of the Civil War, when he returned to Texas and was appointed Adjutant General and chief of staff to Albert Sidney Johnston and was near him when he was killed at Shiloh. Later he was on special duty in the Confederate Army, mainly with General Hood.

When peace came, he returned to Texas and resumed the practice of law at San Antonio and continued until 1883, when he accepted the appointment to the office of Commissioner of Insurance, Statistics, and History tendered by Governor Ireland, and was in the active discharge of his duties, when on the 17th day of November, 1884, he was stricken with paralysis and died. By special request before death, his body was carried to Galveston, taken out to sea and buried in the waters of the Gulf.

COLLINGSWORTH

This county was named for James T. Collingsworth, first Chief Justice of the Republic of Texas, who was born in Tennessee in 1804. He was educated in the common schools, studied law and began the practice 1826. From 1830 to 1834 he was United States District Attorney in Tennessee and at the expiration of his term came to Texas and located in Matagorda.

He was a member of the Constitutional Convention of 1836 and a signer of the Texas Declaration of Independence. President Burnet appointed him one of the Commissioners to the United States, and upon the organization of the judiciary system of the Republic of Texas, in 1837, Collingsworth was appointed Chief Justice. He became a candidate for the Presidency of Texas in 1838 and during the canvass was drowned in Galveston Bay. Historians differ as to the manner of his death, some alleging that he committed suicide by jumping from a steamer, but others alleging that it was accidental drowning.

DALLAM

This county was named for James W. Dallam, who was born in the city of Baltimore on the 24th day of September, 1818. He was educated at Brown University, Rhode Island and later studied law under Reverdy Johnson in Baltimore.

In 1839 he removed to Matagorda, Texas, went to Washington, D.C., in 1844, and there complied *Dallam's Digest* of the decisions of the Supreme Court of the Republic of Texas, which were published in 1845. In the fall of that year he returned to Matagorda and married the daughter of S. Rhoads Fisher. In 1847 he was induced to undertake the establishment of a newspaper in Indianola. He went to New Orleans to make arrangements for its publication and was there stricken with yellow fever, of which he died, August 20, 1847.

DONLEY

Stockton P. Donley was born in Howard County, Missouri, May 27, 1821. He was educated at Transylvania University, Kentucky, and came from there to Texas in 1846, locating at Clarksville, in Red River County.

In 1853 he was elected District Attorney. In 1860 he removed to Tyler and in 1861 enlisted as a private in Gregg's Regiment. He was promoted to a Lieutenancy for gallantry at Fort Donaldson and was captured there. He was exchanged and, finding that his health would no longer permit him to serve in the field, returned to Tyler, and resumed the practice of law. In 1866 he was elected to the supreme bench, but was superseded in 1867 by the military. He resumed the practice of law in partnership with Judge Roberts, and died in Kaufman, Texas, February 17, 1871.

FRANKLIN

Franklin County was named for Hon. Benjamin C. Franklin, who was born in Georgia, April 25, 1805, and was educated at Franklin College, Athens, Georgia. He was admitted to the bar in 1827 and began the practice of law at Macon, Georgia. He removed to Texas in April, 1835, and immediately joined a company in pursuit of Indians.

Later he enlisted as a private in Captain Calder's Company and was in the campaign from Gonzales to San Jacinto, in which latter engagement he participated. After the war he was appointed District Judge of the Republic, served three years, and in 1840 retired from the bench and located in Galveston, entering the active practice of his profession. He represented Galveston in the Legislature for four years.

At the beginning of the Civil War, being physically un-fitted and too old for military service, he retired to his farm in Montgomery County, where he remained until 1870, when he returned to Galveston. He died December 25, 1873, just after being elected to the State Senate.

GRAY

Peter W. Gray was born at Fredericksburg, Virginia, April 10, 1819, and removed with his father's family in 1837 to Houston, Texas, where he was reared and educated. In 1846 he was a member of the First Legislature of the State and later served many years as District Judge of the South Texas District. He was elected a member of the Confederate Congress and served throughout the Civil War.

After the close of the war he returned to Houston and began the practice of law, and in a few years built up one of the largest practices in the South. In 1874 he was appointed to the supreme bench, but he resigned on account of feeble health. He died in Houston, October 3, 1874.

He was a scholar and highly cultured gentleman and a patron of letters. It was largely due to his financial and other aid that Mr. Yoakum was enabled to complete his excellent history of Texas.

HANSFORD

Judge John M. Hansford came to Texas in 1837 and settled near Jonesville (Scottsville), in what is now Harrison County, and took a leading part in the politics of that section. In 1838 he was elected to the lower house of the Congress of Texas from Shelby County and was chosen Speaker of that body. On January 31, 1840, he was appointed Judge of the Seventh Judicial District of Texas and served in that capacity until January 19, 1842, when he resigned.

The Regulator-Moderator War was at its height during this period in that section, and Judge Hansford was not entirely able to steer his way clear through the warring factions. At one time he abandoned his court because of the strength of the assembled mob. Articles of impeachment were at one time preferred against him, but to solve all difficulties he resigned his office and the articles were withdrawn.

After leaving the bench, he retired to his farm near Jonesville. In 1844, while he and his wife were absent, attending church one Sunday morning, a mob took possession of his place and demanded possession of some slaves he was holding under a writ of sequestration. Upon his refusal to comply with their demand he was shot and killed in the presence of his wife.

HARTLEY

Oliver Cromwell Hartley was born in Bedford County, Pennsylvania, March 31, 1823, and was educated in that state at Franklin and Marshall College, from which he graduated in 1841, with the added honor of being the valedictorian of his class. He studied law and was admitted to the bar in 1844.

In 1846 he came to Texas, landing at Galveston. He volunteered as a private in the Mexican War and was later made a lieutenant, but he was disabled in the summer of 1846 and returned to Galveston and began the practice of law. He then prepared a brief digest of the statutes of Texas, beginning the work in 1848, and in 1850 the Legislature subscribed for one thousand and five hundred copies. He was elected to the Legislature in 1851, and in that year was appointed reporter to the Supreme Court and held the office until his death in Galveston on the 13th day of January, 1859. In addition to his work as reporter he was, in 1854, appointed one of a commission of three to codify the laws of Texas.

HEMPHILL

Judge John Hemphill was born in Chester District, South Carolina, in 1809. He may be justly styled the "John Marshall" of Texas jurisprudence. He was educated at Jefferson College, Pennsylvania, where he graduated in 1826. He came to Texas in 1838 and was made judge of the Fourth Judicial District of Texas in 1841, and in 1842 Chief Justice of the Republic, and held the office until annexation.

For a brief period in 1842, there being little business in the Supreme Court, he was appointed Adjutant General of Somervell's Expedition. He was Chief Justice of the Supreme Court of the Republic in 1845, and then was elected a member of the first state Constitutional convention. After annexation he again held the office of Chief Justice. In 1857 he was elected United States Senator, and in 1861 he was sent to the Confederate Congress. He died in Richmond, Virginia in 1862. His body was brought back to Austin and interred in the state cemetery.

HUTCHINSON

Anderson Hutchinson was born in Greenbrier County, Virginia, in 1805. He removed to Knoxville, Tennessee, in 1826, where he began the study and practice of law, and in a few years achieved a fine reputation at the bar. From Knoxville he removed to Raymond, Mississippi, in 1835. In 1840, with Volney E. Howard, he published a digest of the laws of Mississippi, for which they were paid $10,000.

He removed to Texas in 1841 and was soon made one of the District Judges of the Republic. While engaged in holding court in San Antonio in September, 1842, he was, with other officers of the court and citizens of San Antonio, surprised and captured by General Woll on his raid into Texas. He was carried to Castle Perote and subjected to great hardships, but was released in 1843. He returned to Mississippi and began his practice in co-partnership with Henry S. Foote. He died there in 1853.

★

LIPSCOMB

Abner S. Lipscomb was born February 10, 1789, in Abbeville District, South Carolina. He was educated in the common schools and studied law in the office of John C. Calhoun. In 1811 he was licensed to practice law and removed to St. Stephens, Alabama, where he became a member of the territorial Legislature of Alabama, and at the age of thirty, one of the Circuit Judges of the new state. In 1823 he was made Chief Justice of the Supreme Court of the state and held the office eleven years. He resigned in 1835 and removed to Mobile, where he was again elected to the Legislature.

In 1839 he removed to Texas and immediately secured a large clientage. At the urgent solicitation of President Lamar he accepted a position of Secretary of State in his Cabinet. He was also elected a member of the first State Constitutional convention, in 1845. In 1846 Governor Henderson appointed him one of the Judges of the Supreme Court, which position he held for nearly eleven years. He died at Austin, November 30, 1856.

MILLS

Hon. John T. Mills was born in County Antrim, Ireland, November 12, 1817. He came with his parents to America and settled at Beach Island No. 3, Beaufort County, South Carolina, where he was educated and studied law.

About 1837 he came to Texas and located at Clarksville, where he practiced law, and immediately took a leading position in the profession. Recognizing his eminent fitness for the bench, President Lamar appointed him Judge for the Third Judicial District of the

Republic of Texas, January 23, 1839, but he resigned in December, 1840. Upon the redistricting of the Republic he was again appointed District Judge of the Seventh District, January 28, 1842, and served in that capacity until after annexation, in 1845. On August 14, 1846, he was appointed Judge of the new Eighth District, which position he held for several terms.

He was married in Clarksville, Texas, in 1843, to Mary Jane Vining, who died in 1854. He afterward married Mrs. Adair of Marshall, Texas, and removed to that city, where he resided until 1861. He then moved to his plantation on the Brazos River in Robertson County, and lived there from 1861 to 1865, and in the latter year moved back to Marshall and became associated with Judge W. B. Ochiltree in the practice of law. He died at Marshall November 30, 1871. Judge Mills was a consistent member of the Cumberland Presbyterian church, a Mason in high standing, and a profound lawyer. He was a liberal and public-spirited citizen, and aided in many benevolent enterprises.

OCHILTREE

W. B. Ochiltree was born in the vicinity of Fayetteville, North Carolina, October 18, 1811. He moved to the territory of Florida when quite a youth, and there secured his education. In 1830 he removed to Alabama, was admitted to the bar and began the practice of law.

In 1839 he came to Texas and located at Nacogdoches, where he soon obtained a large clientage. In 1842 he was appointed District Judge of the Fifth Judicial District of the Republic. In 1844 he was appointed by President Jones as Secretary of the Treasury in his Cabinet, and early in 1845 transferred to the office of Attorney General, and was the last Attorney General of the Republic of Texas. He was elected a delegate to the Constitutional convention of 1845, and after annexation was again appointed Judge of the Fifth District.

He soon resigned, however, and achieved great success as a practitioner. He was known by the sobriquet of "Buffalo Head" on account of his very large head. He was one of the most prominent members of the Legislature in 1855. In 1859 he moved to Marshall, and was in the Secession Convention of 1861, and was also a delegate to the Provisional Congress of the Southern Confederacy at Montgomery, Alabama. He resigned and raised a regiment and was attached to Walker's Division and led it with conspicuous gallantry. Owing to declining health he resigned in 1863, returned home, and his health continuing to decline, he died in Jefferson, Texas, December 27, 1867. He was exceptionally profound and eloquent as a lawyer and discriminating as a judge.

OLDHAM

Williamson S. Oldham was born in Franklin County, Tennessee, June 19, 1813. He was educated in the common schools of the country; taught school in Tennessee and became clerk of the District Court of Franklin County. Under the direction of Judge Nathan Green he studied law and obtained a license. In 1836 he moved to Fayetteville, Arkansas, and formed a partnership with S. G. Sneed. He was soon sent to the Legislature and elected Speaker of the House of Representatives of Arkansas, and in 1844 was made one of the Justices of the Supreme Court of that state.

His health requiring a change of climate, he resigned in 1848 and in 1849 came to Texas and formed a partnership with General James Webb, former Attorney General. Afterward he formed a law partnership with J.

F. Marshall and A. W. Terrell, and later with Judge White. In 1858 he and Judge White were employed by the state to digest the laws, and for the subsequent ten years *Oldham & White's Digest* was in universal and almost exclusive use in Texas as a digest.

In 1861 he was a delegate to the Provisional Government of the Southern Confederacy at Montgomery, Alabama, and later became a member of the Confederate States Senate from Texas. At the close of the Civil War he went to Mexico, and upon the downfall of Maximilian started for Canada, but before reaching there he learned of the amnesty granted to officers in his position, and returned to Houston and began the practice of law and died there May 8, 1868.

ROBERTS

This county was named for "John S. Roberts, and other distinguished Texans by that name," by which it is presumed the Legislature meant O. M. Roberts.

John S. Roberts was born in Virginia in 1796 and removed to Louisiana in 1826, and came to Texas about 1833. He was a member of the Constitutional Convention of 1836 and a signer of the Declaration of Independence.

Oran Milo Roberts was born July 9, 1815, in Laurens District, South Carolina. In early life he moved to Alabama, where he was educated, graduating from the University of Alabama and entering upon the profession of law in that state in 1838. He served one term in the Alabama Legislature. He came to Texas in 1841 and located in San Augustine and began the practice of his profession. In 1844 he was appointed District Judge. After annexation he resumed the practice of law and continued in the practice until appointed to the position on the Supreme bench in 1857.

He was later colonel of a regiment in Walker's Division, C. S. A. While in the army he was elected Chief Justice of the Supreme Court and was relieved by the results of the war. In 1866 he was in the first Constitutional Convention. He was elected to the United States Senate, but was denied his seat. Upon his return from Washington he established a law school at Gilmer, Texas, and in 1874 was again appointed Chief Justice of the Supreme Court of Texas. In 1878 he was nominated and elected governor, and was re-elected in 1880. In 1883 he became law professor in the University of Texas and held the place until 1888, when, owing to the infirmities of age, he resigned. He died four years later in Austin, Texas.

WEBB

General James Webb was born in Fairfax County, Virginia, in 1792. He received a liberal education in his native state, and was admitted to the bar there in 1816. He removed to Jones County, Georgia, in 1819, and to Florida in 1821. In 1832 he was appointed United States District Judge for Florida, holding court at Tallahassee and Key West. In 1838 he came to Texas and located in Houston. Shortly afterward he was made Attorney General, then Secretary of State, by President Lamar, and was sent by him on a mission to Mexico. At the expiration of Lamar's term of office he located in Austin, and practiced law, and in 1841 was elected to the Senate. Upon the organization of the state judiciary he was appointed Judge of the Fourteenth District. He died November 1, 1856, while on his way to court at Goliad.

WHEELER

Royal T. Wheeler was born in Vermont in 1810 and early in life moved with his father's family to Ohio, where he received a good education. In 1837 he moved to Fayetteville, Arkansas, where he formed a partnership with W. S. Oldham.

He soon afterward moved to Texas and began to practice law in partnership with Kenneth L. Anderson. In 1842 he was elected District Attorney and in 1844 to the District bench. Upon the organization of the state judiciary in 1846, he was appointed one of the Associate Judges of the Supreme Court, and was successively re-elected until his death. In 1858, upon the election of Judge Hemphill to the United States Senate, he was made Chief Justice and held that position up to the time of his death, in Washington County, Texas. He died by his own hand, in a fit of mental aberration, April 9, 1864, in Washington County, Texas.

CHAPTER XI,
COLONIZATION UNDER THE REPUBLIC OF TEXAS

CASTRO

It was the policy of President Lamar to encourage the extension of settlements on the frontier and beyond the settlements made under the laws of Coahuila and Texas, and with this in view, colonization laws were enacted in 1841 and subsequently, whereby Castro, Mercer, Peters, the German Emigration Society and others introduced settlers. The only one of these empresarios, or contractors, whose name has found a place on the county map of Texas is Henry Castro.

Henry Castro was born in France in 1786. After the fall of Napoleon Bonaparte he came to the United States, and in 1827 became a naturalized citizen. Later he returned to France and in 1842 was Consul for the Republic of Texas at Paris. A contract was made by him with the Republic of Texas in 1841 to colonize the following territory:

> Commencing at the Laredo crossing on the left bank of the Rio Frio; thence along the Laredo road to the dividing ridge of the Rio Frio, and Rio Medina; thence with that range to a point twenty miles north of the upper Presidio-Rio Grande road; thence in a direct line to the point of confluence of the Arroyo de Uvalde with the Rio Frio; thence down the left bank of the main branch of the Frio to the beginning.

> Also a fourth part of a tract to the east bank of the Rio Grande, commencing at the Salt Lakes of the

San Patricio (Hidalgo) five miles between the crossing of the road from the salt lakes to Comargo, and
stretching upward along the left bank of the Rio
Grande to a point ten miles above Dolores Ferry.

At great labor and expense he succeeded in introducing 485 families and 457 single men, between 1843 and
1845, and was in the midst of his work at annexation,
over the protests of Mexico to France. In 1845 he settled
the town of Quihi; in 1846 that of Vandersburg, and in
the same year that of D'hanis, and located his colonists
in Medina, Frio, La Salle, McMullen and Uvalde. He
was a man of large means and a publicist of international reputation. He was on his way to France when
death overtook him at Monterrey, Mexico in 1861.

He was the founder of Castroville, in Medina County.
His principal published works are his *Memoirs on Texas*, in French and German, with maps, November 12,
1845, and his work on Mexico.

★ ★ ★

CHAPTER XII,
THE ANNEXATION OF TEXAS
AND THE MEXICAN WAR

After one of the most acrimonious contests in the history of American politics, Texas became a State of the Union in 1845. The sentiment in Texas in favor of the measure was practically unanimous. The political parties in the United States were divided upon the question, but it was decided in the presidential election of 1844, in which James K. Polk was elected president, and George M. Dallas, vice president.

The states voting in favor of the measure were Maine, New Hampshire, New York, Pennsylvania, Indiana, Illinois, Michigan, Virginia, South Carolina, Georgia, Alabama, Mississippi, Louisiana, Arkansas and Missouri. Those voting against it were Vermont, Massachusetts, Rhode Island, Connecticut, New Jersey, Ohio, Delaware, Maryland, North Carolina, Tennessee, and Kentucky.

Mexico was violently opposed to the measure and on several occasions previous to 1845 had, in most unmistakable terms, threatened to wage war against the United States in the event of annexation. The position of Mexico was that Texas was a part of that Republic, that the whole territory of Texas belonged to Mexico, not simply that between the Nueces and the Rio Grande, but the whole territory extending to the Sabine, and that any attempt by the United States to take possession of it was robbery.

President Polk's message of December 2, 1845, accurately and clearly stated the case of the United States in these words:

Texas has declared her independence and maintained it by her arms for more than nine years. She has had an organized government in successful operation during that period. Her separate existence as an independent state has been recognized by the United States and the principal powers of Europe. Treaties of commerce and navigation have been concluded by different nations, and it has become manifest to the whole world that any further attempt on the part of Mexico to conquer her or overthrow her government would be vain.

The successive steps taken by Texas and the United States after the annexation resolution was approved by President Tyler, March 3, 1845, were:

(1) The Congress of Texas was called to meet June 16th to consider the terms of annexation. On the 23rd the terms were accepted and a convention called to meet July 4th to ratify the terms of annexation and to frame a constitution for the state.

(2) This was submitted to a vote of the people and ratified by a practically unanimous vote in October.

(3) On the 29th of December the final act admitting Texas as a state was passed by the United States Congress.

While these things were going on the steps taken by Mexico were:

(1) The Mexican minister at Washington, on the 7th of March, severed the friendly relations existing between the United States and Mexico by demanding his passports and leaving the country.

(2) In May the Mexican Congress decreed that a loan of two million dollars be negotiated to meet the expenses of what they called "the impending war."

(3) On the 4th of June the President of Mexico decreed that Mexico would oppose with all the strength at her command, and would put the whole strength of her army in the field.

(4) On the 12th of July the War Minister issued a circular announcing that the government had decided on a declaration of war, and on the 16th he ordered the filling up of contingents of troops, "for the war which she wages against the United States."

(5) On the 20th of July the supreme government of Mexico decided, with the unanimous consent of the Council, that "from the moment when the supreme government shall know that the department of Texas is annexed to the American Union, or that troops from the Union have invaded it, it shall declare the nation at war with the United States."

At this juncture the United States, upon the suggestion of Texas, ordered General Taylor to move his command from Western Louisiana to Corpus Christi, Texas, and he arrived there on August 12, 1845. After remaining six months at Corpus Christi he was ordered to proceed to the Rio Grande, but to make no attempt to occupy any place in possession of the Mexicans and to avoid any collision, if possible.

Without meeting any opposition he reached the Rio Grande opposite Matamoros in April, and immediately sent General Worth with a courteous note to the Mexican commander at Matamoros, expressing the desire that their respective armies maintain peaceable relations pending any adjustment that might be reached by the civil authorities of their respective governments. He received a curt reply, stating that his movement was considered an act of war. General Ampudia sent him a note a short time afterwards demanding that he move back beyond the Nueces. On the 26th of April a squadron of United States cavalry was ambushed and captured by a Mexican force that had crossed the river, and with this and the siege of Fort Brown and the Battle of Palo Alto, on the 8th of May, the Mexican War began.

No such question as a boundary line between Texas and Mexico, or between the United States and Mexico had ever been raised or disputed. After the treaty of Guadalupe Hidalgo in 1848, the government of the United States and the State of Texas had a serious controversy as to the dominion of Texas over that part of New Mexico east of the Rio Grande, the United States contending that the effort made by Texas in sending the Santa Fe Expedition there in 1841 and failing in its purpose, Texas had no right to claim that portion of the republic. After a long and angry controversy the matter was finally compromised in 1850 by the United States paying to Texas ten million dollars for all of the territory claimed not within her present limits.

In recognition of the services of the statesmen in the United States bringing about annexation and of soldiers who served in the Mexican War the Legislature of Texas named in their honor the following counties:

Baylor	Polk
Calhoun	Tyler
Cass	Upshur
Dallas	Walker
Gillespie	Wise
Hays	

BAYLOR

Dr. Henry W. Baylor was born near Paris, Kentucky, in 1818. He attended the common schools of Paris, and later entered Transylvania University, taking both a literary and medical course.

After his graduation he came to Texas and located in La Grange, where he practiced his profession, while occasionally he joined expeditions in pursuit of marauding Indians. He volunteered in the war with Mexico in 1846 and was surgeon of Hay's First Regiment. Upon the organization of Hay's Second Regiment he was chosen Captain of a company and accompanied it in the campaign from Vera Cruz to the City of Mexico, participating in all its movements.

When peace was declared and he saw his adopted state safe under the protection of the American flag, he returned to Texas and settled near Independence in Washington County, where he resumed the practice of his profession and engaged in farming until his death. He died August 4, 1854, and upon his tombstone is the inscription, "Keep my memory green."

There were two younger brothers, John R. and George W. Baylor. Both brothers became noted in the Indian warfare that was kept up until the Civil War, and both rose to distinction in the war between the states. They were nephews of Hon. R. E. B. Taylor, a member of the United States Congress before coming to Texas, a District Judge of the Republic and State, and a distinguished Baptist minister whose name is commemorated in Baylor University and Baylor Female College.

CALHOUN

John Caldwell Calhoun was born in Abbeville District, South Carolina, March 18, 1782. His parents were Scotch-Irish and his father, a Revolutionary patriot, died soon after John C. was born. Attending school at intervals, he began to prepare for college when eighteen years old. In two years he entered Yale College and after pursuing the course of study there was graduated with high honors. He studied law diligently for three years, a year and a half in the native state and a year and a half in Connecticut. He began the practice of law in South Carolina and was soon elected to the State Legislature.

In 1811 he was married and was elected to the United States Congress. Speaker Henry Clay immediately placed him upon an important committee. During the war of 1812 he worked hard for the United States Army, and after the war, favored a tariff to encourage home manufactures. President Monroe appointed him Secretary of State in his cabinet. He was elected vice president under John Quincy Adams, and again in 1828 under Jackson. In that year, what was called by Mr. Calhoun the "Tariff of Abominations," was enacted into law. In 1832, the nullification troubles took place, and in 1833, a compromise tariff bill was passed.

In February, 1844, there being a vacancy in the cabinet of President Tyler, Henry A. Wise suggested Calhoun to him, saying, "Your most important work is the annexation of Texas, and the man for that work is Mr. Calhoun." Although not the choice of Tyler he was appointed to the position, and his first act was to prepare a treaty of annexation. This treaty was rejected by the Senate. At the expiration of President Tyler's term he again entered the United States Senate and continued in that position up to his death in Washington, D. C, March 31, 1850.

He was one of the great triumvirate of the statesmen of the United States, a great thinker and logician, orator and publicist. He was the author of *A Disquisition on Government* and *The Constitution and Government of the United States*, and other writings. While the treaty of annexation he prepared failed to pass the Senate, he had the satisfaction of seeing Texas safe in the Union soon afterward.

CASS

General Lewis Cass was born in Exeter, New Hampshire, October 9, 1782. In 1799 he removed to Marietta, Ohio, where he studied law and in 1802 was admitted to the bar. He entered the United States Army in 1812 as colonel of the Third Ohio Volunteers. He urged the invasion of Canada, crossed over and was in the Battle of Toronto, and later was surrendered a prisoner at Detroit. He afterwards became major general of Ohio Volunteers and brigadier general of the United States Army. He was appointed military governor of Michigan and held that office from 1815 to 1831.

He was appointed Secretary of State by President Jackson, and in 1836 Minister to France. He was elected United States Senator in 1841 and was a warm advocate of the annexation of Texas, carrying Michigan for that measure in 1844. He was nominated by the Democratic party for President in 1848, but was defeated by Zachary Taylor. He was appointed Secretary of State in the cabinet of President Buchanan in 1857 and held the position until 1860. He died at Detroit, Michigan, June 6, 1868. He authored *An Inquiry Concerning the History, Traditions and Languages of the Indians in the United States*, also of *France, Its King, Court and Government.*

DALLAS

George Mifflin Dallas was born in Philadelphia, July 10, 1792. He was the son of Hon. A. J. Dallas, Secretary of State under President John Adams. He graduated at Princeton College in 1810, and was admitted to the bar in Philadelphia. His father at that time being Secretary of the Treasury under Madison, he spent most of his time in assisting him. At the expiration of his father's term of office, he returned to Philadelphia and actively and successfully engaged in practicing law.

In 1825 he was elected mayor of Philadelphia and in 1829 was elected District Attorney. He was elected to the United States Senate in 1831 and re-elected in 1837, when he was appointed Minister to Russia. In 1844, being a leading advocate of the annexation of Texas, he was elected Vice President of the United States. He was appointed Minister to Great Britain in 1857 and served during the entire term of President Buchanan. In May, 1861, he returned to the United States and died in Philadelphia, December 31, 1864.

GILLESPIE

This county was named for Richard Addison Gillespie, a native of Kentucky, who came to Texas in 1837, and began the business of merchandising. He was in the War of the Republic of the Rio Grande in 1839; in 1840, in the battle of Plum Creek; and in 1841, a lieutenant in Tom Green's company of rangers; was in Somervell campaign in 1842; was seriously wounded in an Indian fight in 1844, and in 1846 he was elected a captain in Hay's Regiment. He greatly distinguished himself at Monterrey, where he led a charge in which ten Mexican guns were captured. A few days later he was mortally wounded while leading a charge on the Bishop's Palace, September 22, 1846.

HAYS

This county was named for John Coffee Hays, familiarly and affectionately known to old Texans as "Jack" Hays. This remarkable man was born on the 23rd day of February, 1817, on a farm in Wilson County, Tennessee, about twelve miles east of The Hermitage, the home of Andrew Jackson. He was reared in his native county with such educational opportunities as were then afforded, and at the age of fifteen he went to Mississippi and secured employment with surveyors and learned and adopted that profession. At the age of twenty he left Mississippi and came to Texas, and while waiting for the opening of the Land Office and the resumption of surveying lands, he joined the rangers, enlisted as a private, where his splendid qualities as a scout and a daring fighter soon attracted public attention to him.

At intervals, he did some surveying, but upon the organization of a larger force of rangers in 1840, he was offered and accepted the captaincy of one of the companies. He was assigned to duty in Southwest Texas and patrolled the basin of the Nueces from Corpus Christi to its headwaters. One of his first exploits was the pursuit of about two hundred Comanche horse thieves. With only twenty men he drove the Indians off and recovered the stolen horses. His defeat of the Mexicans at Laredo in 1841 and the services performed during the Vasquez and Woll raids in 1842 are too familiar to the reader of Texas history to warrant special notice here.

Upon the outbreak of the Mexican War in 1846, Hays was commissioned as colonel of the first regiment of

Texas' mounted troops and attached to General Taylor's army. He did conspicuous service at the capture of Monterrey. In his report of the storming of the fort on Independence Hill, General Worth said, "The General feels assured that every individual in the command unites with him in admiration of the distinguished gallantry of Col. Hays and his noble followers. Hereafter they and we are brothers, and we can desire no better guaranty of success than by their association."

His command being only six-month volunteers, he returned to Texas in the spring of 1847 and organized another regiment. When the time came for assigning the regiment, it was divided; six companies under Lieut. Col. P. H. Bell were assigned to service on the Rio Grande; the other five were assigned to General Scott's army, and in the campaign against the City of Mexico won national fame. Hays' command was the last to leave the City of Mexico. He returned to Texas in 1848 and was mustered out of service. Later he received an important commission to New Mexico to deal with some of the delicate situations there, arising by reason of the opposing claims of the United States and Texas to that territory.

He was again in New Mexico in 1849, and when the great gold excitement seized the people of Texas, he joined and was placed in charge of a large caravan to California. His fame preceded him there, and he was made sheriff of San Francisco shortly after his arrival. The distorted condition of affairs in that embryo city required the services of just such a leader. He served four years in that capacity, and in 1853 was appointed by President Pierce, Surveyor General of California. In the interim, he, with several others, purchased from Vicente Peralto a large Spanish grant on the opposite shore of the bay. After his appointment as Surveyor

General, he moved to the land, laid out a city and named it Oakland.

After the expiration of his term as Surveyor General, his growing young city and his business interests required all his attention, and he retired from public life. He amassed considerable wealth, was president of one bank and the largest stockholder of another, and built one of the most palatial homes in Alameda County. Besides these, he owned considerable real estate in Oakland. His last public service in politics was as a delegate to the National Democratic convention which nominated Samuel J. Tilden to the presidency in 1876.

He died April 25, 1883. His funeral was conducted under the auspices of the veterans of the Mexican War in San Francisco and Alameda County, the pioneer associations, and other military and civic organizations.

POLK

James Knox Polk was born in Mecklenburg County, North Carolina, November 2, 1795. His parents moved to Tennessee in 1806, where he was reared and educated. In 1814 he entered the University of North Carolina at Chapel Hill and graduated from that institution in 1818. He studied law and was admitted to the bar in 1820 and in 1823 was elected to the Legislature of Tennessee. In 1825 he was elected to the United States Congress and was a member of that body for fourteen years and for two years was Speaker of the Lower House.

On the expiration of his congressional term he became the candidate of the Democratic party for governor of Tennessee and was elected by twenty-five hundred majority, made two efforts for re-election but was defeated both times, and in May, 1844, was nominated for president at the convention held at Baltimore and was elected. His administration was a successful one. The annexation of Texas and the Mexican War soon followed, resulting in a treaty of peace extending the area of the United States to the Pacific Ocean. He declined a renomination, after his term of four years, and retired to his home in Nashville, Tennessee. He died and was buried there June 15, 1849.

TYLER

John Tyler was born at Greenway, near Charles City Courthouse, Virginia, on the 29th day of March, 1790. He entered the grammar school of William and Mary College in 1803 and in 1804 entered William and Mary College, from which he graduated in 1807, and upon reaching his majority he was elected to the Legislature of Virginia and served in that capacity five years. In 1816 he was elected a member of the United States Congress and served two terms. In 1823 he was again elected to the state legislature and in 1825 was elected governor. In 1827 he was elected a senator of the United States and re-elected in 1833. In 1835 he was again elected to the state legislature and in 1840 was elected vice president on the ticket with William Henry Harrison. By the death of President Harrison he became President of the United States and qualified as such April 6, 1841. The party which elected him was composed of all the elements hostile to Van Buren. His administration was a stormy one, but its climax was the signing the resolution for admitting Texas into the union of states.

At the close of his term he retired to his estate near Williamsburg, Virginia. In February, 1861, he was called from retirement, selected a delegate to the peace congress, of which he was president, at Washington, was afterward elected delegate to the Virginia convention, which passed the ordinance of secession in April, 1861, and was then elected a member of the Confederate Senate. He died January 17, 1862.

UPSHUR

Abel Packer Upshur was born in Northampton County, Virginia, June 17, 1790. He was educated in the common schools and at William and Mary College and later at Princeton College. He studied law in the office of William Wirt and was admitted to the bar in 1812. He first settled in Richmond, Virginia, and practiced his profession there, but with a view to obtaining a seat in congress, he moved to Northampton, his native county, on the eastern shore of Virginia. Failing in the election, he was afterward elected to the state legislature and there became highly distinguished as a debater and orator. He was a member of the state convention of 1829-30, to amend the Virginia constitution. His review of Judge Story's theory of constitutional law fixed his fame. He was judge of the court of appeals of Virginia for twelve years. In 1841 he became a member of Mr. Tyler's cabinet as Secretary of State and in 1843 began negotiations for the annexation of Texas. He was killed by the explosion of a gun on the steamer *Princeton*, February 28, 1844. Wise in his *Seven Decades of the Union*, says of him, "He was a finer rhetorician and orator than Webster and a closer logician, his style purer and his power of expression clearer."

WALKER

Robert John Walker, in whose honor this county was named April 6, 1846, was born in Northumberland County, Pennsylvania, July 23, 1801.

He graduated from the University of Pennsylvania in 1819, studied law, and began the practice of his profession in 1822 in Pittsburgh, and remained there until 1826, when he moved to Mississippi, and located at Madisonville where he became eminent at the bar.

He was elected as a Democrat to the United States Senate in 1836, and was re-elected in 1842. He resigned his position in that body March 5, 1845, to accept the position of Secretary of the Treasury in the cabinet of President Polk. He declined the mission to China, tendered by President Pierce in 1853 and was appointed governor of Kansas April 10, 1857, but resigned in 1858. He was financial agent of the United States in Europe in 1863, and 1864, where he negotiated a loan of $250,000,000, returned to the United States and acted in an advisory capacity to the government in financial matters, and died in Washington, D.C., November 11, 1869.

One of his first acts in the Senate was the introduction of a resolution acknowledging the independence of the Republic of Texas, He championed the resolution with great zeal and ability, and it was finally adopted by a vote of 23 to 22, and approved by President Jackson March 2, 1837, the first anniversary of Texas Independence.

Messrs. Wharton and Hunt, in a letter to him, expressed on behalf of the people of Texas, their profound thanks for his great work and Hunt proposed to him that he would have a bust made for him and placed in the Capitol of Texas. In his reply, after modestly declining the offer, Walker wrote:

> I marked with many a rising hope and ebbing fear, your trembling solicitude and I beheld the overflowing joy, with which your bosoms throbbed when you saw our country inscribe the name of Texas on the scroll of independent nations. Your star is now beaming with all of the brightness of new born liberty.
>
> The history of your struggle is a history of a series of actions of commingled valor and clemency, worthy of your glorious parentage, unrivaled in moral sublimity which exalt and dignify the character of man. You are a child of our free institutions, the first born of that race, which carries onward and onward, our language, laws, and liberty throughout our old America.
>
> Go on patriotic Americans; go on my countrymen, for such I call you; go on noble and generous people, and may the great dispenser of the destiny of nations so order the course of events, that the single luminary, which now shines from your country's standards, be one of a great constellation of lights, beaming and burning, with our own red stars in perpetual brightness from the banner of the American Union.

From that time until nine years later, when the resolution to annex Texas to the Union was passed, he was instant in season and out of season in behalf of that consummation. No man in all of the Union was more exultant, when he read the elegant address of Anson Jones, the last President of the Republic of Texas, which, among other things, said, were the following:

The Lone Star of Texas, which, ten years since arose amid clouds, over fields of carnage, and obscurely seen for awhile has culminated, and following an inscrutable destiny has passed on, and become fixed forever, in that glorious constellation, which all free men and lovers of freedom in the world must revere and adore, the American Union. Blending its rays with its sister states, long may it continue to shine, and may generous heaven smile upon the consummation of the wishes of the two republics now joined in one. May the Union be perpetual, and may it be the means of conferring benefits and blessings upon the people of all the states, is my ardent prayer.

The first act in the great drama is now performed. The Republic of Texas is no more.

The Legislature of Texas adopted the following joint resolution December 10, 1863:

Whereas it is the opinion of several persons in and out of the County of Walker, in this State, that said county was named in honor of Robert J. Walker, then a distinguished citizen of Mississippi, and who had rendered himself popular with the people of Texas by his warm advocacy of the annexation of Texas to the United States.

And whereas the said Robert J. Walker ungrateful to the people who honored him and nurtured him in political distinction, had deserted that people, and leagued with Abraham Lincoln in his vain efforts to subjugate the Southern States, now struggling for their liberties and independence, thereby rendering his name odious to the people of Texas and to the Confederate States of America; Therefore:

(1) Be it resolved by the State of Texas, that the County of Walker in this State be and the same is hereby named Walker County in honor of Captain Samuel H. Walker, the distinguished ranger, who fell in Mexico, while gallantly fighting for the rights of Texas, and that no honor shall attach to the name of Robert J. Walker, in consequence of a County in the State bearing the name of Walker.

(2) That this joint resolution take effect and be in force from and after its passage, approved December 10, 1863.

When the Mexican War was imminent he devised a tariff system, which proved to be, probably, the most successful and popular the United States have had before or since. It is widely known in the history of tariff legislation as the Walker Tariff. Its main features contemplated a tariff for revenue only. With it, the Mexican War was tided over without the issuance of a single bond. It brought large revenue and in ten years enabled the government to pay off four-fifths of the expenses of the Mexican War debt and almost paid the entire current expenses of administering the government.

In 1857 he accepted the delicate responsibility involved in the office of Governor of Kansas. His official course met with a violent opposition from his party in the South, where he was denounced in various legislatures. This and the aid rendered the United States in negotiating a loan in Europe and afterwards acting in an advisory capacity in financial matters for the government of the United States during the Civil War were the occasion for the action of the Legislature of Texas above mentioned.

WISE

Henry A. Wise was born at Drumnondtown on the eastern shore of Virginia on the third day of December, 1806. He was educated at Washington College, from which he graduated in 1826. After serving a term in the state legislature, he was elected to the United States congress and served eleven years, consecutively. He was in the midst of the storm of the Jackson administration and was the leader of the Whig minority during Tyler's administration. He was a zealous advocate of the annexation of Texas, championing the cause and defending the people of Texas from the fierce onslaughts of her enemies in congress.

He was appointed minister to France in 1842, but the Whig majority of the senate refused to confirm his appointment. He was appointed minister to Brazil in 1844 and the appointment was confirmed. In 1855 he was nominated for Governor of Virginia and in the canvass achieved a national fame in his speeches against Know-Nothingism. He was elected governor and was such when John Brown was captured, imprisoned, tried and hung for murder. He was a member of the peace congress in February, 1861, and when all hope for peace was at an end he was elected delegate to the convention which passed the ordinance of secession in April, 1861. He then joined the Confederate Army, and was made brigadier general. After the war he located in Richmond, Virginia, and died there, September 12, 1876.

A forcible debater and orator, many of his epigrammatic sentences have come down to us. He authored of *Seven Decades of the Union*, and a *Memoir of John Tyler*, two most entertaining works, which deserve to be read for the light they give on the periods of which they treat.

CHAPTER XIII,
FORTS ON THE FRONTIER

After the termination of the Mexican War and the signing of the treaty of Guadalupe Hidalgo, the United States stationed troops in Texas and built a cordon of forts along the frontier. Settlements grew up around them in many places and towns sprang up which have taken their names, i.e., Fort Worth, Fort Davis, etc., but no county name commemorates that feature of our history except Mason.

MASON

Fort Mason was established July 6, 1851, by Companies A and B of the Second Dragoons, under the command of Capt. Hamilton H. Merrill. The fort was named Mason after Richard B. Mason, who was born in Fairfax County, Virginia in 1791. He entered the army as second lieutenant of the infantry, September 2, 1817, was immediately advanced to the rank of first lieutenant, and on the 31st of July 1818 advanced to the rank of captain. On March 4, 1833, he was appointed major of the First Dragoons, and on the 4th of July, 1836, made lieutenant colonel, and then colonel, June 30, 1846. He reached the rank of brigadier general May 30, 1846. He took part in the Black Hawk War, and during the war with Mexico was stationed in California, where he acted as civil and military governor until superseded by General J. W. Reilly. He died in St. Louis, June 26, 1850. The village and settlement grew up around Fort Mason. When the fort was abandoned and the county organized, it retained the name and the county was given the same name.

Gov. Richard Coke (1829-1897)

CHAPTER XIV,
OTHER DISTINGUISHED MEN ON THE MAP

Statesman, jurists, journalists, historians, ministers and others who are commemorated on our county map:

Brooks	Jim Hogg	Runnels
Coke	Jim Wells	Schleicher
Crane	Kendall	Terrell
Culberson	Morris	Willacy
Foard	Reagan	Yoakum
Hudspeth	Real	

BROOKS

Hon. J. S. Brooks was born on a farm near Paris, Kentucky, November 30, 1855, and received a common school education. He came to Texas in January, 1877, was employed as a cowboy in the spring of that year and went up the trail to the northeast with cattle. In 1880 he located in San Antonio, enlisted as a ranger in 1882 and continued in that service until 1906, rising to the rank of captain.

In 1906 he resigned and located at Falfurrias and engaged in farming and stock raising. In 1911, when a new county was created, he was elected to the Thirty-First and Thirty-Second Legislature. He still (as of 1912) lives in the county that bears his name.

COKE

Richard Coke was born in Williamsburg, Virginia, in 1829. He was educated at William and Mary College, graduated in 1849, and studied law. He came to Texas in 1850 and located in Waco, a town at that time less than one year old, and continued to practice law there up to 1861, when he joined the Confederate Army. He was appointed District Judge in 1865, and in 1866 one of the Associate Justices of the Supreme Court. In 1873 he was elected governor and re-elected in 1875. In 1877 he was elected to the United States Senate and was successfully re-elected, and held the office up to his death in 1896.

CRANE

William Cary Crane was born in Richmond, Virginia, March 17, 1816, and was a lineal descendant of Robert Treat, governor of Connecticut. In early boyhood he was sent to a boarding school in King William County, Virginia, six miles from Hanover courthouse. At the age of fifteen he was sent to Mount Pleasant Academy in Massachusetts. He joined the Baptist Church and was baptized at Richmond, Virginia, July 27, 1832, and afterward attended the Richmond College and Columbia College in Washington and was also a student at Hamilton College, now Colgate University. He then went to Talbotton, Georgia, where he taught school and was pastor of the church there. On June 18, 1838, he was married. He was ordained to the full work of the ministry in Baltimore and engaged as pastor of the church in Montgomery, Alabama. He lost his voice in 1839 and in 1842 returned to Virginia and traveled for the American Tract Society. For a short time he was employed as editor of the *Baptist Recorder* at Nashville, Tennessee. In July, 1844, he was called to the Baptist Church at Columbus, Mississippi, where he remained three years.

From there he removed to Vicksburg, and from there was called to the presidency of the Mississippi Female College at Hornado, serving from 1857 to 1860. Later he became president of Simple Broadway College at Jackson, where he also edited a Baptist paper. From there he was called to the presidency of the college in Louisiana, and in 1863 was called to the presidency of Baylor University at Independence, Texas. He died at Independence, Texas, February 26, 1885. He was a voluminous writer, his last and principal work being *The Life and Literary Remains of General Sam Houston.*

CULBERSON

David B. Culberson was born in Troupe County, Georgia, September 29, 1830. He was educated at La Grange, Georgia, then removed to Alabama and studied law under Chief Justice Chilton, and removed to Texas in 1856, locating at Jefferson.

He was elected a member of the Legislature in 1859. He entered the Confederate Army as a private and rose to the rank of colonel of the Eighteenth Texas Infantry. He was appointed Adjutant General of Texas November 17, 1863, and served one year, when he was elected to the Legislature and was a member of that body when the war closed in 1865. After the war he resumed the practice of law at Jefferson and in 1873 was elected State Senator. In 1878 he was elected Representative in Congress from the Fourth District of Texas and by successive re-elections served as a member of Congress until 1902, when he retired and died at Jefferson in 1903.

He was chairman of the Judiciary Committee of the lower house for several terms and achieved a nation wide fame as a constitutional lawyer. At the time of his death he was one of the commissioners to revise the United States Criminal Code, under appointment of President McKinley.

FOARD

Robert J. Foard was born in Cecil County, Maryland, in 1827. He was a nephew of Senator Bayard of Delaware. He graduated at Princeton College and thereafter came to Texas.

He located at Columbus, in Colorado County, and immediately took a leading position at the bar. At the beginning of the Civil War in 1861 he enlisted and rose to the rank of major. At the conclusion of the war he resumed his profession and continued in the practice up to his death in 1898. He was a lawyer of great ability and one of the kindest, most charitable, modest, and reserved men of his generation. This county was named in his honor by his junior partner while a member of the Senate, in recognition of his great qualities, professional and social, and entirely without solicitation or suggestion from Major Foard.

HUDSPETH

Claude Benton Hudspeth, born in 1877 to H. S. and Elizabeth Anna Hudspeth in Medina, Texas, received his education in the family's log cabin on the banks of the Medina River. He began working on ranches in the area as a teen, moving to Ozona in his sixteenth year to edit and publish the town's first newspaper with his brother

Roy. By 1902, he had moved to El Paso and married Marie Cliborne. In that year he was also elected to the state House of Representatives. In 1906, he was elected to the state Senate where he served for twelve years. He was admitted to the bar in 1909 and began practicing law in El Paso.

In 1918, Hudspeth was elected to the United States House of Representatives and was an ardent supporter of the Secretary of War's decision to send American troops into Mexico against Pancho Villa. He served in the House until 1931.

Hudspeth was active in the cattle industry for much of his life and in 1926 opted to drive 1,400 head of cattle from Crockett County to Brewster County rather than ship them by train. His account of the three weeks' drive was published in *Cattlemen* magazine.

After retiring his seat in the House of Representatives, he became director of the Texan Oil and Land Company, and relocated to San Antonio. He died there on March 19, 1941 and was interred in Mission Burial Park.

JIM HOGG

This county was named in honor of James Stephen Hogg, who was born in Cherokee County, Texas, March 24, 1851. He was a son of General James Lewis Hogg, a brigadier general of the Confederate Army, who died at Corinth, Mississippi, in 1864.

General Hogg had been a conspicuous figure in the politics of Texas since the days of the Republic. He came to Texas in 1839, and in 1843 represented his district in the Congress of the Republic. He was a member of the Constitutional Convention of 1845 and State Senator in 1846. He entered the Volunteer Army of the United States and served in the Mexican War.

Upon his return to Texas he was again elected to the Legislature and in 1861 was a member of the Secession Convention. After his death his son, James Stephen Hogg, entered a printing office at Tyler, and later established a newspaper at Longview, which he removed to Quitman, in Wood County and there established the *Quitman News*.

He served as justice of peace from 1873 to 1876, studied law and was admitted to the bar in 1875, and in 1878 was elected county attorney. Two years later he was elected district attorney of the Seventh Judicial District composed of the counties of Gregg, Rains, Smith, Upshur and Wood, and while acting in that capacity moved to Tyler, Texas, and at the expiration of his term began the practice of law. In 1886 he was nominated by the Democrats of the state for the office of Attorney General. He held this office for two terms and in 1890 was nominated and elected Governor of Texas. He served two terms as governor and when his last term expired, began practicing law in Austin, Texas. Later he removed to Houston and practiced his profession there up to the time of his death, March 7, 1906.

From the time he entered state politics in 1886, up to his retirement as governor his career was rather a stormy one. He instituted many wholesome reforms in the public policies of the state, in the face of strenuous opposition by the more conservative element of the Democratic party, so that in 1892 the convention which met at Houston divided, the conservative element withdrew and nominated a full state ticket in opposition. There followed perhaps the most noted political campaign in the history of Texas, but Hogg was triumphantly elected by a large majority. Among the most important reformatory laws were those restricting alien ownership of land, the regulation of railroads by commission, and the prevention of the issuance of fictitious bonds and the restriction upon the issue of all bonds by corporations. He was the most conspicuous leader in the life of progressing democracy in Texas. He was buried in the City Cemetery at Austin.

JIM WELLS

Hon. James B. Wells was born on St. Joseph Island, Aransas Bay, about the year 1852, his father having been in the naval employment of the United States at the time of his birth. He obtained a good education, and in 1873 entered the law department of the University of Virginia, where he graduated in 1874. He located at Rockport and practiced law for a time and then moved to Brownsville, where he has since lived.

He is a prominent lawyer, and although he has taken active interest in the politics of the State he has never held any political office. He was for several years a District Judge in that district by appointment, and after serving one term resumed his practice at Brownsville.

KENDALL

George Wilkins Kendall was born on the 22nd day of August, 1809, in the village of Mount Vernon, New Hampshire, about five miles from the then small village of Amherst, the birthplace of Horace Greeley. He was of Puritan ancestry, both parents having descended from early settlers who came to New England previous to 1630. His father served as a soldier in both wars against Great Britain.

About the year 1827, Kendall went to New York City and learned the art of printing with Horace Greeley, who had just become a journeyman printer. Kendall afterwards went to Boston, but remained only a short time, when he drifted south and obtained employment as a printer, on the Raleigh *Register,* owned by Seaton and Gales. Here he met E. A. Lumsden, his future partner, who was employed on the *Register,* and both left and went to Washington, D. C, where they were employed on the *National Intelligencer.* In 1882, Lumsden left Washington and came to New Orleans and Kendall came a few years later.

In 1836 they formed a partnership under the firm name of Lumsden and Kendall, and on the 25th of January, 1837, issued the first number of the New Orleans *Picayune,* the whole value of the plant at the beginning, not exceeding four hundred dollars. It grew rapidly in public favor, and in a few years was one of the leading newspapers in New Orleans.

In 1841, when Kendall learned of the contemplated expedition to Santa Fe, desiring to see the country and report his observations to the *Picayune,* he set out from New Orleans to Texas and arrived in time to join the expedition, on June 28, 1841. He was taken prisoner and suffered all the hardships of the Texans for about two years, although he was a citizen of the United States, and his mission that of a newspaper correspondent only.

After his release from prison he returned to New Orleans to resume work on the *Picayune.* His contributions to this paper on his adventures created a widespread demand for their publication in book form. The result was his publication of the *Santa Fe Expedition,* by Harper Brothers in 1844, and another edition in London in 1845. It consisted of two volumes, and within eight years 40,000 copies were sold, according to a note in Raines' *Bibliography of Texas.*

Although his assured him an ample fortune, Kendall was ready and anxious to accompany the United States

Army into Mexico, and in 1846 he promptly attached himself to General Taylor's army on the Rio Grande, and was tendered by General Taylor a position on his staff. He actively participated in the battles of Taylor's campaign, and after the Battle of Buena Vista joined General Scott's army at Vera Cruz and accompanied it as aide-de-camp of General Worth, captured a Mexican flag during a charge in one of the main engagements, and was complimented in an especial manner. This flag was on exhibition at the New Orleans Exposition in 1884.

These battles were reported to the *Picayune* in a most vivid manner. Becoming enamored of the climate of Western Texas he made his home at New Braunfels, where he carefully compiled accounts of the principal battles of the Mexican War. He then went to Paris, France, and engaged a celebrated artist to illustrate his work. While in Paris he met Miss Adeline de Valcourt, a lady of rare accomplishments and great beauty. They were married in 1854, and made an extensive tour of Europe, and, never losing an opportunity of giving the benefit of his observations, he sent vivid letters to the *Picayune*.

The building occupied by the *Picayune* was destroyed by fire in 1850. It had then grown to be easily the leading paper of the South. A new four story building of solid granite was erected in its stead. Upon his return with his bride after a short stay in New Orleans, devoting his time to the interests of the paper, he returned to Texas and made his home at New Braunfels. In 1857 he purchased a large tract of land situated in what is now Kendall County, about twenty-five miles northwest of San Antonio, to which he moved with his family in 1857 and improved it according to his own taste, regardless of expense. Here he spent the remainder of his days, going back and forth to New Orleans in the interest of the

Picayune, in which he retained a proprietary interest. He engaged in farming on a small scale, and in livestock. He spared no expense in introducing into Texas the best bred animals of Europe, principally sheep, and soon became the most successful sheep raiser in the Southwest. He contributed many articles to the *Picayune* and the *Texas Almanac* on farming and livestock.

He was urged by friends to allow the use of his name as a candidate for governor, but promptly declined to enter the political arena. Being past the age of fifty at the beginning of the Civil War, he remained on his ranch during the conflict, and took no part in it, directly or indirectly. His communication was cut off from the *Picayune* during the latter half of the period. He devoted most of his means and time to supplying the needs of families of men absent in the Confederate Army, and organizing and arming the old men and boys of the region for protection against marauding Indians.

At the first opportunity after war was over, he went to New Orleans, to find the equipment of the *Picayune* much run down, and immediately went to New York and purchased a new outfit. While on this visit he saw Horace Greeley, who warmly received him and entertained him while in the city. He then visited the scenes of his boyhood in Hillsboro County, New Hampshire, where he met his kinsman and old friend of the Mexican War memory, ex-President Pierce, living in quiet retirement.

He then returned to Texas and died on his ranch, October 21, 1867, and was buried there. His partnership in the *Picayune* had continued for more than forty years. The paper survived until April 25, 1914.

Upon his tomb is inscribed, "He was Poet, Journalist, Author and farmer; eminent in all." He lived to see his name honored by the creation of Kendall County in 1862.

MORRIS

W. W. Morris was born in Halifax County, North Carolina, in 1805, and he was there reared and educated. About the year 1840 he removed to Alabama, where he taught school and studied law.

After practicing his profession in that state he came to Texas in 1849, and located near Henderson in Rusk County. He practiced in the courts of Marshall, Gilmer, Quitman, Nacogdoches, San Augustine, Carthage and adjoining counties, and in the higher courts of Texas. He served two terms in the Legislature, and in his later years gave much of his time and money to the construction of railways in that part of Texas. He died at his home near Henderson in Rusk County, June 3, 1883.

The writer's authority for the naming of this county for Hon. W. W. Morris is Sayles, in a note to his article on counties and county boundaries. Since it has been stoutly contended that the county was named for another eminent jurist, and since there is nothing in the act creating the county to determine the matter, a sketch of Hon. Richard Morris is given.

Richard Morris was born in Hanover County, Virginia, December 27, 1815; was educated at the Brooks High School in Richmond and in the University of Virginia and admitted to the bar of that state in 1838, and in the same year came to Texas and located at Galveston. In the fall of 1841 President Lamar appointed him to the office of District Judge, which at the time made him a member of the Supreme Court ex-officio. He died August 19, 1844, during an epidemic of yellow fever in Galveston.

★ ★ ★

REAGAN

John Henninger Reagan was born October 8, 1818, in Sevier County, Tennessee. He was a student at Nancy Academy in Sevierville, Boyd's Creek Academy, and at the Southwestern Seminary at Marysville.

He came to Texas in 1839, joined General Rusk's regiment and, July 15-16, participated in the battles with the Cherokees and other Indians. In the fall of 1839 he was appointed deputy surveyor in that land district and held the position four years, alternating his duties as surveyor with work as a tutor for the children of a private family. He was elected captain in the militia and justice of the peace in 1842. In 1843 he was with General Tarrant in an expedition to the cross timbers against the Indians, and in the same year was captain of a company organized to suppress the trouble between the Regulators and Moderators in East Texas.

He engaged in farming and stock raising in Kaufman County in 1844, at which time, having studied law, he obtained a temporary license to practice. When the County of Henderson was organized he was elected chief justice of the county and lieutenant colonel of the militia, and in 1847 was elected to the Legislature. In 1849 he was given full license to practice law and was in the active practice until 1852, when he was elected district judge for a term of six years.

While holding court at Kaufman he was prevailed upon to accept the nomination for a seat in the United States Congress, with Judge Lemuel Dale Evans for an opponent on the Know-Nothing ticket. There ensued one of the most exciting canvasses in the political history of the state. He was triumphantly elected. He was re-elected in 1859 and was in the discharge of his duties when the Civil War began. He was a delegate to the State Secession Convention in 1861, and was at the Provisional Congress which met at Montgomery, on March 6, 1861. He was chosen Postmaster General of the Southern Confederacy and held that position until 1865.

After abandoning Richmond he and other members of the official family of Jefferson Davis were pursued and captured by federal troops near Irwinville, Georgia. He was imprisoned in Fort Warren, in Boston harbor, and was released in the summer of 1865.

He returned to Texas and went to work at manual labor on his farm. While so engaged he was tendered the position of Military Governor of Texas, but declined. Upon the restoration of the courts he resumed the practice of law at Palestine. His political disabilities having been removed, he was elected to Congress in 1874 and was a member of the Constitutional Convention in 1875. He was successively re-elected to Congress from 1874 to 1888, and was elected to the United States Senate in 1887. He took the lead while in Congress in the interstate commerce legislation, and at the earnest request of Governor Hogg, accepted the chairmanship of the Railroad Commission of Texas.

He voluntarily retired from political life in 1903, went to his home at Palestine and spent the remainder of his life in writing his memoirs. He died on his plantation in the suburbs of Palestine March 6, 1905.

REAL

This county was named in honor of Justus Real, Senator representing the Twenty-fourth Senatorial District of Texas, composed of the counties of Bexar, Bandera, Kendall, Kerr, and Gillespie. He was born in Kerr County, Texas, May 7, 1860. After taking advantage of such educational opportunities as this part of the sparsely settled county afforded, he entered the Southwestern University of Georgetown, Texas, and attended the sessions of 1883 and 1884. Since that time he has been a successful businessman and in 1911 was elected to the State Senate as a Republican against a popular Democrat.

RUNNELS

Hiram G. Runnels was born in Hancock County, Georgia, December 17, 1796. He moved to Mississippi Territory at an early age and taught school. He served for a short time in the army, fighting Indians. In 1817-18 he was a member of the convention that framed the first constitution of the state of Mississippi. In 1822 he was elected Auditor of Public Accounts and served several years in that capacity. In 1829 he was elected to the Mississippi Legislature, and in 1830 was appointed receiver of public revenues. In 1831 he was a candidate for governor, but was defeated by a small majority. He was again a candidate for governor in 1833 and was elected. In 1835 he was a candidate for re-election and defeated. In 1836 he became president of the Union Bank for a year, and for some animadversion upon his management, he caned Governor McNutt upon the streets of Jackson. For a similar reason he fought a duel with Volney E. Howard, editor of the *Mississippian*, in 1840.

In 1842 he came to Texas and engaged in planting on the Brazos. Later he represented Brazoria and Galveston Counties in the State Senate. He moved to Houston about the year 1855 and was again elected to the State Senate. He died in Houston, Texas, December 17, 1857, and was buried in Glenwood Cemetery in that city.

SCHLEICHER

Gustave Schleicher was born in Darmstadt, Germany, November 29, 1823. He was educated at the University of Giessen and chose the profession of civil engineer, and after graduation was engaged in several works of internal improvement in Europe. In 1847, in company with thirty-nine former students of German universities, he formed what was known as the "Colony of Forty," and purchased a large body of land in what is now Llano and other counties, where they engaged in farming and stock raising upon the most scientific methods. But the location was then beyond the settled portion of the country, and Indian depredations and other causes soon rendered the enterprise impracticable.

With a number of his associates he moved to San Antonio in 1850, and there he soon mastered the English language. In 1853 was elected a member of the lower house of the Legislature, more to get an inside view of American institutions and customs than for any honor or emolument on his part. At the close of his term, in 1854, he was chosen surveyor of the Bexar land district, an area of country larger than New England.

After serving in this capacity five years he was, in 1859, elected a member of the State Senate. When the Civil War began in 1861, he entered the engineer corps and served in the Confederate Army with the rank of captain throughout the war. At the close of the war he engaged in railroad work, laying out and superintending the construction of the railroad from Cuero to Indianola.

He was elected to the Forty-fourth Congress, re-elected to the Forty-fifth and again to the Forty-sixth. He died January 10, 1879, in Washington, D. C. His remains were removed to San Antonio and buried there.

He was one of the most cultured men in the history of Texas. Being a close student of political economy, his carefully prepared addresses were always educative and upon a high plane and models of literary form. In summing up his qualities, President Garfield said, "He has done justice to the scholarship which Germany gave him and the large and comprehensive ideas with which life in the new world inspired him." Senator Bayard of Delaware said of him, "It has been said to me more than once how admirable would Schleicher have been as a cabinet officer, and what a loss to our country it is that his powers and talents for administration could not have been exemplified in the highest office of the government."

TERRELL

Alexander Watkins Terrell was born in Patrick County, Virginia, November 23, 1827. His parents moved to Cooper County, Missouri, in 1832, and he obtained his primary education there. He entered the University of Missouri and, finishing his course there, he began the study of law at Booneville and was admitted to the bar in 1848. He located at St. Joseph and practiced law until 1852, when he came to Texas and located at Austin.

Five years later he was elected district judge of the Second District and served as such until his term expired. Being a judicial officer, he took no prominent part in the political agitation immediately preceding the secession of the state.

At the expiration of his second term as District Judge, in 1863, he entered the Confederate Army as lieutenant colonel of the Thirty-fourth Texas Regiment (cavalry) and was soon promoted to the rank of colonel and commanded the regiment until near the close of the war, participating in the Battles of Mansfield, Pleasant Hill, and other engagements in the campaign against Banks, in Louisiana. In 1865 he was promoted to the position of brigadier general and was in command of a brigade at the close of the war. In company with General Magruder and many other prominent Confederates he went to Mexico, but soon returned.

He entered the practice of law at Houston, but owing to the unsettled condition of the courts, he retired to his plantation on the Brazos in Robertson County, and for four years was eminently successful as a planter with the new system of free labor. In 1872 he moved to Austin and formed a partnership with Judge A. S. Walker in the practice of law. In 1875 he was selected to the State Senate and re-elected in 1879 and 1882. At the urgent solicitation of his fellow citizens he was later elected as a member of the lower house of the Legislature, in all serving sixteen years as a legislator.

He was the author of many of the most salutary laws now on our statute books, two of the most conspicuous and far-reaching being our jury law and what is known as the "Terrell Election Law." His portrait hangs in the Hall of Representatives at the State Capitol. By a standing vote of that body, in presenting his portrait, the chairman of the Judiciary Committee voiced the sentiment of the people of Texas when, among other things, he said, "Judge Terrell has been the author of more good laws for Texas than any other man, living or dead."

Besides his active career as a lawmaker, he was for some years reporter of the Supreme Court decisions, and reported the decisions of that court embraced in Volumes 52 to 76 inclusive, and in connection with Judge A. S. Walker, in Volumes 38 to 51, inclusive. During the last administration of President Cleveland he represented the United States as Minister to Turkey. He died while on a visit to Mineral Wells, Texas, September 9, 1912, and was buried in Austin.

WILLACY

This county was named in honor of J. G. Willacy, who was born in Kentucky. He removed to Texas and located at Corpus Christi. He represented this district in the lower house of the Twenty-sixth and Twenty-seventh Legislatures, and the Senate in the Thirtieth, Thirty-first, Thirty-second and Thirty-fifth Legislatures. He is a farmer.

YOAKUM

Henderson Yoakum was born in Claiborne County, Tennessee, September 6, 1810. He studied in the common schools until prepared to take a collegiate course, and on July 1, 1828, entered the United States Military Academy at West Point. He graduated and was made a brevet second lieutenant July 1, 1832. After serving in the Black Hawk Expedition, he resigned from the army March 31, 1832, and was married in the same year in Roane County, Tennessee, and removed to Murfreesboro, where he studied law and entered the active practice of the profession. In 1836 he entered the military service again as captain of a company in General Gaines' command in Louisiana. In 1839 he was elected to the State Senate of Tennessee.

In October, 1848, he came to Texas and located at Huntsville. In May, 1846, he enlisted in a company of riflemen and was elected first lieutenant. He went to the front and served throughout General Taylor's campaign in the Mexican War. At the close of the Mexican War he returned to Huntsville and resumed the practice of law.

In 1853 he established a country home a few miles from Huntsville and devoted himself to completing his history of Texas. In November, 1855, he visited Houston for the purpose of delivering a Masonic address, and on the 30th of that month died suddenly at the old Capitol building. Yoakum's *History of Texas* is known and consulted by writers of history the world over, and regarded as the standard for the period which it covers.

The unveiling of the Confederate monument on the Capitol grounds, 1903

CHAPTER XV,
THE WAR BETWEEN THE STATES

The soldiers and statesmen of the Southern Confederacy who have been honored by county names are:

Camp	Randall	Terry
Ector	Reeves	Tom Green
Gregg	Scurry	Upton
Hood	Stephens	Val Verde
Jeff Davis	Stonewall	Winkler
Lee	Sutton	Young

CAMP

John Lafayette Camp was born on a farm adjacent to Elyton (now a suburb of Birmingham), Alabama, in 1820. He attended the common schools and at the age of twenty graduated from the University of Tennessee at Knoxville.

He removed to Texas and located at Gilmer, in Upshur County, where he taught school and practiced law. He married in 1851 and continued the practice of law up to 1861. He was then elected Captain of a company from Upshur County and joined the Confederate Army. When the Fourteenth Texas Regiment was organized he was elected colonel, and in that capacity served through the entire period of the war. He was twice wounded severely, first at Murfreesboro, Tennessee, in the right shoulder, and afterward at Altoona Heights, Georgia, was seriously wounded in the right leg. He was twice captured and imprisoned for many months.

After the war he returned to Texas and was elected a member of the Constitutional Convention of 1866 and state Senator in 1874. He became District Judge in 1878, and was appointed a member of the Board of Regents of the State University, but owing to ill health could not serve. In 1884 he was appointed Land Commissioner to Arizona. At the end of his term he moved to San Antonio and after a lingering illness died in July, 1891.

ECTOR

M. D. Ector was born in Putman County, Georgia, February 28, 1822. He was educated at La Grange, Georgia, and at Center College, Kentucky. He began the practice of law in his native county in 1845, and in the same year was elected to the Legislature in that State.

He came to Texas in 1849 and located at Henderson, where he practiced law. He was elected and served in the Texas Legislature in 1855. In 1861 he enlisted as a private and soon afterward was appointed adjutant by Colonel (afterward General) Hogg. After the Battle of Shiloh he was made a colonel for gallantry on the field, and two weeks later was made a brigadier general. He was in the battles of Chickamauga, Murfreesboro and other engagements, and while fighting near Atlanta on the 28th of July, 1864, he received a wound which necessitated the amputation of his left leg. When sufficiently recovered from the operation he reported for duty and was assigned to the command of troops at Mobile.

He returned to Texas after the war. He was elected district judge, but after about a year's service he was removed, along with other officers in the Throckmorton administration, upon the pretense of his being an impediment to reconstruction. He then removed to Marshall and practiced law. In 1874 he was appointed district judge by Governor Coke. When the Court of Appeals was created, in 1875, he was made a justice of that body, and in 1876 selected as Chief Justice by his associates. During a session of the court at Tyler he died in that city October 20, 1879.

GREGG

General John Gregg was born in Lawrence County, Alabama, September 28, 1828. He attended the celebrated school of Professor Tutwiler, from which he graduated in 1847, and after graduation was employed as professor of languages and mathematics in the same school. In 1851 he studied law in the office of Judge Townes at Tuscumbia, Alabama, and in 1852 removed to Texas and located at Fairfield, in Freestone County.

After practicing law four years he was elected district judge of that district and was holding that office in 1861, when elected a delegate to the Secession Convention. He was then chosen as a delegate to the Provisional Congress of the Southern Confederacy, holding sessions at Montgomery, and went with that body to Richmond, Virginia. Immediately after the Battle of Manassas, July 21, 1861, he resigned, returned to Texas and organized the Seventh Regiment of Volunteers, of which he was made colonel. The command went to Kentucky, and he was captured at Fort Donaldson. When exchanged he returned to the Confederacy and was promoted to the position of brigadier general and joined the army in Mississippi. He was in the engagements of the Western army until the Battle of Chickamauga. He was then transferred to Virginia and placed in command of

Hood's old brigade, and was killed near Fort Harrison
on the Charles City road, October 7, 1864.

HOOD

General John B. Hood was born in Bath County, Kentucky, June 29, 1831. At an early age his parents moved
to Fort Starling, Montgomery County, Kentucky, where
he was reared and educated in the common schools.
He entered the United States Military Academy at West
Point, from which he graduated in 1853, and was made
second lieutenant in the army, being assigned to duty
with the Fourth United States Infantry in California. He
was later transferred to the Second United States Cavalry.

In 1855 he served on the frontier of Texas. On the 16th
of April, 1861, he resigned his commission in the United
States Army and tendered his services to the Southern
Confederacy and was ordered to report to General
Magruder on the peninsula, below Richmond, with a
captain's commission. He was soon promoted to the
rank of Major, and on the 30th of September, 1861, was
made colonel and placed in command of the Fourth
Texas Regiment of Infantry. On the 3rd of March, 1862,
he was made brigadier general, and in hotly contested
battles of the different campaigns in Virginia in 1862,
his brigade became famous. In 1863 he was made a
major general.

At the Battle of Gettysburg, July 2, 1863, he was so
severely wounded in his right leg as to necessitate amputation. Later he was appointed lieutenant general. On
the 17th of July, 1864, he was put in command of the
army near Atlanta and commanded in a severe engagement on the 20th and again on the 27th. He abandoned
Atlanta on September 1, and in command of an army

of forty thousand men he marched back into Tennessee and fought the disastrous Battle of Franklin on the 30th of November, and again, on the 15th of December, attacked and was defeated at Nashville. This practically ended his military career. After the close of the war he located at New Orleans and embarked in the insurance business. He was stricken with yellow fever and died in that city in 1879. A handsome monument to his brigade has been erected on the Capitol grounds at Austin.

He, like many other Confederate officers, died leaving little property to support his family. He left a family of nine young orphan children, his wife having previously died.

JEFF DAVIS

Jefferson Davis, in whose honor this county was named, was the grandson of Eben Davis, who came from Wales to America about the year 1748 and settled in Georgia. His son, Samuel, did honorable service in the war of the revolution, and at its close settled near Augusta. Later he moved to Christian County, Kentucky, where Jefferson, his ninth child, was born, June 3, 1808.

Young Jefferson attended St. Thomas' College, in Kentucky, a Catholic school, for two years; Jefferson College in Mississippi, and Transylvania University at Lexington, Kentucky, for two years. He was then appointed a cadet at West Point Military Academy and graduated in 1828 and commissioned as second lieutenant in July of that year, and on March 4, 1833, was promoted to first lieutenant of dragoons. He served in the Black Hawk War and later was stationed at Fort Gibson, Arkansas, where he married the daughter of Colonel Zachary Taylor in 1835.

He then resigned his commission and engaged in cotton planting in Warren County, Mississippi, where his wife soon afterwards died. He was a presidential elector on the Polk and Dallas ticket in 1844, and was elected to the lower house of the U. S. Congress in 1845, and served until June, 1846, when he resigned to take command of the First Regiment of Mississippi Riflemen in the Mexican War. He was with Taylor's Army at Monterrey in September of 1846, where he greatly distinguished himself, as he afterwards did at Buena Vista.

Three months later he was appointed brigadier general, but declined it to accept the appointment to the U.S. Senate from Mississippi. He was subsequently elected to the same position and served from August, 1847, to November, 1851. He was a candidate for governor that year and was defeated, but was again elected to the U.S. Senate. He resigned that to become Secretary of War in President Pierce's cabinet March 3, 1853, and served four years. He was then elected to the United States Senate and served until January 21, 1861, when he withdrew from that body with other southern senators.

He was chosen Provisional President of the Southern Confederacy at Montgomery, Alabama, and inaugurated February 19, 1861. He was elected President of the Southern Confederacy for a term of six years and was inaugurated February 22, 1862, at Richmond, Virginia. While attempting to make his escape from the Federal Army, after the surrender of Lee and Johnston, he was captured by Union troops at Irwinville, Georgia, May 14, 1865. He was imprisoned for two years at Fortress Monroe and indicted for treason, but by the direction of the federal government the case was dismissed and he was released in December, 1868. He then returned to Mississippi and settled at Beauvoir and died in New Orleans December 6, 1868.

LEE

Robert E. Lee, son of General Henry Lee ("Light Horse Harry" of the Revolution), the great chieftain of the Southern Confederacy, was born in Stratford, Virginia, January 19, 1807.

He entered the United States Military Academy at West Point and graduated from there in 1829. When General Scott invaded Mexico, in 1847, Lee was appointed Chief of Engineers of the Army. He received three promotions for services in that campaign. He was superintendent of the Academy at West Point in 1852, and afterward served on the frontier of Texas. He was in command of troops that captured old John Brown at Harper's Ferry, in 1859.

He resigned his commission as colonel in the United States Army on April 20, 1861, and was appointed major general by the State of Virginia immediately afterward. He was made commander of the army of Northern Virginia in 1862, and directed all its campaigns afterward. He was made General in Chief of the Armies of the Southern Confederacy January 31, 1865, and surrendered to General Grant at Appomattox, Virginia, April 9, 1865.

After the war he was tendered several lucrative positions, but declined them to accept the presidency of Washington College (now Washington and Lee University) and was acting in that capacity when he died, October 12, 1870.

RANDALL

General Horace Randall was born in Tennessee in 1821. His parents moved to Texas and located in San Augustine County. He was appointed cadet at West Point in 1849, graduated in 1853 and was commissioned second lieutenant of cavalry in the same year. He served in the army on the Texas and other frontiers, but resigned in 1861 to offer his services to the Southern Confederacy. He organized a regiment in East Texas and went to the front, commanding in various engagements, first as colonel, then as brigadier general, in the Trans-Mississippi Department, and was killed at Jenkin's Ferry, otherwise known as the Battle of Saline, in Arkansas, on the 30th of April, 1864.

REEVES

George R. Reeves was born in Hickman County, Tennessee, July 3, 1826. At the age of nine years his parents moved to Arkansas and he resided there until he came to Texas in 1845, and located in what is now Grayson County, about seven miles north of the present site of Sherman, and engaged in farming and stock raising. He was sheriff of that county and assessor and collector of taxes from 1845 to 1856. He was elected a member of the Legislature and was serving in that body when the Civil War began. He organized Company C, Eleventh Texas Cavalry, and was chosen captain of the company, serving east of the Mississippi. He was promoted to the position of colonel in 1863. He was elected to the Legislature in 1873, and successively re-elected up to 1881, and was Speaker of the House of Representatives at the time of his death, September 5, 1882.

SCURRY

William R. Scurry was born in Gallatin, Tennessee, February 10, 1821. He was reared, educated and studied law in that county and came to Texas in 1840, locating in Washington County.

He became a full-fledged lawyer before he was twenty-one years old. He was elected a member of the Ninth and last Congress of the Republic, and at the breaking out of the Mexican War he promptly enlisted and was elected Major of Wood's Regiment. He was conspicuous for gallantry in the engagement of Monterrey.

After that he moved to Clarksville, in Red River County, where he actively engaged in the practice of law and became one of the most popular orators in the state. He then located in DeWitt County, at Clinton, then the county seat, and was engaged in his profession when the Civil War broke out in 1861.

He promptly enlisted in the Confederate Army, and was elected lieutenant colonel and accompanied Sibley's Brigade to New Mexico and participated in the Battles of Peralto, Valverde, and Glorietta. Upon his return to Texas he was appointed to the command of the Eastern Military sub-district. In 1863 he was commissioned brigadier general and assigned to duty under General Dick Taylor in Louisiana, and was killed at the Battle of Saline (Jenkin's Ferry), April 30, 1864.

STEPHENS

Alexander H. Stephens, Vice-President of the Confederate States, was born at Crawfordsville, Taliaferro
County, Georgia, February 11, 1812. He graduated from
Franklin College in 1832, and from 1836 to 1842 served
in both branches of the Georgia Legislature. In 1843
he was elected to the lower house of the United States
Congress, and by successive elections was a member
of that body to the close of the Thirty-fourth Congress.

At the first stage of the secession movement he was
opposed to the policy, but when secession became
inevitable he joined his native state and was chosen
Vice-President of the Confederate States in 1861.

At the close of the war between the states, he was
arrested by the United States authorities but was soon
released, and in 1866 was chosen United States Senator
from Georgia, but was refused admission to the Senate.
He was elected to and served in successive Congresses
from the Forty-third to the Forty-seventh. In 1882 he
was elected governor of Georgia. He died at Atlanta
before the expiration of his term as governor, March
4, 1883. He was an author of note, his *History of the
United States* and *A Constitutional View of the War Between the States* being his principal published works.

STONEWALL

Thomas Jonathan Jackson was born in Clarksburg,
Virginia, (now West Virginia) January 21, 1824. He was
educated in the common schools of his section of Virginia and entered the United States Military Academy
at West Point in 1841. Graduating in 1845 he was made
a second lieutenant, and in 1847 actively participated in

the campaign from Vera Cruz to the City of Mexico in General Scott's Army.

After the close of the war he served upon the frontier of the United States, but resigned in 1855 to accept the position of professor of mathematics at the Virginia Military Institute, and was engaged in the duties of that position when the Civil War began in 1861.

He offered his services to his native state and was immediately commissioned colonel and soon afterward brigadier general. While commanding his brigade at the first battle of Manassas, Colonel Barnard E. Bee, whose regiment was confused by the enemy, pointed out to his command General Jackson, saying, "There stands Jackson like a stone wall," and he was ever afterward called "Stonewall Jackson." He was afterward made major general, and after his wonderful campaign in the Valley of Virginia, and the rapid movements by which he was enabled to come to the rescue of Lee at Richmond in 1862 his fame became worldwide.

He was killed at Chancellorsville by his own men through mistake, May 10, 1863. His rapid marches earned for his command the title of "Jackson's Foot Cavalry."

SUTTON

John S. Sutton was a native of Newcastle County, Delaware, where he was born September 12, 1821. At the age of eighteen he was appointed to a cadetship at West Point Military Academy, but left in January, 1840, and came to Texas, making his home at Austin.

Soon after his arrival he joined the ranger service and was actively engaged in that capacity when the Santa Fe Expedition was organized. He organized a company and joined this expedition and was one of those who surrendered and was carried prisoner to Castle Perote, where he shared all the hardships of his fellow prisoners. After his release from prison he returned to Texas and again joined the army in time to take part in the Somervell Expedition, but did not accompany that portion of the army that crossed the Rio Grande. He shortly afterward joined the ranger service and was an active participant in various conflicts with the Indians.

When Texas was annexed to the United States and the Mexican War followed, he again joined the army and remained with it until the war closed. He was actively engaged in the ranger service until 1849, when, with the many other gold hunters, he went to California, and from time to time served under Jack Hays, sheriff of San Francisco. Upon the expiration of Hays' term as sheriff, Sutton returned to Texas, and for a short period was again in the ranger service.

Upon his retirement he located at Port Lavaca and was engaged in business there at the commencement of the Civil War in 1861. He then volunteered and was elected captain of a company, and upon the organization of the Seventh Regiment of Texas Volunteers at San Antonio in the summer of 1861 was elected lieutenant colonel and went with Sibley's brigade to New Mexico. While leading the regiment in a charge at Val Verde, February 21, 1862, his right leg was shattered by grape shot. He refused to have it amputated and died from the wound.

★ ★ ★

TERRY

Benjamin Franklin Terry was born on the 18th of February, 1821, in Russelville, Kentucky. In 1831 he, in company with his mother and three younger brothers, also his mother's brother, Major Ben Fort Smith, came to Texas and settled in Brazoria County. He and his younger brother, David S. Terry, ran away from home just before the Battle of San Jacinto to join Houston's army, but learning of the overthrow of Santa Anna at San Jacinto, returned home. He married Mary Bingham, Oct. 12, 1841. Her father was one of Austin's original three hundred colonists.

In 1849, he and his brother, David S. Terry, went to California. David remained and became chief justice of the Supreme Court of that state, but Ben F. Terry remained only eighteen months. He returned to Texas and located in Houston. In 1852 he purchased the Oakland sugar plantation in Fort Bend County and was there engaged as a sugar planter in 1861. He was elected as a delegate to the Secession Convention in 1861 and after the adjournment of that body he, in company with Thomas S. Lubbock, repaired to the seat of war in Virginia, both participating in the Battle of Manassas, July 21. Immediately after that battle they returned to Texas and organized at Houston a regiment of cavalry which became famous in the annals of the Confederacy as "Terry's Texas Rangers."

Terry was chosen as colonel and Lubbock lieutenant colonel. Immediately after the organization and equipment of the regiment they went to the seat of war in Kentucky. In an impetuous charge upon the enemy Terry was killed at Woodsonville, Kentucky, December 17, 1861.

TOM GREEN

Gen. Thomas Green was born in Amelia County, Virginia, June 8, 1814. In 1817 his father's family moved to Tennessee, where his father was for many years a justice of the Supreme Court. Tom Green received a liberal education in the common schools, Princeton College, Kentucky, and at the University of Tennessee. He studied law in 1834 and in the fall of 1835, when he learned of the conditions of Texas, came and joined the army as a private. He arrived in March, 1836, and was in the campaign that culminated April 21, at San Jacinto. He was promoted to a lieutenancy for gallantry in this battle.

He then went back to Tennessee, but returned to Texas in 1837, held the position of clerk in the Congress of 1838 and in that year was elected Surveyor of Fayette County. In 1841 he was appointed clerk of the Supreme Court of the Republic and held that office continuously up to 1846, and was re-elected to the same position after annexation and held the office until 1861, when he enlisted in the Confederate Army.

In the early days of this court there was not enough business to employ his entire time, and on repeated occasions he left the office in charge of a deputy and joined military organizations when the exigencies of the country seemed to demand it. In 1841 he joined the expedition against the Indians up the Colorado River. In 1842 he joined the Somervell Expedition as Inspector General and in 1846 he volunteered in the Mexican War and commanded a company in the famous regiment of John C. (Jack) Hays. Early in 1861 he was made colonel of a regiment in the Sibley expedition into New Mexico and performed conspicuous service in the Battle of Val

Verde. On the 31st of December, 1862, he was in immediate command of the forces that captured Galveston,
and from that time up to his death he was in the various
campaigns in Louisiana.

On the 12th day of April, 1864, he was killed at the
Battle of Blair's Landing, on the Red River, in Louisiana.

UPTON

John Cunningham Upton was born on a farm near
Winchester, Franklin County, Tennessee, January 22,
1828. He attended the common schools of his county
and attended the University of Lebanon, Tennessee. He
left Tennessee in 1850 and went to California, where he
remained until 1859. His family having moved to Texas
in the interim, he removed from California to Texas in
that year and settled in Fayette County and took charge
of his mother's plantation.

Early in 1861 he raised a company, was chosen captain
and went to the seat of war in Virginia and was attached
to the Fifth Texas Regiment of Hood's Brigade, and was
in the numerous engagements of that brigade up to his
death. He was promoted to major and then lieutenant
colonel of the regiment, and while at the head of the
regiment in a charge at the second Battle of Manassas,
August 30, 1862, he was killed.

William Felton Upton, John Cunningham Upton's
brother, was born near Winchester, Tennessee, August
30, 1832, and was reared and educated there. In 1853
he moved with his mother and family to Fayette County, Texas, and engaged in farming in that county until
1861. In that year he enlisted in Nichol's Regiment and
was successively promoted from captain to lieutenant
colonel and served during the entire war. He returned

to Fayette County in 1865 and began, in connection with his farming operations, a mercantile business and soon became the leading merchant at Schulenberg. He served several terms in the State Legislature and died at Schulenberg, Texas, February 7, 1887. Upton County was named in honor of these brothers.

VAL VERDE

This county was named in honor of the battle fought at Val Verde, near Fort Craig, New Mexico, on the 19th of February, 1862, under the command of General Tom Green, General Sibley, the commander, being unwell. This was the culmination of what was called the Sibley Expedition into New Mexico, the object of which was to bring New Mexico under the dominion of the Southern Confederacy.

WINKLER

C. M. Winkler was born in Burke County, North Carolina, October 19, 1821, but moved with his father's family to Indiana in 1831. He was educated there and came to Texas in 1840. He settled at Franklin, county seat of Robertson County, and prepared himself for the bar while acting as deputy clerk of the District Court. In 1844 he was elected District Clerk, held the office two years and went into the active practice of his profession. In 1848 he removed to Corsicana and was in the same year elected to the Legislature. After serving one term he devoted his entire energies to the practice of his profession up to 1861.

Early in 1861 he was elected captain of a company in the Fourth Texas Regiment and was successively promoted until he was made colonel. He was seriously wounded at Gettysburg.

After the war he resumed his practice in partnership with Colonel (afterward United States Senator) Mills; was elected a member of the Legislature in 1873, and in 1876 was elected one of the Judges of the Court of Appeals, and after holding this office he was re-elected, and while serving died on the 13th of May, 1882, at Austin, Texas.

YOUNG

W. C. Young came to Texas about the year 1841 and settled in Red River County. He was in the service as a Ranger for some time, and in 1845 was elected a delegate to the convention which framed the first state constitution. He afterwards served in the State Legislature and was in the ranger service in northwest Texas from time to time up to 1861. In that year he was elected a delegate to the Secession Convention and after adjournment entered the service of the Southern Confederacy and was chosen colonel of the Fourth Texas Regiment of Cavalry and went with his command into the campaign in Arkansas and Missouri. He was killed in the Indian Territory in 1862.

Texas Comanche Indian family, circa 1900

CHAPTER XVI,
THE INDIANS OF TEXAS

Five counties of the State have been named for Indian tribes: Cherokee, Comanche, Nacogdoches, Pecos and Wichita.

CHEROKEE

This tribe of Indians played a somewhat conspicuous part in the history of the United States, not only in the usual and ordinary Indian way, but in the politics of the United States, and in the politics of Texas as well.

They began to settle in the region north of the old San Antonio Road, between the Sabine and Trinity Rivers, as early as 1819, and continued for five years to arrive from the region they occupied in Tennessee, Alabama, Georgia, and the Carolinas. They sought to obtain a grant from Mexico to this region in 1822, but failed to obtain anything beyond its permissive use, until the subject of colonization of Texas was definitely fixed and regulated by laws providing for the settlement of the country which were enacted several years later. No provision was made for granting titles to land, except in severalty or to the individual, and not to a community or tribe in solido. This, of course, the Cherokees did not desire, and matters remained in this way, they continuing in possession until the revolution of Texas against Mexico, when, by some understanding, their permissive use and occupancy was continued. Their persistent claim of title to the country and the friction that increased as the neighboring country was settled, together with undoubted evidence of disloyalty to the

Republic of Texas, culminated in what was known as the Cherokee War in 1838, which resulted in their expulsion from Texas in 1839.

COMANCHE

The connection of this tribe with the history of Texas dates back to about 1750, when they came down from the north and vanquished that other warlike tribe, the Apaches. They were more than a match for the Spanish settlers and troops, and were the virtual masters of Texas until the Anglo-Americans came. They stubbornly resisted every advance of the new settlers, stealing and murdering, and they did not finally leave the borders of the state until railroads and barbed wire fences obstructed their way, and there were no longer buffaloes and other available wild game for them to subsist upon. In 1882 they gave up the contest and retired to Indian Territory.

NACOGDOCHES

This was the name of one of the Texas tribes in the Hasinai Confederacy for which a mission was established in 1716. If the term "prehistoric" means the period embraced before Columbus discovered America we may call it a prehistoric name, as a tribe of Indians of this name was encountered by the remnant of De Soto's followers under Moscoso in 1542, and they were referred to by that name in the narrative of that expedition.

The mission established there in 1716 was abandoned in 1719, when the French invaded that country. But the Indians, such as were left there and were willing to go, were transferred to the Mission Espada about 1731, and they seem to have lost their identity afterwards. In the meantime some Spaniard settlers had settled on the Trinity and about 1775 re-established this old mission, and in 1785 there were two Spanish friars and a few settlers around there. The old Spanish fort recently demolished was the last relic of the old mission.

After this American traders began to visit the place and to settle in the vicinity. When Edwards obtained his contract in 1825 to introduce 800 families into this region it was found to embrace many of these old Spanish claims, and the friction that arose resulted in the Fredonian War. It was made a municipality by Coahuila and Texas and became one of the first counties of the Republic of Texas.

PECOS

This county took its name from the Pecos River. Banderier's report on the Pueblo of Pecos (in the papers of the Archaeological Institute of America), American Sur., Vol. 1, Page 114, note, says: "The name Pecos itself belongs to the Qq'ueres language of New Mexico, and is pronounced Pae-qp. It is applied to the inhabitants of the Pueblo, the place itself being called Pae-qog-one. The first mention of it under the name of Pecos is found in the documents of the year 1598, after the general meeting of Juan de Onate with the Pueblo Indians in the Estufa of Santo Domingo (a Qq'ueres village)." This village, or pueblo, was on the headwaters of the stream which now bears this name. As far back as Coronado's expedition (1542) this tribe, if one may call it such, had a tradition of its own, for their boast then was that it had never been conquered and could conquer any of its neighbors. The name, therefore, is, as is Nacogdoches, of prehistoric origin.

WICHITA

This was a common name for a number of tribes of Indians who occupied the headwaters of Red River and its tributaries. They came down into Texas from the north after the Spaniards first came to the country and lived in villages of the upper Brazos and Red Rivers. Like the Cherokees, they were peaceably inclined as a rule, practiced agriculture and remained in Texas long after the Anglo-American settlers came, but disappeared on the reservation after the Civil War.

CHAPTER XVI,
PHYSIOGRAPHIC NAMES

Twenty-nine counties take their names from the land and waters of Texas.

Atascosa
Blanco
Bosque
Brazoria
Brazos
Colorado
Concho
Comal
Delta
El Paso
Falls
Fort Bend
Freestone
Frio
Lampasas
Lavaca
Limestone
Live Oak
Llano
Matagorda
Midland
Nueces
Orange
Palo Pinto
Panola
Red River
Rockwall
Sabine

ATASCOSA

This word means "boggy." We have no historical account of its application to this region, but there would seem to be no doubt as to why it was called Atascosa before the Anglo-Americans began to traverse it. Brown's *History of Texas* says:

> On a pleasant November day, 22nd, 1842, all the camps (of the Somervell Expedition) around the Mission Concepcion...took of march on the road from San Antonio to El Presidio Rio Grande. They encamped two nights and a day on the Rio Medina, then crossed that stream and after following the road several miles, to the astonishment and mortification of everyone, turned to the left southerly... and a few miles brought them to a sandy post-oak country where horses and mules sank to their bodies in quicksand...That locality became known as the "bogs," or "The Devil's Eight Leagues."

Green, in his *Mier Expedition*, gives a somewhat more minute and picturesque description. He says:

> This kind of land, with much appearance of firmness to the eye, and sufficiently firm to bear a man's weight, will let horses' feet through, and after once through the grass sod the soft quicksand beneath will carry the animal down...Two days were employed in five miles of this kind of land...The whole seven hundred and sixty men, horses and packs were scattered over the country as far as the eye could reach, some floundering and plunging forth; some with their bodies down upon the ground, their legs entirely out of sight and their noses upon the ground, in perfect quietude, as well as to say

to their owners, "You put me in here, now get me out," while the owner would be standing by giving utterance to all manner of curious oaths; some would be lying on their side, afraid to trust their legs under them, while the poor pack mules, with their little feet, stood the worst kind of a chance. The coffee pots and frying pans would go one way and the aparajos and other camp appurtenances another...Here one would strike a fire and go to cooking, as he would say, while the animal could blow, etc.

The name, first applied to a circumscribed area, was soon given to the stream, and in 1856 the Legislature created a county with more than one thousand square miles of area and applied "Atascosa" or "boggy" to it.

BLANCO

The Aguayo Expedition of 1721 was composed of a larger body of men and better equipments and traveled a greater distance than any other of the Spanish expeditions to Texas. It traveled entirely across the country from the Rio Grande to and beyond the Sabine. From San Antonio it went by what is now New Braunfels, San Marcos, and Austin until it reached Georgetown, Belton, and Waco, where it crossed the Brazos, then in a southeasterly direction until it reached the old San Antonio Road; thence in a northeasterly direction to the Texas villages, and from there across the Sabine to Natchitoches, Louisiana. After leaving San Antonio Aguayo gave names to many streams and other natural objects, some of which names have long since disappeared, and only a few have survived to become county names.

Blanco means "white." It was given to that stream, which flows almost its entire length through a white, chalky limestone region.

BOSQUE

The whole course of the Aguayo expedition from Monclova to the Brazos was through a sparsely wooded region, and when they reached the Brazos, at the junction of the Bosque, they encountered a dense growth of larger trees than they had ever seen, and called that stream the "Bosque" or "Woody" River, the word meaning "woody."

BRAZORIA

Brazoria is simply a derivative of "Brazos."

BRAZOS

This word means "arms." Brazos de Dios—Arms of God. Applied to streams it means forks.

The river was probably named in 1690 or 1691. As to the circumstances of the application of the name, there are various accounts, but as far as the author was able to learn, none of them have any historical foundation.

The county was named for the river in January, 1842.

COLORADO

This word means "Red Water." When it was first applied to the present stream is not definitely known. It was applied to several streams by different expeditions.

COMAL

This word means "basin." It was probably applied to this stream during the Aguayo Expedition. It had its source in numerous springs a short distance above the town of New Braunfels, which formed the Comal River, one of the most rapid and steady streams in the state. The river is only about three miles long and furnishes the best natural water power in the state.

CONCHO

This word means "shell," from the Spanish *concha*. The River Concho, from which the county took its name, has a history extending back to 1650, when an expedition went there from New Mexico and found pearls in the streams, which they sent to the Viceroy. A want of knowledge of the geography of Texas on the part of Mr. Bancroft deprives his history of what would be one of its greatest values. Appreciating the importance of this, Dr. Bolton, in his researches in Mexico, found a diary of another expedition, undertaken in 1683, and was able to make out in detail the route of this last expedition, and with accuracy to trace it to the site of the modern city of San Angelo. The Indians in that region induced the authorities at El Paso to undertake the establishment of a mission there and a large expedition was fitted out and marched there. They encamped on the banks of the stream and awaited the gathering of the Indians. They waited in vain for many months, and while waiting engaged in fishing in the river for pearls, with some success.

A half century ago there were some traces of large beds of shells (mussels) near the banks of the stream. The finding of so many shells in the river at different times caused the Spaniards to identify it as the Concho (Shell) River. The shells or mussels are still abundant in this and other streams of the upper Colorado, and valuable pearls are taken from them, the value of some reaching as high as two hundred and fifty dollars.

DELTA

So named because of the county's boundaries being in the shape of the Greek letter Delta. It is situated between the north and south branches of the Sulphur Fork of Red River, the two joining on the extreme eastern end.

EL PASO

"The Pass," one of the first, if not the first, geographical names applied by the Spaniards to any part of Texas. It is a natural gateway through the chain of mountains, and from its peculiar situation all routes of that region converge there, and in modern times all railways in that region converge there.

FALLS

About thirty miles southeast of Waco the water of the Brazos River has a fall of about twenty feet over the rocks and shoals, hence the name of the county through which the river flows.

FORT BEND

This county was named for an old fort on the bend of the Brazos River at the present county site of this county. The fort was built about 1818, when Lafitte had his headquarters on Galveston Island and when the interior was infested by wild Indians. In that year William Andrews established a trading station there and to protect it built a fort. It was well known as old Fort Bend several years before Austin's first colonists began to arrive.

FREESTONE

Was created out of the territory of Limestone County in 1850, Limestone having been created in 1846. The totally different soil formation and character of water prompted the authors of the bill to make the boundary between the new and the old county represent in a general way the line between the freestone and the limestone regions. This line, in a general way, is a part of the western line of the great lignite belt of Texas.

FRIO

"Cold," applied, according to Bancroft, to the River Frio in 1689, during De Leon's expedition, as a testimonial to the low temperature of the water.

LAMPASAS

The origin of this name is not definitely known. The river, after which the county took its name, was named Lampasas more than a century before the county was created, and was supposed by some to be of Indian origin, having particular reference to the Sulphur Springs which supplied most of its water. The most plausible theory is that it was borrowed from the name of the Mexican town, Lampazos, and the stream first became known to the Spaniards in 1721, when the Aguayo Expedition crossed it going to eastern Texas. This expedition crossed it where three streams come together and formed what was known at different times Primeria Brazos or San Andress, and is now known as Little River. Spanish names were given to these three rivers, namely: Salado, Lampasas and Leon. About twenty years later three missions were established on the San Gabriel River near its mouth. These missions were maintained about twelve years and the geography of the region doubtless became familiar, as there are evidences of attempts to find several silver and gold mines in various places near what is now known as the town of Salado. Evidences of old shafts sunk near the Williamson and Bell County lines are still in existence.

Mr. Gannett says the word means "water lily," but the standard Spanish dictionaries do not so define it. The

word *lampazos* is defined as "Burdock,", "common burdock" or "cockleburr," "pimples on the face," "swab or
mop used to clean off the decks of ships." The Spanish
word for water lily is *nenúfar*. This name was given to
the stream probably in 1721.

LAVACA

This word is composed of the two Spanish words *la*,
"the," and *vaca*, "cow." It is named for the river, near
whose mouth La Salle built Fort St. Louis, and was
first named by the French because of the large herds
of buffalo seen in the vicinity. When the Spaniards took
possession of the country they transformed the French
name given to the river La Vaca, and the practical Anglo-
American took the two words and ran them together in
the one word Lavaca.

LIMESTONE

See Freestone.

LIVE OAK

This county takes its name from the trees. It marks
the end of the great postoak belt and the beginning of
the scattered live oaks, extending up through the lower
coastal plain.

LLANO

"Plain." This is a very common geographical term wherever the Spaniards settled. The river, from which the county took its name, has its source among the plains in Schleicher and Sutton Counties, and flowing through a region of broken country empties into the Colorado River. There is another theory as to an Indian origin, but only a theory.

MATAGORDA

There is some controversy as to the origin of this name. It is made up of two Spanish words, *mata*, which is defined as "small brush, shrubs, sprigs, blades, etc.," and *gorda*, which is defined as "fat, coarse, thick, dense, etc.," as Cerrogorda, Alamogorda, etc. In Matagorda the meaning is "dense canebrake." The most conspicuous geographical feature of this county is the dense cane-brake through which flows Old Caney Creek, an ancient bed of the Colorado River. Having its source within less than a mile of the Colorado River, the creek flows about seventy miles through the only considerable canebrake in the state, with a width of bottom lands ranging from three to ten miles wide, in many places through an al-most impenetrable growth of cane. Its general course is parallel with the general trend of the present channel of the Colorado River, and the adjacent lands are the most fertile in the state.

The theory advanced by some is that the word is com-posed of the obsolete Spanish word *mata* ("slaughter") and *gorda* ("fat"). The name first applied to the bay was San Bernardo. It was afterward changed by the Spaniards to Matagorda, and the ancient bed of the Colorado from Matagorda was changed to "Old Caney" by the Anglo-Americans.

MIDLAND

This county is so called because it marks the midland or halfway ground between Fort Worth and El Paso on the Texas & Pacific Railway.

NUECES

"Pecans," so called during De Leon's expedition in 1689, in the diary of which it is said, in writing of the Nueces River, "We call it Nueces because of the many pecan trees on its banks."

ORANGE

All the original thirteen States have the geographical name "orange," except Rhode Island, in honor of the House of Orange. The Gulf States and California have the name fourteen times, given for the fruit of that name. Since the earliest settlements near the mouth of the Sabine River, oranges have been grown for domestic purposes.

★

PALO PINTO

This county takes its name from the principal creek of the area, Palo Pinto Creek, named so by the Spaniards. It is derived from the Spanish words *palo* (stick) and *pinto* (painted), "painted stick." There are varying opinions as to why it was named as such. One notion is that the Spaniards arrived in the fall and were taken by the colors of the autumn leaves. Another is that the name was applied because of a colorful variety of lichen growing on the tree trunks along the creek. Most likely, though, the name Palo Pinto came to be as a result of the colorful markings left on tree trunks by Indians of the area.

PANOLA

This word means "cotton," from the Indian word *ponolo*. No more appropriate name could have been selected by Hon. Isaac Van Zandt, the author of the act creating the county, January, 1841. Of this plant Henry W. Grady said:

> The world waits in attendance on its growth; the shower that falls on its leaves is heard around the world; the sun that shines on it is tempered by the prayers of all the people; the frost that chills it, and the dew that descends from the stars, is noted; and the trespass of a little worm upon the green leaf is more to England than the advance of the Russian army upon her outposts. It is gold from the instant it puts forth its tiny shoot; its fiber is currency in every bank, and when loosing its fleece to the sun, it floats in a snowy banner that glorifies the field of the humblest farmer.

No other agricultural product has so great a commercial value.

RED RIVER

The country through which this river, from which the county took its name, flows, goes through several hundred miles of red soil, which imparts its color to the water. To distinguish it from the Colorado the Spaniards called it Rio Rojo or Roxo, or Red River, of Natchitoches.

ROCKWALL

An underground rock wall, apparently built by a prehistoric race, gives the name to this county.

SABINE

The large cypress forests through which the river flows gave the name, Sabine, a derivative of a Spanish word for cypress, to the stream and the county.

APPENDIX

Prior to the revolution of Texas against Mexico there was no such political subdivision as the county. The state's area was subdivided into departments and municipalities. When the revolution began there were three departments: Bexar, Brazos and Nacogdoches; and eighteen municipalities, viz: Austin, Bexar, Brazoria (formerly called Columbia), Goliad, Gonzales, Harrisburg, Jasper (formerly called Bevil), Liberty, Matagorda, Milam (formerly called Viesca), Mina (afterward called Bastrop), Nacogdoches, Refugio, San Augustine, San Patricio, Shelby (or Teneha), Victoria and Washington. Five additional ones were created by the provisional council in 1835, viz: Colorado, Jackson, Jefferson, Red River and Sabine. The department was ignored as a political unit in the several conventions held, being wholly unsuited to a representative form of government. The representatives came from the various municipalities and those were the nucleus of the counties created by the first Congress of the Republic of Texas, and the following diagram shows the development of the counties from them.

Municipality	Derivatives			Created	Organized	Area	County Seat
Austin	Austin			17 Mar 1836	1837	712	Bellville
	Ft Bend			29 Dec 1837	Jan 1838	897	Richmond
	Waller			28 Apr 1873	16 Aug 1873	510	Hempstead
Bastrop	Bastrop			17 Mar 1836	8 Apr 1837	881	Bastrop
	Lee			14 Apr 1874	2 June 1874	666	Giddings
	Travis			21 Jan 1843	8 Apr 1843	1036	Austin
	Travis	Burnet	Burnet	5 Feb 1852	7 Aug 1854	1010	Burnet
			Blanco	12 Feb 1858	12 Apr 1858	*762	Johnson City
		Brown	Brown	27 Aug 1856	2 Mar 1857	*911	Brownwood
			Mills	15 Mar 1887	12 Sept 1887	604	Goldthwaite
			Callahan	11 Feb 1858	3 July 1877	882	Baird
			Coleman	1 Feb 1858	6 Oct 1864	1302	Coleman
		Comal	Comal	24 Mar 1846	13 July 1846	569	N. Braunfels
			Blanco				
			Eastland	1 Feb 1858	2 Dec 1873	947	Eastland

Municipality	Derivatives			Created	Organized	Area	County Seat
Travis	Gillespie		Gillespie	23 Feb 1848	3 June 1848	*1140	Fredericksburg
			Blanco				
	Hays		Hays	1 Mar 1848	7 Aug 1848	*647	San Marcos
			Blanco				
	Lampasas		Lampasas	1 Feb 1856	10 Mar 1856	*755	Lampasas
			Mills				
		Hamilton	Hamilton	22 Jan 1858	2 Aug 1858	*658	Hamilton
			Mills				
Bastrop			Runnels	1 Feb 1858	16 Feb 1880	1073	Ballinger
			Taylor	1 Feb 1858	3 July 1878	900	Abilene
Fayette			Fayette	14 Dec 1837	Jan 1838	992	La Grange
			Lavaca	6 Apr 1846	13 July 1846	992	Halletsville
			Lee				

Municipality	Derivatives	Created	Organized	Area	County Seat
Bexar	Bexar	17 Mar 1836	1837	1268	San Antonio
	Andrews	21 Aug 1876	1910	1591	Andrews
	Armstrong	21 Aug 1876	8 Nov 1890	870	Claude
	Atascosa	25 Jan 1856	4 Aug 1856	1182	Jourdanton
	Frio	1 Feb 1858	20 July 1871	1064	Pearsall
	McMullen	1 Feb 1858	1877	1180	Tilden
	Bandera	25 Jan 1856	10 Mar 1856	822	Bandera
	Real	3 Apr 1913	1913	701	Leakey
	Bailey	21 Aug 1876	1917	1000	Muleshoe
	Borden	21 Aug 1876	17 Mar 1891	892	Gail
	Briscoe	21 Aug 1876	11 Jan 1892	850	Silverton
	Callahan				
	Carson	21 Aug 1876	26 Jun 1888	860	Panhandle
	Castro	21 Aug 1876	1891	870	Dimmitt
	Cochran	21 Aug 1876	1924	750	Morton
	Collingsworth	21 Aug 1876	30 Sep 1890	867	Wellington

(Sub-derivatives noted in table: Atascosa — Atascosa; Bandera — Bandera)

Municipality	Derivatives	Created	Organized	Area	County Seat
Bexar	Comal				
	Concho	1 Feb 1858	11 Mar 1879	941	Paint Rock
	Crockett	22 Jan 1875	14 July 1891	3004	Ozona
	Schleicher	1 Apr 1887	1891	1355	El Dorado
	Sutton	1 Apr 1887	4 Nov 1890	1517	Sonora
	Val Verde	24 Mar 1885	2 May 1885	3034	Del Rio
	Crosby	21 Aug 1876	11 Sept 1886	1463	Emma
	Dallam	21 Aug 1876	8 Sep 1891	1463	Dalhart
	Dawson	21 Aug 1876	1905	900	Lamesa
	Deaf Smith	21 Aug 1876	1 Dec 1890	1477	Hereford
	Dickens	21 Aug 1876	14 Mar 1891	918	Dickens
	Dimmit	1 Feb 1858	2 Nov 1880	1164	Carrizo Sprgs
	Donley	21 Aug 1876	22 Nov 1882	878	Clarendon
	Edwards	11 Feb 1858	10 Apr 1883	1937	Rock Springs
	Real				

Municipality	Derivatives		Created	Organized	Area	County Seat
Bexar	El Paso	El Paso	3 Jan 1850	7 Mar 1871	*5572	El Paso
		Culberson	10 Mar 1911	1912	3780	Van Horn
		Hudspeth	1917	1917	4571	Sierra Blanca
		Fisher	21 Aug 1876	27 Apr 1886	836	Roby
		Floyd	21 Aug 1876	28 May 1890	1036	Floydada
		Frio				
		Gaines	21 Aug 1876	24 Oct 1905	1590	Seminole
		Garza	21 Aug 1876	15 Jun 1907	821	Post
		Gillespie				
		Gray	21 Aug 1876	27 May 1902	860	Lefors
		Guadalupe	30 Mar 1846	13 July 1846	717	Seguin
		Hale	21 Aug 1876	13 Aug 1888	1036	Plainview
		Hall	21 Aug 1876	23 Jun 1890	868	Memphis
		Hansford	21 Aug 1876	11 Mar 1889	860	Hansford
		Hartley	21 Aug 1876	9 Feb 1891	1460	Hartley
		Hemphill	21 Aug 1876	5 July 1887	860	Canadian

Municipality	Derivatives	Created	Organized	Area	County Seat
Bexar	Hockley	21 Aug 1876	1921	977	Levelland
Bexar	Howard	21 Aug 1876	15 Jun 1882	888	Big Springs
Bexar	Hutchinson	21 Aug 1876	1901	850	Plemons
Bexar	Jones	1 Feb 1858	13 Jun 1881	900	Anson
Bexar	Kent	21 Aug 1876	8 Nov 1892	777	Jayton
Bexar — Karnes	Karnes	4 Feb 1854	27 Feb 1854	*740	Karnes City
Bexar — Karnes	Wilson	13 Feb 1860	6 Aug 1860	784	Floresville
Bexar — Kerr	Kerr	25 Jan 1856	22 Mar 1856	1165	Kerrville
Bexar — Kerr	Real				
Bexar	Kendall	10 Jan 1862	18 Feb 1862	613	Boerne
Bexar	Kimble	22 Jan 1858	3 Jan 1876	*1302	Junction
Bexar — Kinney	Kinney	28 Jan 1850	2 Feb 1874	1269	Brackett
Bexar — Kinney — Maverick	Maverick	2 Feb 1856	13 July 1871	1332	Eagle Pass
Bexar — Kinney — Maverick	Dimmit				
Bexar — Kinney	Zavala	1 Feb 1858	25 Feb 1884	1328	Batesville
Bexar — Kinney	Val Verde				

Municipality	Derivatives	Created	Organized	Area	County Seat
	Lamb	21 Aug 1876	1908	1021	Olton
	La Salle	1 Feb 1858	2 Nov 1880	1707	Cotulla
	Lipscomb	21 Aug 1876	6 Jun 1887	850	Lipscomb
	Llano	1 Feb 1856	4 Aug 1856	*993	Llano
	Lubbock	21 Aug 1876	10 Mar 1891	982	Lubbock
	Lynn	21 Aug 1876	1903	821	Tahoka
	Martin	21 Aug 1876	4 Nov 1884	900	Stanton
Bexar	Mason	23 Jan 1858	2 Aug 1858	*968	Mason
	McCulloch	27 Aug 1856	1876	1110	Brady
	McMullen				
	Medina	12 Feb 1848	7 Aug 1848	1284	Hondo
	Menard	22 Jan 1858	8 May 1871	888	Menardville
	Mitchell	21 Aug 1876	10 Jan 1881	807	Colorado
	Moore	21 Aug 1876	6 July 1892	885	Dumas
	Motley	21 Aug 1876	25 Feb 1891	984	Matador
	Nolan	21 Aug 1876	10 Jun 1881	828	Sweetwater

Municipality	Derivatives	Created	Organized	Area	County Seat
	Ochiltree	21 Aug 1876	21 Feb 1889	814	Ochiltree
	Oldham	25 Aug 1876	12 Jun 1881	1470	Tascosa
	Parmer	26 Aug 1876	1907	873	Farwell
	Potter	21 Aug 1876	6 Sep 1887	874	Amarillo
Presidio	Presidio	3 Jan 1850	1875	3970	Marfa
	Brewster	2 Feb 1887	26 Feb 1887	5006	Alpine
	Jeff Davis	15 Mar 1887	24 May 1887	1922	Ft Davis
	Pecos	23 Jan 1858	2 Aug 1858	*968	Mason
Pecos	Reeves	14 Apr 1883	4 Nov 1884	2610	Pecos
	Terrell	8 Apr 1905	1905	2776	Sanderson
	Val Verde				
	Randall	21 Aug 1876	27 July 1889	872	Canyon
	Roberts	21 Aug 1876	10 Jan 1889	860	Miami
	Runnels				
	San Saba	1 Feb 1856	3 May 1856	1150	San Saba
	Scurry	21 Aug 1876	28 Jun 1884	821	Snyder

Bexar

Municipality	Derivatives	Created	Organized	Area	County Seat
Bexar	Sherman	21 Aug 1876	13 Jun 1876	850	Stratford
	Swisher	25 Aug 1876	11 Nov 1890	850	Tulia
	Taylor				
	Terry	21 Aug 1876	1904	828	Brownfield
Tom Green	Tom Green	13 Mar 1874	5 Jan 1875	1363	San Angelo
	Coke	13 Mar 1889	23 Apr 1889	800	Robert Lee
	Crane	26 Feb 1887	1927	850	Crane
	Ector	26 Feb 1887	6 Jan 1891	976	Odessa
	Glasscock	4 Apr 1887	28 Mar 1893	952	Garden City
	Irion	7 Mar 1889	16 Apr 1889	800	Sherwood
	Loving	26 Feb 1887	1931	873	Mentone
	Midland	4 Mar 1885	15 Jun 1885	972	Midland
	Reagan	7 Mar 1903	1903	1190	Stiles
	Sterling	4 Mar 1891	3 Jun 1891	821	Sterling City
	Upton	26 Feb 1887	1910	1190	Upland
	Ward	26 Feb 1887	29 Mar 1892	858	Barstow
	Winkler	26 Feb 1887	5 Apr 1910	888	Kermit

Municipality	Derivatives			Created	Organized	Area	County Seat
Bexar	Uvalde	Uvalde		8 Feb 1850	21 Apr 1856	1579	Uvalde
		Bandera	Bandera				
		Real					
		Dimmit					
		Frio					
		Zavala					
	Webb	Webb		28 Jan 1848	16 Mar 1848	3421	Laredo
		Dimmit					
		La Salle					
		Zapata	Zapata	22 Jan 1848	26 Apr 1858	*1269	Zapata
		Wheeler		21 Apr 1876	12 Apr 1879	851	Wheeler
		Wilbarger		1 Feb 1858	10 Oct 1881	932	Vernon
		Wilson					
		Yoakum		21 Aug 1876	1907	840	Plains
Brazoria	Brazoria			17 Mar 1836	1837	1438	Angleton
	Galveston			15 May 1838	1839	438	Galveston

Municipality	Derivatives		Created	Organized	Area	County Seat
Colorado	Colorado		17 Mar 1836	1837	948	Columbus
	Fayette					
	Lavaca					
	Lee					
	Wharton		13 Apr 1846	13 July 1846	1137	Wharton
Goliad	Goliad		17 Mar 1836	1837	*817	Goliad
	Bee		8 Dec 1857	25 July 1858	875	Beeville
	DeWitt	DeWitt	24 Mar 1846	13 July 1846	880	Cuero
	Karnes					
	Karnes					
Gonzales	Gonzales		17 Mar 1836	1837	1079	Gonzales
	Caldwell		6 Mar 1848	7 Aug 1848	530	Lockhart
	Comal					
	DeWitt					
	Guadalupe					
	Lavaca					

Municipality	Derivatives	Created	Organized	Area	County Seat
Harris	Harris	17 Mar 1836	1837	1761	Houston
Jackson	Jackson	17 Mar 1836	1837	888	Edna
	Lavaca				
	Wharton				
Jasper	Jasper	17 Mar 1836	1837	*977	Jasper
	Newton	22 Apr 1846	13 July 1846	903	Newton
Jefferson	Jefferson	17 Mar 1836	1837	1109	Beaumont
	Chambers	12 Feb 1858	2 Aug 1858	*648	Anahuac
	Hardin	22 Jan 1858	2 Aug 1858	844	Kountze
	Orange	5 Feb 1852	20 Mar 1852	392	Orange
Liberty	Liberty	1 Mar 1836	1837	*1162	Liberty
	Chambers				
	Galveston				
	Hardin				
	Polk	30 Mar 1846	10 July 1846	1110	Livingston
	San Jacinto	13 Aug 1870	1 Dec 1870	636	Cold Springs

Municipality	Derivatives	Created	Organized	Area	County Seat
Liberty	Tyler	3 Apr 1846	13 July 1846	925	Woodville
Matagorda	Matagorda	17 Mar 1836	1837	1135	Bay City
	Wharton				
Milam	Milam	17 Mar 1836	1837	*1014	Cameron
	Bell	22 Jan 1850	1 Aug 1850	1091	Belton
	Coryell	4 Feb 1854	4 Mar 1854	1115	Gatesville
	Comanche	25 Jan 1856	17 Mar 1856	828	Comanche
	Brown				
	Hamilton				
	Mills				
	Eastland				
	Erath	25 Jan 1856	4 Aug 1856	*1110	Stephensville
	Lampasas				
	Hamilton				
	Mills				
	Mills				
	Burnet				

Municipality			Derivatives	Created	Organized	Area	County Seat
Milam	Burleson		Burleson	24 Mar 1846	13 July 1846	677	Caldwell
			Lee				
			Callahan				
			Falls	28 Jan 1850	5 Aug 1850	*844	Marlin
			Haskell	1 Feb 1858	13 Jan 1885	843	Haskell
	McLennan		McLennan	22 Apr 1846	13 July 1846	903	Newton
		Bosque	Bosque	4 Feb 1854	7 Aug 1855	972	Meridian
			Comanche				
			Eastland				
			Erath				
			Hamilton				
			Jones				
			Palo Pinto	27 Aug 1856	27 Apr 1857	971	Palo Pinto
			Parker	2 Dec 1855	11 Mar 1856	888	Weatherford
			Shackelford	1 Feb 1856	12 Sep 1874	926	Albany
			Throckmorton	13 Jan 1858	18 Mar 1879	871	Throckmorton

Municipality	Derivatives					Created	Organized	Area	County Seat
Milam	McLennan	Bosque	Young	Young	Young	2 Feb 1856	17 Apr 1874	821	Graham
					Wichita	1 Feb 1858	21 June 1882	606	Wichita Falls
				Coryell					
		Johnson	Johnson		Johnson	4 Feb 1854	7 Aug 1854	740	Cleburne
					Hood	2 Nov 1866	25 Dec 1866	*436	Granbury
					Somervell	13 Mar 1875	12 Apr 1875	200	Glen Rose
	Robertson				Robertson	14 Dec 1837	1838	913	Franklin
					Brazos	30 Jan 1841	6 Feb 1843	510	Bryan
					Dallas	30 Mar 1846	10 July 1846	*900	Dallas
		Leon			Leon	17 Mar 1846	13 July 1846	1066	Centerville
					Madison	27 Jan 1853	7 Aug 1854	*488	Madisonville
		Limestone			Limestone	11 Apr 1846	18 Aug 1846	*987	Groesbeck
					Falls				
					Freestone	6 Sep 1850	6 July 1851	947	Fairfield
					McLennan				

Municipality	Derivatives			Created	Organized	Area	County Seat
Milam	Robertson	Navarro	Navarro	25 Apr 1846	13 July 1846	1136	Corsicana
			Ellis	20 Dec 1849	5 Aug 1850	1066	Waxahachie
			Hill	7 Feb 1853	14 May 1853	*1006	Hillsboro
			Johnson				
			McLennan				
			Palo Pinto				
			Parker				
			Tarrant	20 Dec 1849	5 Aug 1850	*900	Ft Worth
	Williamson	Williamson		13 Mar 1848	7 Aug 1848	1169	Georgetown
		Burnet					
Nacogdoches	Nacogdoches			17 Mar 1836	1837	962	Nacogdoches
	Angelina			21 Apr 1846	13 July 1846	880	Lufkin
	Cherokee			11 Apr 1846	13 July 1846	990	Rusk
	Dallas						

Municipality	Derivatives				Created	Organized	Area	County Seat
Nacogdoches	Henderson			Henderson	27 Apr 1846	13 July 1846	940	Athens
		Kaufman		Kaufman	26 Feb 1848	7 Aug 1848	932	Kaufman
				Rockwall	1 Mar 1873	23 Apr 1879	*171	Rockwall
		Van Zandt		Van Zandt	20 Mar 1848	2 Aug 1848	877	Canton
			Wood	Wood	5 Feb 1850	5 Aug 1850	*688	Quitman
				Rains	9 June 1870	1 Dec 1870	252	Emory
	Hopkins			Hopkins	25 Mar 1846	13 July 1846	666	Sulphur Sprgs
				Rains				
				Delta	29 July 1870	6 Oct 1870	266	Cooper
	Houston			Houston	8 Jun 1837	1837	*1192	Crockett
				Anderson	24 Mar 1846	13 July 1846	1060	Palestine
				Henderson				
	Hunt			Trinity	11 Feb 1850	1 Apr 1850	*704	Groveton
				Hunt	11 Apr 1846	12 July 1846	888	Greenville
				Rains				

Municipality	Derivatives			Created	Organized	Area	County Seat
Nacogdoches	Rusk	Rusk		16 Jan 1843	6 Feb 1843	*915	Henderson
		Gregg		12 Apr 1873	28 June 1873	287	Longview
		Smith		11 Apr 1846	10 July 1846	984	Tyler
	Upshur	Upshur		27 Apr 1846	13 July 1846	*587	Gilmer
		Camp		6 Apr 1874	20 June 1874	217	Pittsburg
		Gregg					
Red River		Red River		17 Mar 1836	1837	*1061	Clarksville
	Bowie	Bowie		17 Dec 1840	1841	*907	Boston
		Titus	Titus	11 May 1846	13 July 1846	421	Mt Pleasant
			Franklin	6 Mar 1875	30 Apr 1875	325	Mt Vernon
			Morris	13 Mar 1875	12 May 1875	278	Daingerfield
		Cass	Cass	25 Apr 1846	13 July 1846	945	Linden
			Marion	8 Feb 1860	15 Mar 1860	384	Jefferson
	Fannin	Fannin		17 Dec 1837	Jan 1838	940	Bonham
		Baylor		1 Feb 1858	12 Apr 1879	957	Seymour
		Childress		11 Apr 1876	Apr 1887	660	Childress

Municipality	Derivatives			Created	Organized	Area	County Seat
Red River			Collin	3 Apr 1846	13 July 1846	828	McKinney
			Collingsworth				
			Archer	22 Jan 1858	27 July 1880	960	Archer City
			Hardeman	21 Feb 1858	31 Dec 1884	532	Quanah
	Fannin		Cooke	20 Mar 1848	10 Mar 1849	850	Gainesville
		Cooke	Clay	24 Dec 1857	24 Nov 1875	*1250	Henrietta
			Jack	27 Aug 1856	1 July 1857	858	Jacksboro
			Montague	24 Dec 1857	2 Aug 1858	*976	Montague
			Wise	23 Jan 1856	5 May 1856	*843	Decatur
		Cottle	Cottle	11 Aug 1876	11 Mar 1892	956	Paducah
			Foard	3 Mar 1891	27 Apr 1891	636	Crowell
			Denton	11 Apr 1846	13 July 1846	*865	Denton
			Grayson	17 Mar 1846	13 July 1846	1012	Sherman
			Haskell				
			Hunt				

Municipality	Derivatives			Created	Organized	Area	County Seat
Red River	Fannin	King	King	21 Aug 1876	25 June 1891	928	Guthrie
			Foard				
		Knox	Knox	1 Feb 1858	20 Mar 1886	947	Benjamin
			Foard				
			Stonewall	21 Aug 1876	20 Dec 1888	777	Aspermont
			Throckmorton				
			Wheeler				
			Wichita				
			Wilbarger				
			Young				
	Lamar		Lamar	17 Dec 1840	1841	903	Paris
			Delta				
			Hopkins				
			Titus				

Municipality	Derivatives	Created	Organized	Area	County Seat
Refugio	Refugio	17 Mar 1836	1837	802	Refugio
	Aransas	Sep 1871	1871	295	Rockport
	Bee				
Sabine	Sabine	17 Mar 1836	1837	*577	Hemphill
San Augustine	San Augustine	17 Mar 1836	1837	570	San Augustine
San Patricio	San Patricio	17 Mar 1836	1837	700	Sinton
	Bee				
	Live Oak	12 Feb 1856	4 Aug 1856	1123	Oakville
	Duval	1 Feb 1858	7 Nov 1876	1840	San Diego
	Jim Hogg	31 Mar 1913	1913	1099	Hebronnville
	Brooks	11 Mar 1911	1912	912	Falfurrias
	Jim Hogg				
	McMullen				

Duval; Brooks; Live Oak

Municipality	Derivatives					Created	Organized	Area	County Seat
San Patricio	Nueces		Nueces			11 Apr 1846	12 July 1846	592	Corpus Christi
			Jim Wells			11 Mar 1911	1912	856	Alice
			Kleberg			27 Feb 1913	1913	1012	Kingsville
		Cameron	Cameron			12 Feb 1848	7 Aug 1848	1670	Brownsville
			Willacy			11 Mar 1911	1912	1800	Sarita
			Hidalgo	Hidalgo		24 Jan 1852	7 Aug 1852	1583	Edinburg
					Brooks				
					Willacy				
		Duval	Duval						
					Jim Hogg				
			Live Oak						
		Starr	Starr			10 Feb 1848	7 Aug 1848	1223	Rio Grande
			Brooks						
			Duval	Duval					
					Jim Hogg				

Municipality	Derivatives	Created	Organized	Area	County Seat
San Patricio	Nueces				
	Starr				
	Zapata				
	Zapata				
	Brooks				
	Webb				
Shelby	Shelby	17 Mar 1836	1837	*814	Center
	Harrison	28 Jan 1839	18 June 1842	873	Marshall
	Marion				
	Upshur				
	Panola	30 Mar 1846	Sept 1846	814	Carthage
	Panola				
Victoria	Victoria	17 Mar 1836	1837	883	Victoria
	DeWitt				
	Calhoun	4 Apr 1846	13 July 1846	592	Port Lavaca
	Lavaca				

Municipality	Derivatives			Created	Organized	Area	County Seat
Washington	Washington			17 Mar 1836	1837	568	Brenham
	Brazos						
	Burleson						
	Lee						
	Montgomery			14 Dec 1837	1837	1064	Conroe
	Grimes	Grimes		6 Apr 1846	15 July 1846	*770	Anderson
			Madison				
			Walker	6 Apr 1846	13 July 1846	754	Huntsville
		Walker	Walker				
			Madison				
			San Jacinto				
			San Jacinto				

www.ingramcontent.com/pod-product-compliance
Lightning Source LLC
Chambersburg PA
CBHW020339100426
42812CB00029B/3186/J